A Time
of
Tears

Llanharan and Brynna
the story of two mining villages where coal
reigned supreme at the turn of the century

WHITCHURCH BOOKS LTD.

First Published 2000

Published by Whitchurch Books Ltd.
67 Merthyr Road, Whitchurch,
Cardiff CF14 1DD

© Whitchurch Books Ltd.

ISBN 0 9539771 0 2

Printed by J & P Davison
3 James Place, Treforest, Pontypridd, Mid Glamorgan CF37 1SQ

This book is inspired by the life and times of my grandparents,
Nimrod and Margaret Witts, of 3, William Street, Brynna.
My grandfather was killed at South Rhondda Colliery,
Llanbad, Brynna on 2 May 1919

Nimrod William Witts 1877 - 1919
Margaret Royal Witts 1883 - 1924

T.J. Witts
(Llanharan 2000)

FOREWORDS

Bryan Riddleston,
Former Chief Executive,
Celtic Group Holdings.

It gives me great pleasure to write this foreword for Terry's latest work. As Celtic Energy, the newest and largest coal mining company in South Wales, we have inherited the work of completing the opencast site at Llanharan.

By the end of coaling in 1996, we won over 600,000 tonnes of prime coal for use by the steel and cement manufacturers in England and Wales. This continues the proud and honourable tradition of coal mining in the locality and I would like to thank all of the men and women who have strived to keep the industry alive today.

It was interesting to read Terry's history of the collieries in the Llanharan area, and it is sad that these once bustling places of work are now no longer with us. However the opencast site carried on with the work and is just one more episode in the history of coal mining. No doubt Llanharan will be associated with coal for years to come.

When the first opencast site started in Llanharan, we had the task of removing the old colliery waste tips and reclaiming the land for agriculture and social amenity. Two sports pitches and a cricket pitch have been formed on this very area, which is a fitting conclusion. When the present site finishes the land will be restored once again to agriculture, and the south shaft of Llanharan Colliery will be filled and capped, sealing up the old workings and making way for whatever the future may hold.

I wish Terry good fortune with his book and am sure that it will be regarded as an important work on the history of the area and its inhabitants.

Jill Craigie,
Writer-Producer-Director
'Blue Scar'

My visit to Llanharan and Abergwynfi in 1947 taught me more than all the history books read during my early schooldays. The knowledge gleaned in South Wales has since served me well in my approach to other social situations. At the time of my film location visit, it came as a shock to discover how one- sidedly the miners and mining communities had been portrayed. Descriptions which were far from the truth, taught from my school, the national press and, indeed, in most of the standard works on the Industrial Revolution.

It was nice to learn that there are still a number of people at Llanharan who remember and recall my visit, especially the officials at the colliery who helped my team immensely. It was certainly a memorable occasion, never to be forgotten. I am sure that if I came to Wales today to make 'Blue Scar' I could have made much more of the film.

I can only wish Terry Witts the best of luck with this book "A Time of Tears", he obviously has a warm and close affinity with miners and their way of life. Sadly, a way fast disappearing from the industrial scene. This work will, no doubt, be a valuable contribution for future generations.

Note: *Jill Craigie died in 1999. This foreword is published with the permission of her husband, Michael Foot, formerly MP for Ebbw Vale.*

Mr. Alan Reed M.E., Manager

1957 - Glenhafod Colliery, Port Talbot
1958 - Tonmawr Colliery, Pontrhydyfen
1959-60 Llanharan Colliery, Llanharan
1961 - St. Johns Colliery, Maesteg
1978-84 Wyndham/Western, Ogmore Vale

It was with pleasure that I accepted Terry Witts' invitation to write a foreword to his latest literary effort. I have read his earlier works and would like to congratulate the author on continuing his style of presentations of interviews with important contributors, and also the unique pictorial records he has managed to obtain from a large number of people over a long period. These photographs have obviously been available in isolation, but the driving enthusiasm highlighted in the author's research and collation of events has resulted in an excellent record of the development of not only the mining industry of Llanharan and district, but also the development of the community spirit of the area during that important period. Sadly, the deep mining industry

has disappeared from the South Crop area and many changes have taken place.

My father, Joe Reed, came to Llanharan in 1929 and settled at the Powell Duffryn housing site at Bryncae, and I understand that, at the time, there were still up to ten empty houses available for occupation.

I was born in 1931, and as I grew up was aware of the distinct 'Forest' accent which was prevalent amongst the older residents in the village of Brynna. Since that time, Llanharan has attracted its workforce from many neighbouring communities and when I started work at Llanharan Colliery, I recall workmen travelling from Bridgend to the west, Llanharry to the south and Tonyrefail and Gilfach Goch to the north.

When I lived at Westbourne Terrace, our next door neighbours were Mr. Richard Roberts and his wife Kate. They had been born and bred in North Wales, but Richard Roberts senior had settled in Llanharan where he carried out his trade as a colliery carpenter after leaving North Wales due to the decline of the slate industry.

Included in this book are prints showing Richard Roberts' five sons. One son went to London to live but Ben, Evan, Dick and Glyn became popular lads in the village. Ben was a notable scout leader in his earlier days and eventually became a mining engineer. Evan was an excellent singer and joined a number of choirs in the district. Dick was a good footballer and played for Brynna and Caerau (along with Evan Bowen, Brynna). Dick also made a number of appearances with Swansea Town. Yes! the Roberts family I bring to mind with ease, a family held in high esteem by my own during that time at Llanharan.

Over the years other groups arrived and were welcomed into the community, not all of them to work in the mines, and not all arriving on a voluntary basis. During the Second World War I can remember the searchlights being situated on the site of the then derelict Brynna Wood Colliery, manned by a number of soldiers stationed in their wooden hut quarters. About the same time a large number of American soldiers were stationed at St. Mary Hill, and were regular visitors to Llanharan at Saturday dancing venues. Also, British servicemen from R.A.F. stations at Llandow and St. Athan were regular visitors.

Another group of settlers at Llanharan during the war years were the evacuees, torn away from their homes and families, but fortunate to be distributed to the homes of many resident families who went to extraordinary lengths to make them as happy as possible during their stay. Recently my sister Betty, in answer to an advert in the local press, contacted a Mr. Colin Manley who, with his younger brother Ivor, was billeted at our home in Westbourne Terrace fifty years ago. A further group of incomers about that time were the 'Bevan Boys' directed to the mines during wartime.

When the war was over a further group of people were directed into the community. They were, of course, the Poles, Yugoslavs and other European allies whose nations had been overrun in the war. These people were billeted at a number of hostels in the area, the main being at Rhydyfelin, Pencoed and Brynmenin. Many of these men were recruited into the mines, a large number taken into our own Llanharan Colliery.

Once again these people received the best of welcome. Many sought lodgings privately, and some still reside in the area today. It says much for the community that so many people from such different backgrounds were accepted, welcomed into, and in time, made such a worthy contribution to Llanharan.

In closing I would like to reiterate the importance to present and future generations of the untiring and enthusiastic efforts made by the author in documentation and presentation of the varying and interesting articles recorded in this fine and well researched record. The views expressed in this foreword are, of course, my own, but they have been prompted by the many excellent reports published here and in the author's previous works. One article cited in this collection of important memories was of particular interest to me. That was the article in which Mrs. Laura Pearce of Brynna describes the accepted procedure carried out following a fatal accident at the mine. It was of course, management's responsibility to inform the next of kin. During my twenty seven years as a colliery manager four fatalities occurred (one is one too many) and I will be forever indebted and grateful to the respected union officers, who, on every occasion, undertook to organise the dreadful task of informing the deceased's family.

The last chapter in the transfer of labour at Llanharan was the sad closure of Llanharan Colliery in 1962. By this time I had transferred to St. Johns Colliery, Maesteg, and was delighted to welcome to that pit former Llanharan colleagues (management, officials and workmen). Many of the Llanharan workmen were transferred to other pits, mainly in the Garw Valley.

I shall close this foreword quoting the words from a famous Bob Hope song: 'Thanks for the memory'. Keep up the good work Terry Witts, today's action forms tomorrow's history.

Cliff Jacobsen
Prestatyn
(Son of photographer Victor Jacobsen)

There can be no doubt that the appetite that Mr. Terry Witts has for the history of Llanharan and its people is insatiable. After his trilogy of "The Forgotten Years" he has researched and collected sufficient material for yet another book on the subject.

Through his love of the district and his devotion to the task he has set himself, he is held in high regard by his contemporaries, as a dedicated and very knowledgeable historian.

Those who live in the village, and indeed those who have moved away, are indebted to him for his extensive research and the detailed account he has given us of life in the area, from before the days of coal, through the mining era, to the present day.

He has ensured that the name Llanharan is immortal and that its people will be remembered, not for years but for centuries, not just in Wales but in many countries throughout the world.

Historians of the future, endeavouring to create interest in their subject, may very well point to Terry's works and say "That is how it should be done."

With "The Forgotten Years" and this new work "A Time of Tears" Terry Witts has made certain that Llanharan is not just another village, but something a little bit special to us all.

DEDICATION

This list is a tribute to all the miners of Llanharan and Brynna who paid the ultimate price during the exploration for coal. Sadly, it has proved impossible to record a full and comprehensive list as not all mine fatalities were recorded, especially prior to the 1920s.

Willie John	Brynna Wood Drift Mine
David John Matthews	Brynna Wood Drift Mine
William Mounter	Brynna Wood Drift Mine
Wilfred Tomlins	Brynna Wood Drift Mine
William Williams	Brynna Wood Drift Mine
Robert Jones (brother of John Jones, Contractor)	
	Llanbad Drift Mine, Brynna
Thomas Perkins	Llanbad Drift Mine, Brynna
Caleb Tomlins	Llanbad Drift Mine, Brynna
Thomas Barkle	Llanbad Colliery, Brynna
Patrick Donovan	Llanbad Colliery, Brynna
John Pyne	Llanbad Colliery, Brynna
Nimrod Witts	Llanbad Colliery, Brynna
Vivian Boulton	Llanharan Colliery
Raymond Coles	Llanharan Colliery
David Evans	Llanharan Colliery
Gwyn Evans	Llanharan Colliery
William John Harris	Llanharan Colliery
Kenneth Hanson	Llanharan Colliery
Cyril Jobbins	Llanharan Colliery
David Llewellyn	Llanharan Colliery
Dilwyn North	Llanharan Colliery
Bill Richards	Llanharan Colliery
Owain Glyndwr Richards	Llanharan Colliery
Percy Smith	Llanharan Colliery
Jack Summers	Llanharan Colliery
Trevor West	Llanharan Colliery
Michael Williams	Llanharan Colliery
Tom Cox	Meiros Colliery
Thomas Davies	Meiros Colliery
Henry Evans	Meiros Colliery
John Limebeer Hole	Meiros Colliery
Daniel Lewis	Meiros Colliery
John Morgan	Meiros Colliery
Thomas Owen	Meiros Colliery
Rees Owen	Meiros Colliery
John Parsons	Meiros Colliery
Samuel Shillabeer	Meiros Colliery
Matthew Snook	Meiros Colliery
Ben Taylor	Meiros Colliery
Jenkin Williams	Meiros Colliery
Thomas Williams	Meiros Colliery
Will (Toasty) Davies	Wern Tarw Colliery
George Green	Wern Tarw Colliery
Jim Plant	Wern Tarw Colliery
John Shillabeer	Wern Tarw Colliery
George Frederick Tasker	Wern Tarw Colliery
William Wetherall	Wern Tarw Colliery
Fred Wills	Wern Tarw Colliery
William Young	Wern Tarw Colliery
Will McIntyre (Manager)	Wern Tarw Drift Mine

"I see people around me touched by
the ecstasy of new beginnings."

Gwyn Thomas.

This book is dedicated to those early pioneering mining families who came and settled into the tiny areas of Llanharan and Brynna at the turn of the century. Here, these new immigrants from such areas as the Forest of Dean and Cornwall were to change the scene of places which were nothing more than primitive agricultural hamlets. They created a coalmining bonanza which was to open up a new world of unforeseen challenges......

T.J. Witts

T.J. Witts with his dogs Spot, Raq and Tara outside the Llanbad South Rhondda Colliery power house ruin. The author holds a deep affection for the mining communities that once surrounded his village Llanharan. His grandfather, Nimrod Witts was one of those early pioneers who flooded into Brynna from the Forest of Dean, when the mining engineers struck the famous Rhondda No. 3 seam in 1886. Nimrod himself was killed in an underground accident in 1919 at the early age of forty two years. The author's father, William Robert, continued in his father's footsteps and started in the Llanbad pit. Having worked at Llanbad for seven months he went to Brynna Wood and worked in the No. 3 drift there until its closure in the mid thirties. From Brynna Wood he worked in Llanharan Colliery for seventeen years.

–THE MINERS –

The men in black are gone –
And the shafts are lost within the intercourse
    of grey and green.
The empty mining shells of anarchy –
Are hiding beneath the blankets of nature's
    courage.
Where is the reality of those earthly shrines –
Where has the richness gone! From this now
    inferior world.
The miner – whose heart paved a militancy –
On a darkened stage of disciplined dedication.
In masses they came to mould the village –

Changing the scene into an ebony repentance.
Some died – giving their souls to the
    loathsome earth –
While others fought for a grim respectability.
Watching the toiling heroes – gravestones
    shivered nervously
Anticipating that sudden call.
Women's ears rode swiftly on the wind –

Dreading the screaming hooters pain.
The agonising fight went on and on –
Man against creation.

Dreading the screaming hooters pain.
The agonising fight went on and on –
Man against creation.
A time of tears –

As they writhed in the sanctums cursing
    humanity.
There were no stars in their sky –
Only dark subdued restlessness.
The miner – played hide and seek with death –
And won the early imperfections.
But now! Time has destroyed their very
    existence –
And only passion can save their pride.
The silent dreamers sit behind curtained walls –
Looking back through days of careless security.

The pit-head wheels are dead –
And the mine's heart is buried in humiliation.
The men in black are gone –
And the shafts are lost within the intercourse of
    grey and green.

T.J. Witts

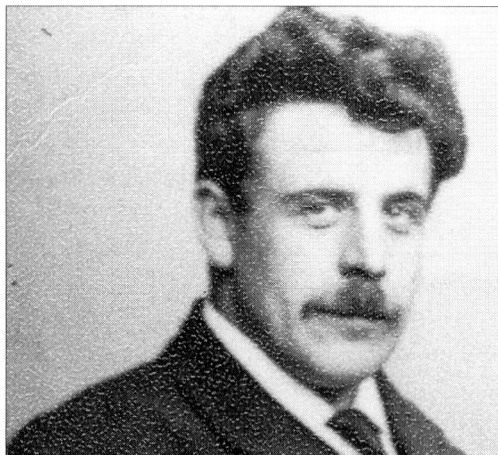
Mr. Thomas Russell

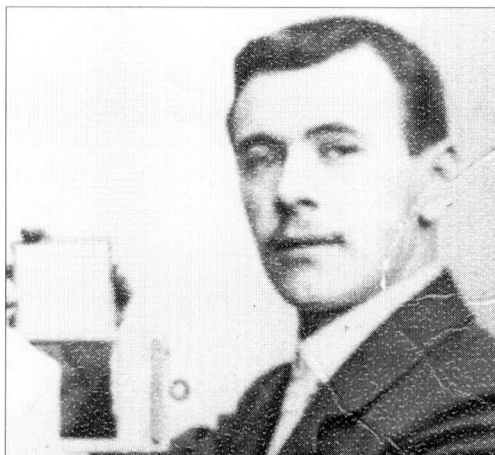
Mr. Frederick Russell

Mr. Victor Jacobsen

Armed with a Thornton Pickard camera, Mr. Victor Jacobsen took many village and colliery scenes during the 1920s and early 1930s. Likewise, the Russell brothers established their photographic expertise during the early 1900s. The work of our three photographers gave me the opportunity of creating a living encyclopaedia of life in our villages during the days when coal was king.

The three gentlemen were excellent cameramen. Their celluloid images gathered over the years have left us with a true and effective historical record.

T.J. Witts at the coalface of the Coed Bychan No. 3 drift mine at Brynna. The drift was featured in a London Weekend T.V. Production entitled 'Black Goddess' which featured the late actors Talfryn Thomas, David Davies and Ronald Lewis. The mine closed down during the mid 1970s.

AUTHOR'S PREFACE

Compiling the "Forgotten Years" series was, for me, an exhilarating experience. My trilogy took me nearly thirty years to complete and I have been asked on numerous occasions what inspired me to undertake such a long and arduous task. My reason, of course, is simple, a love of my community.

When I stop to think about those early researches I made during the 1960s, I realise that the driving force behind my inspiration was gleaned from that mining bonanza which occurred at the turn of the century, when new and talented families flooded into Llanharan and Brynna, to create, not only one of the largest coal mining areas on the South Crop, but to change the whole way of life in both communities. I am proud to say that my family was part of that early influx. Llanharan and Brynna, before the coming of coal, were nothing more than primitive agricultural hamlets. The introduction of the mines not only brought a new way of life, but a creation of two new villages. From the human invasion of 1886, we witnessed the birth of choirs, musicians, carnival bands, soloists, writers and most of all, characters and personalities on a grand scale. The rich Anglicising influences saw the introduction of new religious denominations in massive proportion. Schools in both parishes became a priority, and housing development escalated. In truth, it is from the outbreak of coalmining and the Forest of Dean influence, that the Brynna community at least was developed and progressed.

My late father, William Robert, started work at Llanbad Colliery, Brynna, as a lad and later went into the Brynna Wood Drift mining complex. When Brynna Wood closed down in 1935, he went to Llanharan Colliery where he remained for seventeen years before ill health forced him out of the pits altogether. His service in the mines covered 31 years. It was at my father's side as a young lad that I learned about all that was telling and traumatic during his early years in the Brynna pits. Just like many other families in the area, my father was drawn into the bitter class conflicts, protracted strikes and abject poverty that beset every mining community during those early days.

I am one of three brothers who were stopped entering the mining industry. Keeping us out of the colliery was a promise which my father had set upon himself. I started my working life with the Great Western Railway on 12 November 1954. My job was number checker on coal wagons which - yes, contrary to my father's beliefs, put me immediately into the local collieries. However, as it was surface work and not underground, my first job was acceptable. I worked four years in the local colliery coal transport programme, the first two at Wern Tarw before moving on to Llanharan. I am convinced that those early experiences at both pits inspired this present book. There was so much magic about those working days of the fifties. At Wern Tarw, individuals like Cliff Yaw (weighbridge), Bill Dacey (steam locomotive driver), and Harry Burt (sidings roadman), were outstanding people who made my working days rich and memorable. In fact, I can honestly say that while working at both collieries I actually looked forward to going to work.

I wonder how many people would say that today.

The working day started for me at 7.30 a.m. It was my job to call at Llanharan railway station to collect time sheets which I would distribute to the 'gangers'* who were working along the length of the Ogmore branch line leading to Wern Tarw. I can remember vividly calling into the various huts en route. On cold wintry mornings you could see the smoke rising from the chimneys of the huts. On opening their doors you would be hit by a rush of smoke as the gangs of men were smoking their pipes and cigarettes sat around the old steel stove, supping their tea from old enamel mugs. I always had the best of welcome from the men because they relied on me to see that their time sheets were taken back to the station daily. After a quick mug of tea I would continue my way along the line for Wern Tarw. For the record the 'ganger' on that branch line during my days at Wern Tarw was Mr. Jim Troakes, Pencoed. He was a man who demanded respect, and got it. Another golden memory of walking that line was during the warm summer months. I used to stop at Llangorse Ucha farmhouse, which was situated right on the side of the line near Pencoed, here Mrs. Downes used to give me a mug of ice cold milk whenever I passed. In turn I arranged for the fireman on the U.5 train travelling to Llanharan daily to throw off a lump of coal occasionally. Sadly, both the family and farmhouse have long passed into history.

At Wern Tarw I worked from a small zinc sheet shed which was situated at the side of the Tondu line. From the old shed we controlled all coal traffic leaving Wern Tarw. My boss was Mr. Donald Sully who came from my own village, Llanharan. He organised all traffic for the trains and was head shunter for the railways. I can say honestly that I learned to respect him immensely. I remember that near our shed there was a large house adjacent to a crossing gate. Here, a family named Lane lived. They were lovely people who kept the key to our shed hanging inside their outhouse from where I retrieved it every morning. I became very friendly with them and occasionally Mr. Lane used to give me some beans, lettuce and various garden produce from their large garden, which my parents appreciated. I learned later that they were relatives. At Wern Tarw people like Jim Lewis and Bill Davies, steam loco drivers who came from Tondu, evoke a deep and lasting memory. I have heard in recent years that both men have passed on. God Bless.

In 1956, I was transferred to Llanharan Colliery. There I was guided and influenced by the likes of Mr. William Charles (railway signalman, colliery box), Mr. Stan Hughes, M.E. (colliery manager), Mr. Ivor Prosser (colliery engineer), and most of all, Mr. Ivor Trotman, Mr. Emrys Edmunds and the boys of the Carriage and Wagon Company there. It was in the wagon shed that I was informed by Mr. Trotman that smoking fags was definitely a bad thing to do, and that if I had to smoke, then it should be a pipe. Mr. Trotman convinced me and brought a well used pipe into work to start me off. At Ivor's side I smoked my first pipe of St. Bruno tobacco, and I can say openly now that it nearly killed me, I became sick and had to go home dizzy and a little bit the worse for wear. However, I stuck to cigarettes and smoked for thirty years before giving up smoking altogether in the mid eighties. Other influences from those early colliery days came from Mr. Bill Thomas and Mr. Peter Matthews of the Llanharan transport weighbridge team. I would like to think that a little of their charisma rubbed off on me. They were two genuine and helpful individuals.

Who will ever forget Billy (Willie) Ellis. Billy was the colliery screens coal shunter. He was a small man with a large heart. Everyone loved him, his personality brimmed right throughout his working day, he loved life and showed it. To watch him dropping wagons of coal down into the sidings was a sight to behold. For a small man his strength and expertise with a brake stick had to be seen to be believed. On one occasion an assistant was having trouble with the wagons and they were beginning to run away from him. Fortunately Billy saw what was happening and rushed to take over the impending runaway. Chasing the wagons, he swung like a monkey on each brake as the trucks passed. He stopped the run only yards from the siding gates. They say that he had covered fifty yards fighting with the run. Such people will never be seen again. It was ironic that we were both talking about the old days at the colliery in a house at Brynna. One hour after I had left him on that day in the April of 1993, I received a telephone call informing me that he had collapsed and died. The memory of Billy and the timing of his demise will live with me forever.

I will always bring to mind those early meetings with the old and now forgotten mining people of both parishes. They were an exceptional breed. I thank them all for taking me through those hard and bitter years. Those men and women faced death head on and accepted it as a formality. They believed in survival and battled bravely through that time of tears.

---

* (gangers) men in charge of railway track repair team.

Llanharan in 1919, reproduced from the 1919 Ordnance Survey Map

Childhood Memories
of Llanharan

by Cliff Jacobsen.

It is a fine autumn day, the low sun is casting long shadows over the landscape, and the cold nip in the air heralds the oncoming winter. I am standing on the concrete cap that seals the pit shaft on the old Meiros Colliery, a site that I have not visited since I was a young lad of fourteen. It all seems rather bleak, as nature reclaims what is rightfully hers, and Meiros Colliery disappears into the pages of history.

It was in this small mining village of Llanharan, more than seventy two years ago, I was born. It was here I went to school, and it was from here that I left, as a young lad, to join the Army. Now I have come back many years later, to renew my acquaintance with the village that has given me an abundance of memories to enjoy in my twilight years.

Gazing across to the remains of the old engine house, its walls still standing as a memorial to days gone by, I am transported back in time, to my childhood.

Smoke ascends from the stack, and again the old colliery is working bringing coal from the bowels of the earth to the surface. My grandfather is in the engine house, tending and operating the engines that provide power for the mine. I can hear the gates being opened and closed as full drams are taken out of, or empty ones pushed into, the cages. I can see a load of Norwegian pit props waiting to be taken below. The wheels at the top of the headgear spin as the cages are lowered or raised. Grime-faced colliers go about their

tasks oblivious to the noise. A train of empty coal wagons, bearing the name of the colliery, is being hauled up the incline from the sidings at Llanharan station, soon to be filled with the coal being mined below. They will carry the coal, to all corners of the lands. It will be burnt, in black-leaded grates, providing warmth for the home, and heat with which to cook, for firing boilers of steam locomotives, and other industrial purposes.

I recall my father telling me the story of when he first worked in the pit. How in those days you worked for a gaffer who was responsible for your pay. The colliery manager paid him for the coal mined by his team and he in turn paid his men. In my father's case he worked at the face hewing coal for the late Mr. David Jenkins of 57 Bridgend Road, a very much respected man, who died in the early nineteen thirties.

Standing here, I can see my mother coming, carrying a basket in one hand and holding me with the other. We are bringing my father's snap. He returned to the colliery after losing the lower part of his left arm in World War 1, and is working as a hitcher at pit bottom, using a hook in an artificial arm for his left hand. He is able to do all that a normal two handed person can do, but approaches each task in a different way.

Today he is on the morning shift and will soon be coming to the surface for his breakfast. Mother has cooked his meal at home, placed it between two hot plates and wrapped it in clean tea towels to keep warm. We have brought it to the pithead and soon father will ascend the shaft and have his breakfast in a corrugated iron hut.

This hut, as I have said, is constructed of corrugated iron and has no windows. The only light is from the open door. Three of its sides are used for seating and on the other there is a combustion stove providing warmth. It would be stretching one's imagination to call it a canteen, for it certainly is not. Nevertheless, it is a dry place for surface workers and those able to come to the surface to enjoy their well earned break, warm and sheltered from the elements.

As I watch my father eating I can see Mr. Tommy Gardner of Llanharry sitting in the corner close to the stove. He has bought, on his way to work, a fresh load of bread and half a pound of butter from Richardson's bakery. He is busy toasting a thick slice of bread in front of the open stove, spreading on a generous amount of butter, devouring one slice and toasting another. His walrus moustache glistens with melted butter like dew in the morning sun.

From the other side of the hut comes the sound of snoring as another old timer snatches forty winks before returning to his tasks. Two others are discussing the merits of using steel for supporting the roof instead of the traditional wood pit prop. "But" says the one, "wood can talk and you can't say that for steel. At least you get some kind of warning with wood." The other agrees and I am left wondering how wood can talk.

My father takes out his pocket watch, bearing the inscription "We require eight hours for work, eight hours for our own instruction and eight hours for repose," notes the time, and then lights his cigarette. Snap time over, he returns to the pit bottom to continue his shift. As mother and I are leaving, Mr. Owen Parry of Park Terrace comes along and we stop for a moment to chat, before paying my grandfather a visit in the engine house.

Entering the engine house was to enter another world for there was no grime or dust here. Everywhere was spotlessly clean and all the metal shone like jewels in a crown. To touch any metal without an oily rag between flesh and metal, was to commit the cardinal sin. Woe betide anyone who did so.

Grandfather had spent more than thirty four years at sea, surviving being torpedoed three times, and once spent seven days in an open boat floundering in the Bay of Biscay. He sailed as a second class, first class and chief engineer, before taking the job of looking after the engine at Meiros Colliery. To anyone watching, it was obvious that he loved the power of steam and that he had done so all his life.

He explains how this and that works, what this lever does and what that wheel is for, I listen intently and am spellbound. Brought back to reality by the call of my mother, a reluctant child, fascinated by the working engine, has to say goodbye to his grandad.

One evening there is a knock on the door and the caller tells my mother that my father has had an accident at pit bottom and has suffered a crushed foot. She puts on my hat and coat and we hurry to the pithead seeking news of him. We find he has been brought to the surface, had his foot dressed by the mine's doctor and was ready to be taken home.

He is lying on a stretcher fitted with a pair of large wheels, and covered with blankets. It was on this primitive ambulance that my father finished his last shift in the Meiros Colliery. He was

Johann Adolph Jacobsen, 1858 - 1944

Johann Adolph Jacobsen came to Llanharan in 1918 to work in the steam engine house at Meiros Colliery. However, before that he worked as Chief Engineer from 1884 until 1918 for Messrs. Evans, Thomas & Radcliffe, Baltic House, Mount Stuart Square, Cardiff, sailing the seas carrying coal to ports all over the world. When he came to Llanharan in 1918 he lived at the 'Castle Cottage' above the Mill.

wheeled home by a couple of colliers, one pushing at its head, the other pulling at its foot, and mother and me walking alongside. After a long period of convalescence he became the village postman, taking over from his friend Harry Wyatt. He never descended a pit shaft again.

Accidents were not news in those days, and very often passed unnoticed, unless of course they were of major proportions. They were just a part of everyday life for the families of those men who toiled below ground. The blue battle scar was carried by most colliers of that era. Thankfully it is less prevalent today.

A cold breeze, or maybe the ghosts of those who laboured beneath my feet, sends a shiver down my spine, bringing me back to reality and the present time. Whichever, it is time to move on and refresh old memories. Taking the path down over the tip, now not so easy to find, I arrive at the old Mill.

Where is Mill Row? I ask myself. Where is number eleven? The cottage where the Cottrell family once lived and in which four of my cousins first came into the world. They have gone, disappeared in the wake of the demolition squad, remembered in the future only in history books and by those, like myself, who had an association with someone who once lived there.

No longer the sound of Mr. Cogbill's pigs can be heard snorting away in their sty. No longer will the smell of pig swill being boiled permeate the surrounding area, and thankfully no longer will the slaughter house emit the sound of squealing pigs.

I look passed the old Mill building, and expect to see the white washed "Castle Cottage", where once my grandparents lived, still standing, but it too has gone,

and no doubt one day its existence will only be remembered as a subject for a quiz question.

A stroll along Church Terrace brings me to the path leading to Llanharan House along which I often walked, after my father became the village postman. I wonder if the tree, one of two growing near the wicket leading to the house, and struck one night by lightning, still stands. My father and I used it as shelter on several occasions when taking mail to Llanharan House and getting caught in a shower of rain. It was lucky for us that we were not sheltering when the lightning struck, as it was split from top to bottom.

The other path led to the mountain, and was one that most children in the village used at some time of other. Setting off with a bottle of "pop", lemonade powder dissolved in water, we would climb along the path and up through the fields. In some places we would test our skill at balancing, by walking on the large blast pipe that ran from the Powell Dyffryn colliery up over the mountain to the Ynysmaerdy colliery. We kept a wary eye open for snakes, especially adders basking in the sun, as they, unlike the common grass snake, are poisonous.

Picking wimberries was a long and laborious job but the taste of a freshly baked tart was so good, that it made the chore worth while. Arriving on the mountain we commenced to fill our chosen container with ripe juicy wimberries, and soon all present would be sporting mauve lips as the picking drill became, one for me and one for the pot.

Having filled our containers, we headed for the "Egg Well" where water smelling of rotten eggs oozed from the ground. It tasted foul but was prized by many in the village for its medicinal properties. Refilling our empty lemonade bottles with the water, just in case someone should need it, we returned home with our thoughts on the mouth watering wimberry pie that our mothers would bake. The day on the mountain in the fresh air, enjoyed by all.

As I pass the old school room I remember the time when I joined the "Cubs", and was taught the morse code, and how to tie the knots that I have found useful in my everyday life. Lessons learned within that building have served me well.

Passing the parish church I think of the members of my family, lying in peace in its hallowed ground. I remember also the weddings that took place there, the solemn vows that were exchanged and in those days kept. How we as children waited for the bride and groom to emerge from the church and throw a handful of pennies into the street. After scrambling for them, the lucky ones would run to Mrs. Hole's shop, just down the road, to buy sweets.

I wonder if the custom still exists or has it fallen by the wayside. Of course it would need to be fifty pence pieces today and they would neither roll like the old penny or buy as many sweets, so perhaps the custom has gone forever.

Looking around The Square I sense that something is missing but I am unable to recall just what it is. It's not the buildings for they remain the same as I remember them in my childhood. Names have changed, Mr. Gower's name no longer on the chemist shop, the Post Office now here, and not on Bridgend Road, Mrs. Hole's shop now used by the gambling fraternity, but otherwise there seems little change.

It's not the trees for they went when the war memorial was deported to the far end of the recreation ground in the early nineteen thirties. I see that at long last it has now been restored to its rightful place, in the centre of the village. I glance towards the blacksmith's shop and realise that the small ever present group of men that once stood on the corner is missing.

One could always find at least half a dozen men wearing mufflers and brass-buckled leather belts standing on the corner throughout the day. Perhaps reading the daily paper, and trying to pick a "winner", or discussing last Saturday's match, and simultaneously puffing on their Club or Woodbine cigarette. Some would have their whippets with them, and perhaps would be trying to assess their prospects for the next racing session. It seemed that whatever the weather, they were a part of The Square.

Whippet racing was in vogue at this time, and it was not uncommon to see men training their dogs in one or other of the neighbouring fields. This was usually done by using an upturned bicycle, with a modified back wheel, drawing a piece of sacking attached to a long line, and representing the hare, across an open field. On the dog handler giving a signal the person at the bicycle started turning the driving wheel. The dog was released to begin its chase of the hare, the commencement and finishing time over a measured distance noted and used to assess the dog's ability. I cannot imagine much money ever changing hands, but the sport did provide pleasure for many.

Crossing to the blacksmith's shop, I think back to the days when one could stop and watch Mr. John Beard at work. Hammering on his anvil making horse shoes, or perhaps with a horse's hoof between his knees fitting a new shoe. At times he would make those steel "bowlies" with which the children often ran around the village.

My favourite memory is of him fitting new spokes and a new steel rim to a cart wheel. The spokes had been fitted and the wheel was lying on the ground in the yard. Mr. Beard himself was in the forge, heating and expanding the rim. At the appropriate time, handling the rim expertly with huge metal tongs, he slipped the rim over the wheel and immediately drenched it with cold water. This sent clouds of hissing steam into the air and caused the rim to contract rapidly. As the contraction took place one could hear the spokes being forced into the hub and into the wooden rim, tightening all the components and making the wheel one solid structure. As always, Mr. Beard had completed another excellent job and his expertise was beyond doubt.

Glancing along Chapel Road I remember that as children there was little to interest us in this area. There was, of course, the sweet shop, and Morgan's Chip Shop.

Along the road at the Llanharan Primary school my early school days began. The old school is another building that has passed into the pages of history and has been superseded by a modern new school at Llwynybrain.

The last house in the road was that of Dr. Tucker, a combined house and surgery. It was in that surgery I once stood, and had a wound in my scalp stitched. I was given a penny by the doctor for not crying and promising not to throw stones again.

Turning the corner into Bridgend Road, by the grocery shop of Mr. D. Hopkins, brings me to what was once the surgery of Dr. Patterson. Many older folk still living in the village will remember Dr. Pat better than I. My lasting memory of the doctor is of seeing him pedalling furiously down Bridgend Road on an old bicycle, dressed in the same old navy blue suit that he always seemed to wear, and clutching his gladstone bag containing the tools of his trade.

The colliery siren was sounding continuously, signifying an accident at the pit. The doctor was on his way, not knowing what faced him, or how many needed his help. The urgency of his mission could always be assessed from the manner in which he pedalled that old bicycle. A very different life from that led by the modern-day doctor.

Across the road I find the old Post office is now the office of a solicitor. Something that was rarely needed when I was a child, for there was little or no crime and buying homes was beyond the means of most. This building was the only one, as far as I can remember, to carry the name of Llanharan spelt with a double letter "R". It was on the name plate above the entrance door to the office. I wonder if it was ever changed.

The postmaster was Mr. Walker, a gentleman who lived in Chapel Road. The postmen were Mr. Victor Jacobsen, Mr. Humphries and Mr. Wilmington, the latter two lived in Miskin, and the post lady was Miss W. Sheppard also of Chapel Road. She walked many miles every morning delivering the mail to many outlying farms in the area. Mr. Bert Lanyon was employed from time to time to cover for holidays, sick leave, and helping at Christmas time.

I wonder how many remember the "distressed area parcels" delivered to the children of the village on Christmas Day nineteen thirty six. Parcels provided through a scheme, funded by the daily newspapers of the day, to ensure that every child had a present on that Christmas morning. I remember them, for I helped to deliver them.

Crossing the railway bridge leading to the south side of the village, I arrive at the station approach road. Whilst making my way towards the station entrance, I wonder how often I have trod this path to school, and on various outings.

Visions of those wonderful school trips we had in the early thirties come to mind. Visiting London Zoo and the sights of London, Piccadilly Circus, Buckingham Palace, Westminster Abbey. Travelling to Windsor Castle and Kew Gardens, or to Hampton Court and a trip on the river to Runnymede where the Magna Carta was signed. They were paid for by our parents saving from the beginning of the year, and over a period of six months a few pence a week in the school saving fund.

Where I wonder, are all the boys and girls, who over the years caught the ten past eight train in the morning, six days a week, to Cowbridge Grammar School, returning home on the six o-clock train in the evening.

No longer is the platform covered with tomato baskets filled with blackberries, as the pickers wait for the "Blackberry Special" on a Saturday morning. No longer will they take their fruit to Chivers jam factory in Ely, and have a day out in Cardiff. It is worth noting that the price on that train was just ninepence return (approximately three and a half pence in today's currency). Thankfully we now live in better times and there is no need to pick blackberries all week to pay for a trip to Cardiff.

Gone are those magnificent green and black engines of the Great Western Railway, drawing their cream and chocolate coaches, and thundering through the station, on their way to Fishguard or London. The end of the steam locomotive meant the thrill of standing on the footbridge and being enveloped in smoke has gone. No more will we see those long goods or passenger trains pass through the village.

The sight of a diesel train passing by brings back memories of the experimental diesel car, front and back looking like the bows of a ship, passing through the village on its trial runs. It was later introduced on the Cardiff to Birmingham service, and was the forerunner of the modern diesel car. Sadly the station is now closed and these sights have disappeared forever.

Turning I see that the C.W.S. Dairy has also gone. The sound of milk churns being loaded on, or off, the milk lorries, and of the crates of empty bottles being thrown from one place to another has disappeared. When it opened in nineteen thirty two some children that attended Dolau School, where I was a pupil, were taken on a conducted tour of the factory. I suppose the same must have happened for the children of the Llanharan Primary School. They were shown how the milk was heated and how foreign matter was extracted from the milk. We were all encouraged to drink only pasteurised milk but many older people still preferred to buy direct from the farm milk churn. Old habits die hard and sixty years on, not all are convinced of the value of pasteurisation.

Moving on to the site of the cinema I note that it, and the police station, have disappeared. The cinema is now a bakery, and the police station has been demolished. I have no memories of the police station, never having been inside its walls, but the cinema was different.....

I, like many others, saw my first films there, sitting on wooden benches, listening to the piano, and watching the silent films. My mother once told me of how, when I was a baby, she would undress me, and get me ready for bed before going to the picture house with my father. I would be wrapped in a shawl, taken along to sleep through the show, and then placed in my cot on their return home. This was the only way that families with young babies could pay a visit to the local cinema, for there was no such thing as a baby sitter in those days.

My first "talkie" was called "The Vagabond King", and I remember marvelling at the sound of the music, and the voices. Friday night became picture night for most children, as the admission was only twopence. It soon became known as the "Tuppeny Rush", and one went armed with a pea shooter and plenty of shot, or else plenty of elastic bands to use with one's fingers to make a sling. Neither Tom Mix nor Roy Rogers ever fired as many shots as was fired in the cinema on a Friday evening.

My most lasting memory of Llanharan cinema has nothing to do with films but more with football. The year was nineteen twenty seven and Cardiff City had won the F.A. Challenge Cup by beating Arsenal one goal to nil. Later that year, at an evening performance, the lights in the cinema went up and there was "The Cup" on display for all to see. It was passed along each row and all in the cinema that night handled it. To a six year old lad, mad on football, it was fantastic. I have never been to Wembley, but I, along with many others, did hold the F.A. Cup on that night.

Parked alongside the cinema was a maroon coloured, ornately decorated caravan, not the kind we see today being drawn by motor cars, but an old horse-drawn type. It belonged to Mrs. Phillips, a member of the family who owned the cinema. She lived in it throughout the year. During the winter months it was parked alongside the cinema and in the summer taken to Porthcawl.

I was once privileged to view the interior of this caravan, and found it really wonderful. Beautifully decorated, fine bone china on the shelves, lovely porcelain ornaments and sparkling mirrors all conspiring to make a palatial home for Mrs. Phillips. It was no wonder she was happy living in her mobile home.

Reaching Oakland Terrace I think back to the days when Reuben Owen, working in the gent's hairdressing saloon, cut my hair. After leaving to work in Cardiff, he came to our home on a Sunday morning to give my brother and me a short back and sides. I last saw him in nineteen sixty five when he was living in Llanharry and working as a postman in Cowbridge.

Living next to the hairdresser's shop was Mrs. Barkle. She had two sons, Gomer and Douglas. It was Doug Barkle who, in his mother's front room, opened the very first shop in the village to sell wireless sets. Today, of course, they are known as radios. Unfortunately, the business did not prosper, so closing the shop he found employment with the Hoover Company in Birmingham. He maintained his interest in radio throughout the remainder of his life.

Looking in at the recreation field I am amazed to find it deserted. How things have changed. Again I travel back in time and see it in a completely different light.

Someone has brought a football, and soon there is a match being played with twenty or thirty players on either side. There was no shortage of players then with so many young men out of work. The six Cogbill brothers are playing for Llanharan Rugby Club and the spectators are shouting and urging them on. It is carnival day, and two teams of burly men are playing "Push Ball" with a ball that must be at least eight feet in diameter. They are trying to push the ball over the opposing side's goal line and are expending much energy in doing so. There is the pretty ankle competition for the ladies, the slow cycle race for the men, the egg and spoon, and sack races for the children, along with many side-shows of various descriptions.

A cricket match is in progress and Dyson North, with the bat looking like a match-stick in his hands, is hitting the ball out of the ground or "Mog" Evans stonewalling his way to a century. In due course, the opposition will face big Fred Callow hurling the ball down at them in an attempt to win the match.

In the evening the sound of the Silver Band practising in the band room could be heard. I can see my uncle playing the bass and the young Derek Redman and Stan Howe on the cornet stand.

On the swings the children are playing a game, swinging as high as possible, and then on the forward swing sliding off the seat, and seeing how far they could leap. I suppose today it would be called dangerous, but I have no recollection of anyone ever being hurt. We had lots of fun in the "rec" in those days and it was never deserted.

In the south western corner of the recreation field is the Llanharan Rugby Club, standing on the site of the old Workmen's and Public Institute Hall. We knew it as the Workman's Hall and it was a very popular meeting place.

Here a game of billiards or snooker could be played, the daily papers read, or just a place to sit and chat. It was also used however by the local Drama Society, and from time to time a travelling Repertory Company would call to put on plays for the enjoyment of the local population.

It was the venue for the annual Christmas concert, given by Lady Blandy Jenkins. It was at this concert that a large amount of meat and poultry was distributed to members of the audience. This concert complemented the party given every summer, by the same lady, to the children of the village, and held in the grounds of Llanharan House.

Re-entering Bridgend Road I find the Royal British Legion Club a totally different place to the one standing there when I left the village. Then it was a building constructed in the main of old railway sleepers, and built by volunteers.

The local branch of the British Legion had been formed around nineteen twenty four and their first meetings were held in a shed or garage at the rear of The Square. This early Club Room was approached by using the lane leading from Bridgend Road, and running between the old Post Office and the rear of the shops and houses on The Square.

It was in the early nineteen thirties that it moved to its present site, becoming a meeting place for the ex-servicemen but one with a difference, it sported an air rifle range.

The range was, if my memory serves me correctly, about twenty five to thirty feet in length and the rifles were of B.S.A. manufacture firing lead pellets. The target consisted of a metal disc, six inches in diameter, with a three eighth of an inch hole in the centre for the "bull" and lit by a well protected electric light. The target was covered with white paint and when struck by the pellet would show a black mark, indicating the precise position of the shot. Each shot was painted out before the next was fired. The ringing of a bell, positioned behind the central hole, signified the scoring of a bull. A competitor was allowed seven shots, scoring five for the bull, with the outer rings counting four, three, two and one.

All firing was from the standing position but youngsters, as I was then, were allowed to use a trestle as a support for the barrel of the heavy air rifle.

There were several air rifle clubs in the neighbouring towns and villages and matches were often arranged between them. It was then a popular sport and the club was well supported. Jack Padfield, the local insurance agent who lived near The Square, and my father had many a friendly contest with, over the period of the range's existence, honours being shared.

The same field was the site for the annual visit of Freeman's Fair, and a time for the youngsters of the village to have lots of fun. The chair plane was always the central attraction with its organ music filling the evening air and its many lights creating a kaleidoscope of colour. Paying one's penny, holding on to the seat in front, and then swinging out over the people watching below, was the fun of the fair.

There were the side shows, rolling a penny down a chute to land in a numbered square and clearing the black lines, the coconut shy, the hoop-la and the swinging boats for all ages to enjoy. Inevitably the day of departure would arrive, and the fair be dismantled packed up and hauled away by those beautiful fairground steam engines, leaving the village to look forward to its return the following year.

Across the road I can see the haberdashery shop once owned and run by Miss Powell. In the year that Princess Marina of Greece married the Duke of Kent everything was called after the princess. It was Princess Marina this, and Princess Marina that. I remember buying a Princess Marina apron as a Christmas present for my mother, price one shilling and sixpence, from this very shop. I wonder what seven and a half pence would buy today.

There was a shop just a few doors from that of Miss Powell and known by some as the "Monkey" shop. It was there in the mid nineteen twenties that Mr. & Mrs. Price Evans ran their general store. I know they sold toys so perhaps they had a monkey on a string hanging in the window. I don't know really, but the shop no longer exists.

Mr. Price Evans was a native of Llangollen and had worked in the slate quarries there for many years. When they closed he, like many others, headed for South Wales seeking employment as a collier in one or other of the pits. He settled in Llanharan and with Mrs. Price Evans raised their family of four children. He was a very good watch-maker and a keen motor cyclist.

As I pass Joe David's garage I note the absence of the red "Shell" and green "B.P." hand operated pumps. They are probably collector's items today. The "Redex" upper cylinder lubricant dispenser, that was once on the right hand door, can no longer be seen. The price of petrol has risen somewhat, from the one shilling and sixpence a gallon that my father paid, when buying his from Joe's garage. Folk no longer bring their accumulators here for charging, as they did in the early days of wireless, for just as the acetylene lamp was made redundant by the battery, so was the accumulator, by mains electricity and the battery eliminator.

I move on passing the Arcadia Billiard Hall, where Mr. Sheppard and then Mr. Gwyn Howells were in turn the proprietors. I played my very first game in this hall and although I never progressed beyond the novice stage, the sight of it brings back memories of many a happy half an hour spent trying to play the game. A foot stool was provided to enable youngsters like myself to reach the table.

Passing where once Charlie Basso had his ice cream shop, I am reminded of him pushing his ice cream barrow along the back of Brook Terrace and of buying a halfpenny cornet. It was no mean feat to push a full barrow up Hillside Avenue and around that part of the village. He sold lovely ice cream and it was always a treat to see him.

In this part of the village the aroma of freshly-baked bread was ever present, coming from Richardson's Bakery. Bread and confectionery baked here was delivered to the north side of the village by Mr. Gore. His bread van was drawn by a well groomed horse, and he could be found delivering his orders on most days of the week. Those of us privileged to have known him will remember the wonderful smell, and the warmth that emerged from that van when the rear doors were opened. At Christmas time some people would bring their cakes and puddings to the bakery for cooking. This was a part of the Richardson's service.

Mrs. Dutton's shop where we bought our sweets, one ounce for a halfpenny, was a general store and stocked most household items. The sound of my mother's voice asking me to go to Mrs. Dutton's for this or that still rings in my ears. Crockery was always in demand, with it not seeming so durable then as it is today. There was however always a plentiful supply in her shop. She was a friendly person, and had good relations with all her customers.

I pause as I reach the next shop, closed, and with its windows made opaque. The sign in the window reads the headquarters of the local C.N.D.

movement but for me it is still Lusardi's.

It is where in the early nineteen thirties the then teenagers met to sit and talk, play on the pin table, or drink hot cordials. Mr. Lusardi was thirty years ahead of his time in providing for us a coffee shop meeting place such as those that became popular in the nineteen sixties. A win on the pin table was rewarded with half a dozen bars of Rowntree's "Motoring" chocolate, or some similar type.

It was in this shop that I first tasted the "Milkyway" and "Aero" when they were introduced to the market, and where I bought my first packet of cigarettes. A large variety of tobacco was stocked, all stored in beautiful china pots arranged on shelves at the back of the counter. Of all the shops in the village this without doubt was my favourite.

The gully running alongside the shop and leading to the lane at the rear of Bridgend Road also led to the entrance of Lusardi's Hall, where I sometimes played with Dante and Gloria, Mr. Lusardi's children. The hall at that time was a roller skating rink, built like a deep-sided saucer to make high speed skating easier. I cannot remember it ever being used on a commercial basis so perhaps the venture failed. I hope not. Lusardi's shop and Hall provided me with a host of treasured memories for which I am most grateful.

Looking along the back lane I am disappointed to find that it has received a rough coating of concrete, an attempt I presume to appease the motoring public. Gone is the lane I knew, where we played marbles, cat and doggy, flicked cigarette cards, shot darts from our "Daisy" and "Diana" air guns at targets pinned to a shed door; where we played cricket with a household shovel for a bat, and an upturned ash bucket for a wicket. The chickens that once strutted around clucking loudly would be hard-pressed to find any grit today. Pen-y-Waen field where we shot our bows and arrows, flew kites and held our own sports until chased by the farmer, has gone, buried beneath a concrete jungle. What, and where, do the children of today play? Sad at what I have seen I retrace my footsteps and am glad to be back in Bridgend Road where little seems to have changed.

Passing Dick Freeman's, the butchers shop, I can visualise the brawn, the faggots, the rabbits, the sausage, also the various cuts of meat that once filled the window. At Christmas it was poultry, for it was then that the people scrimped and scraped to afford a chicken, duck or goose. I don't recall anyone being able to afford a turkey.

I find myself thinking of the days that we, my school pal Bill Watkins and myself, went rabbit shooting with Mr. Freeman and his assistants, the men doing the shooting and us collecting and carrying the rabbits on a long pole. How things change, and how different it all is today when we can just trot off to the local supermarket, and buy what we require straight from the deep freeze.

I am now in a very familiar part of the village, where because traffic was light, we were able to play whip and top on the road. Using a leather boot lace on a stick for a whip, it was possible to make the top jump large distances. In winter when the road was frozen over, we made those long slides that were so popular with the children of that era. There was traffic, and from time to time we would have to leave the top and jump out of the way of some mechanical monster.

There were the steam lorries with their loads of bricks or beer casks. The small red solid tyre Brooke Bond's tea van, and the white van of the Phillips's tea company. Then there were the milk lorries that were beginning to use the road, and of course the motor car, with the cumbersome steam roller putting in an appearance from time to time. Traffic was on the increase but speeds were such that danger was really non existent.

Now the family names begin to come back as I pass familiar houses; Pontin, Carter, Childs, Jenkins, Howells, Casley, Marlin, Pascoe, Worgan, Watkins, Riddler and Evans all readily spring to mind. I recall Cyril Rogers living with his grandmother in Jubilee Street, joining the Royal Engineers as an apprentice and going to Chepstow to do his training. Stan Howe taking the King's shilling and joining a Highland regiment as a bandsman. Bill Watkins enlisting in the Royal Air Force as an apprentice, and training at Cranwell. Mrs. Carter's eldest son serving on the battleship "Royal Sovereign", and Mickey Childs, whose parents lived in Chiswick, coming regularly to stay with his grandparents. There was the phantom whistler, a man who could be heard whistling his way to work along Bridgend Road in the early hours of the morning. He was able to whistle most beautifully. However, not all appreciated his talents at that time of the day.

Number fifty seven, the home of Mrs. David Jenkins, aunt "Jane". She had three children, the eldest was I believe a teacher in a London school, and I knew her as Mrs. Forrest; then there was Roy her son, and Nancy her other daughter. Mrs. Forrest spent her summer holidays with her mother and naturally brought her son David. It was on one of these holidays that the young boy, no more than a few years old, was involved in an accident at home and sadly died in Cardiff Infirmary.

His death affected both Bill Watkins and myself very deeply for we had taken him to heart and loved looking after him.

Roy on leaving school started work in Mr. Gower's chemist shop in The Square. He worked there until, one evening in the summer of nineteen thirty six, he set off on his bicycle for London, and presumably a new life. I met Nancy on one of my infrequent visits to the village, she had married and was living in the house that her mother had occupied for most of her life.

Mr. & Mrs. Gwyn Howells resided in number fifty nine, this was before they moved to the Arcadia Billiard Hall. Living with them was Mrs. Howells' brother Morgan Evans, known affectionately as "Mog" Evans. He was a popular member of the Llanharan Cricket Club and Stonewall Mog was usually one of the opening pair of batsmen. Mrs. Edith Howells was very popular and well liked by the children who frequented the lane, for she would often join in many games being played there.

Passing the shops on either corner of Jubilee Street, both of which were grocers' shops and of no interest to me as a child, I reach a door on which I had knocked many times. It was the home of a lady, her name I just cannot recall, who brewed dandelion "pop" and ginger beer. On a hot summer's day there was nothing nicer than quenching one's thirst with a glass of this home made nectar. Her cottage industry was very well supported and priced at just twopence a flagon it was good value for money.

Across the road in number seventy one I was born, my parents then living with my father's eldest sister Mrs. Williams. Not remembering anything about the house I pass on.

Living on the same side of the road, but further along, was the celebrated boxer Sid Worgan and his parents. I wonder if he ever finished building the gymnasium in Pen-y-Maen field, opposite the gully. Sid was a very well-respected boxer of the modern era, and much has been written about his success in the ring, but living nearby was one of the old time pugilists, one who had had many bare-fist bouts.

Mr. William Watkins was my school pal's father, and one who enjoyed telling a tale. We sat and listened in awe at the stories he told of his prize-fighting days. How he tramped many times from Chirk to South Wales, summer and winter, sleeping under hedgerows, washing in streams and shaving with an open razor and no soap, taking fights when and where he could get them. He told of how he had sat with his hands soaking in vinegar for many hours, trying to harden his fists. He recalled the names of many of his opponents as he reminisced about the illegal fights that had taken place in yards at the rear of public houses and other out of sight places.

He and Mrs. Watkins had three sons, the two eldest served in the Welsh Guards and Bill, as mentioned before, served in the Royal Air Force. They were all good athletes and the silverware displayed on their sideboard was proof of their sporting successes.

On reaching the corner of Llanharry Road and glancing across I can see Mr. Pascoe's butchers shop and The Emporium on the corner of Robert Street. The picture in my mind's eye is of Mr. Phillips, the proprietor, standing in the doorway and looking for customers. His shop was the village outfitters, where one went for new suits, usually jacket and shorts, when needed, and when our parents could afford to buy them, which was not very often.

Over the way, on a fine day, the young men of this part of the village would gather to sit and chat, or play a game of quoits. The game was played by driving a metal spike into the ground and throwing old horseshoes from a set distance. The object being to "ring" the spike with the horseshoe.

Sometimes the sound of music could be heard as Jim Riddler strummed his banjo, or as he taught youngsters to play the mandolin. All it needed was a fine day and they would be there.

Llanharry Road made a great children's playground as it carried very little traffic. Roller skating on one or two skates was very popular, and in winter when the road was frozen over it was another ideal place to make slides. Children riding cycles backwards and playing with homemade four wheeled bogies was a common sight. The road led to Primrose Hill where, on a Sunday afternoon, in the spring, children went picking primroses, hence its name.

When the hill was the subject of a road widening scheme a tomb of a Roman soldier was found. An earthenware pot containing Roman coins had been buried with him and this was also unearthed. It is now in the National Museum at Cardiff.

The Meadow was also reached by using the old or new road and it was there that we, as children, braved the geese to get to our favourite blackberry-picking areas. Those geese always seemed to chase us, or so we thought, perhaps it was just that they needed feeding.

Walking by Manchester House, Mrs. John's wool shop, I think of all the tangled skeins of wool that my mother bought from her, and of how winding into a ball was a slow and tedious task. How it managed to become so entangled we never knew. My mother was an avid knitter so my brother and I were glad when she was able to buy balls of ready wound wool. Mother John, as she was affectionately called by us, never knew how much we blessed her.

Reaching the end of Rose Terrace I find the shop that was once a soup kitchen. In the "Good Old Days" as some people still like to think of them, some children ran from school at dinner time hoping to find the kitchen open. If it was, they were given a bowl of pea soup and a hunk of bread. On the days when supplies were not available, the kitchen remained closed and the children returned to school hungry. What would those children have given for school dinners?

I cross to the other side of Harold Street, and again peer into what was Mrs. Sheen's shop window. I can see myself, standing there nose pressed flat against the window, wishing I had this, and wishing I had that. In the window on the right hand side as one enters the shop, was a board displaying all the spare parts for the "Mecanno" sets. Then there were the "Hornby" clockwork train sets, the "Daisy" and "Diana" air guns and pistols, all manner of clockwork toys, as well as dolls, and prams, and a host of other toys of that period.

The boxes of lead soldiers, so popular then, are sought after by collectors world wide today. All mechanical toys were made of tin, others were of wood as plastic had not been invented. Around bonfire night it was fireworks that were the main attraction, and Mrs. Sheen always had a plentiful supply of them. It was a veritable Aladdin's cave. I wonder how many children have pressed their noses against that window and "wished".

Leaving the Gospel Hall in my wake I arrive at what was once the entrance to the Powell Dyffryn Colliery, later called the Llanharan Colliery. It is now closed, and the site is being cleared for other industrial purposes. The history of this colliery is well documented, and stories of the men who once worked there will be told for years to come. For me, a schoolboy on his way to school, it was the sight of bicycles stacked in racks on the other side of the road that I remember.

In those days the bicycle was the main mode of transport, and the only way for some colliers to get to work. They were left in the safe custody of a caretaker while they did their shift. Any punctures or minor mechanical failures sustained while on their way to work were repaired by the time the shift was completed. On collection the cycle would be in a fit state to ride home.

Leaving the colliery I pass the site of a wooden bungalow, long since gone, where an aunt of mine once lived before the family emigrated to Canada. The site was buried beneath a conical tip, which has now been removed under the colliery redevelopment scheme.

On the other side of the road is the farm, remembered by me for the outbreak of foot and mouth disease it suffered in the early nineteen thirties. Consequently there was an absence of cattle from the fields for a very long time. It must have been a heart-breaking time for the farmer and his family as they watched the destruction of their herd of cattle.

Standing at the boy's entrance to Dolau Primary School, I have reached the end of my journey in this direction. Much has been written about this school, of its headmaster, Mr. D. Emlyn Davies of Newcastle Emlyn a former head of Brynna School, and all the teachers who toiled ceaselessly to educate the children of the community.

As I stand now outside its gates, I silently thank Miss Pearl Kingsley and Miss Irene Morris B.A., for my early education and for the valuable lessons that they taught me. There were of course all the other teachers, but these two stand out in my memory.

I fancy I can hear again the strains of "Blaze Away" being played on the gramophone, as we march from the school yard into the assembly hall. The sound of children at play fills the air, the playground is alive with children enjoying themselves, girls skip and chant their favourite ditty, some boys play leapfrog or football while others swap cigarette cards. Varied were the activities of the school playground.

At Christmas we enjoyed making those paper chains and lanterns to decorate our classrooms, receiving some "goodies" such as a Clarnico Bar, Wrigley's P.K. and Spearmint chewing gum, or orange maybe and a paper puzzle or two.

On St. David's Day morning we had a concert in the assembly hall, when individual children performed various acts for the benefit of the school. I wonder where the young ballet dancer who danced the part of the dying swan from the Swan Lake Ballet, the young lad who played a cornet solo and many others are today. When the concert was over the pupils went home, as there was always a half day holiday on our Patron Saint's day.

Standing there outside the gate, I find myself thinking about the boys and girls who attended this school in its early days. Those undernourished children who received a spoonful of Cod Liver Oil and Malt every morning. There were those who received a free issue of boots, distributed to the needy from time to time. No doubt many will have survived the ravages of war, and peace, and can be found today in many countries throughout the world.

Retracing my footsteps, I return to Jubilee Street, and as I pass along its length the names of Mr. & Mrs. Ware and Mr. & Mrs. Pick are brought back from the corners of my mind. I am heading for what was once the ash path that led to Chapel Road. It is no longer an ash path as it has been made up, and now forms a pleasant walk from one part of the village to another.

Crossing the main line I wonder if trains still slow down at this point, and whether the subsidence caused by the colliery working has ceased. Trains arriving at or leaving Llanharan Station travelled at a walking pace, and had done so for as long as I can remember.

The removal of the coal tips, brought about by the closure of Llanharan Colliery, has changed much of the landscape. One day perhaps, after mother nature has healed the scarred land, it will recapture the beauty it must have once held.

Crossing Chapel Road, I climb the footpath leading to Brook Terrace and stand in front of my old home. Through misty eyes I see my father, wearing his artificial arm, digging the front garden. My mother is hanging out the washing and praying it won't be covered in coal dust. In his pram, near the front door, my brother lies sleeping, and there I am, being given a swing by my cousin Elizabeth.

Our neighbours were, on the one side Mr. Perkins, a coal merchant whose hobby was keeping greyhounds, and on the other Mr. & Mrs. Ducker. In the end house lived Mr. & Mrs. Rees with their daughters Megan and Nancy. Unfortunately the passing years have dimmed my memory and I am unable to recall the occupants of other houses.

On a Sunday morning the air was filled with the sound of hymn singing, drifting up from the Welsh Chapel below. There were no children at play, and no washing hanging out to dry. It was on Sunday that a fire was lit in the parlour or front room. The day we put on our best clothes and attended Sunday school. A day to take flowers to the cemetery, and lay them on the graves of loved ones, and a day, during good weather, to go for a walk. Now, it seems that the day itself will eventually become the subject of future history books.

Walking to the end of the path and up School Hill I reach Park Terrace. It was in this road that I kicked my first ball, first grazed my knees, bought my first ice cream cornet from Charlie Basso and first saw Mr. Gore delivering the bread in his horse-drawn van. Again I try putting names to houses. Mr. & Mrs. Evans in number one, number four Mr. & Mrs. Islwyn Jones, five Mr. & Mrs. Cogbill, six Mr. & Mrs. Owen Parry with their eight children, seven Mr. & Mrs. Jones, eight Mr. & Mrs. Austin with their daughters Nora, Phyllis and Enid and number nine Mr. & Mrs. North. Of all these I know the whereabouts of just one, Grace Parry, who on marriage became Mrs. Orchard and lived for many years on the Isle of Wight. She now lives in Saltney, on the outskirts of Chester. Sighing with nostalgia I turn and make my way to the top of the hill.

Standing on the corner of Brynna Road and School Hill, I find myself thinking of those with whom I went to school. David Parry, who lived in the Cemetery House and on whom we could rely to produce a ball with which to play handball in the school "Tally Court" at Cowbridge. There was Dilwyn Cogbill, who lived just across the road on Hillside Avenue, and with whom I played rugby in the under fifteen side at school.

Roy Martin also resided on Hillside Avenue. He had a distinguished flying career with the Royal Air Force during the Second World War, and was awarded the D.F.M. He and I met one evening in Chapel Road, and despite not having seen each other for more than fifty years, greeted each other with a warm handshake, a "Hi Ya Cliff" and "Hi Ya Roy". Since commencing this little story I have been informed that he has passed away. It is sad to think that another life has run its course, but I am sure that Roy will be remembered by all who were privileged to know him.

I have reached my final destination, the War Memorial, standing proudly at the bottom of Hillside Avenue. My father would have been very pleased to see it standing here today, in the heart of the village, in its rightful place. I well remember his disgust when it was moved to the Welfare ground, out of sight, save for one day a year. I slowly read the names of those who fell in the two World Wars, and offer a silent prayer.

Llanharan, like every other city, town, and village throughout the land, is changing, that is inevitable. The sight of new buildings, and the disappearance of some old ones, is evidence of this change. The march of time sees old names disappear, to be replaced by new ones. New businesses flourish where old ones once struggled. The incessant noise of the colliery compressor has ceased, bringing a degree of peace and normality back to those who dwell within the village boundary. However, it still maintains its character, and is easily recognisable by returning expatriates.

We live in more affluent times these days, enjoying the convenience of the motor car, eating out, holidays abroad, the supermarket and increased hours of leisure. There were none of these in my childhood days, nevertheless, the people who walked these familiar streets were happy, complained little and accepted life for what it was, a challenge. Are we today, with all our modern advantages, any happier than they? I somehow doubt it.

C. Jacobsen
Prestatyn. (1997)

The Egg Well

The old 'Egg Well' on Garth Maelwg was at one time one of the most famous sulphur wells in Wales. So much so, that during the early 1900s it attracted visitors from as far afield as London and Birmingham. It was believed that the waters of the old well would cure most ills of the day, including rheumatism. Often the farms in the area were crammed with guests right through the summer.

Meiros Colliery

Most of the early mining exploitation at Meiros consisted of primitive drifts. We know that pack horses were used to convey coal into the village during the 1870s. Most of it would then be carted to nearby Llantrisant and sold while the majority was distributed to the farms and tenants of the district. The sinking of the new pit was to be the major project. In April 1880 a meeting was held between the coal owners and the Llanharan Estate. Various problems materialised from the meeting, but compromises were made by both sides and contracts were made up.

However, one momentous problem lay ahead of the new company. How were they to transport their newly found coal riches down to the Great Western Railway at nearby Llanharan village. The problem was that the land from the new colliery down to the village was owned by the Llanharan Estate then held by Caroline Ann Blandy Jenkins, mother of John Blandy Jenkins, who owned at that time nearby Tregroes house at Pencoed. John was instructed by his mother to handle her affairs with the Meiros Coal Company. It must be pointed out that John Blandy Jenkins was no stranger to the coal trade. Records show that he was in 1880 Agent to the Bute Estate, Cardiff. Much of his work centred around the valley of Gilfach Goch and the Ogmore Valley to name just two areas. It was John Blandy Jenkins who acted on behalf of the Bute Estate in the sinking of the Trane Pit in Gilfach Goch. This was the period when such great names as Archibald Hood and David Llewellyn were the coal barons of the day. Up until recent years the Blandy link with the Ogmore Valley was quite strong with

an inn named Llanharan Hotel and a street named Llanharan Terrace, supposedly named after our squire. (The Llanharan Hotel is now demolished).

The first move by the owners of the new colliery was to lay down a track from the colliery to the siding of the G.W.R. Also, a four track siding to accommodate the coal trucks near the railway had to be set up. Four engineers and sixty men were employed in the venture. A cutting was mooted down through Talyfan field towards Llanharan village, and large wooden bridges were erected over the lanes and roadways. The late Mrs. Sarah Holland Miles (see "Forgotten Years" volume I) told of the Temperance and Chapel movements who rebelled at the building of the bridges on Sundays. The Chapel members rallied with banners shouting down the workers as they went about their labours.

Such was the anger vented by the religious denominations that the colliery owners relented. A letter was addressed to all the local Chapels and an apology was given stating that all work on the Lord's day would cease forthwith. But it was a known fact that the delay was a thorn in the side of the colliery owners. To keep on the time schedule, the men worked double shifts. The undertaking took eleven months to complete. As the years went by various alterations to the route took place (see "Forgotten Years" volume III).

The late Mr. Edgar Hole, Llanharan, who himself was a local historian and former miner at Meiros colliery, remembered the squire during his rare visits to the colliery. Such visits he informed, resembled a Royal occasion, with everyone running about trying to impress him. Such were the powers of the squire of Llanharan House.

By 1888 a clear picture emerges. The colliery plant was now known as The Llanharan Welsh Estates & Property Company Limited, Cardiff, and employed two hundred and twenty eight men. We learn that from the contract between the Llanharan House Estates and the colliery, for all wagons of coal that crossed the bridge on the Square in the village, the Estate received 2d. (old money) per ton. By 1912 the price had risen to 4d. per ton.

The link between squire and colliery was certainly an amicable one. Once a year a lavish dinner and social evening would be arranged at Llanharan House. This saw the gathering of the owners and their families. After the death of our squire in 1915, the practise ceased. Although we learn that Elizabeth Nora, the squire's widow, kept on amicable terms with the owners right up until the closure of Meiros in 1931.

The late Mr. Harry Sheppard, Llanharan, during an interview stated that one of the rules of the contract was that under no circumstances should mining exploration travel under Llanharan House. Although Llanharan colliery mined the area extensively eastward, it is believed today that the House stands on unmined foundations.

Sadly we can but only trim at the edges of history. Without written documentation we are so to speak 'lost in the mists of antiquity'. I have, during my researches, worked to obtain facts on the life and times of people, events and developments appertaining to the growth of our community. Fortunately, most of my work is fully recorded for posterity. I was devastated to learn that the Llanharan House Estate books were burned and destroyed in 1953. Two volumes survived the fire, and I have been most fortunate in reading the contents of both, which I put to good use in my series. These books are now owned by Mr. Dewi Rees, Bryn Farm, Pendoylan, to whom I am greatly indebted.

Sources:
"Glynogwr & Gilfach Goch" by Meirion Davies (1981)

Interviews with:
Mrs. Sarah Holland Miles
– November 3 1965

Mr. Edgar Hole
– January 8 1971

Mr. Harry Sheppard
– May 11 1971.

MEIROS MINES

We know that an early 1825 venture took place at Meiros with small outcrop drift mines. Local business people tried various means of coal exploitation there. Names listed as coal owners are as follows: John Miles, William Holland and Joseph Millard. These mountain drifts were not all that successful but as far as the owners were concerned the business kept them employed covering local needs. A far more adventurous drift came into being in 1826. This drift was called Meirose (Meiros) Coal Works. Owners recorded are: Harry Thomas, Morgan Morgan and Daniel Morgan. Their drift and company worked under various names right up until the opening of the major deep mine at Meiros in 1880. Published records for Meiros begin in 1907.

When the Meiros Deep Mine was sunk in 1880, it had two structural points unique to this area. Firstly, the pit head gear was made of wood. Secondly, the pit shaft was unusual because it was oval shaped. It was mined this way because of the shale and loose ground difficulty during sinking operations.

The Meiros Colliery shafts were two hundred yards deep and penetrating the No. 3 seam and the Pentre seams which proved to be valuable gas coals. The colliery was listed in 1888 as owned by the Llanharan Welsh Estate and Property Company Ltd., and employed two hundred and twenty eight men. By 1908, the colliery became known as Meiros Gas Coal Collieries Ltd.

Meiros Colliery was regarded as a safe pit giving a hard rock roof which has been described to me by many of the former miners as "good conditions". However, Meiros, in its day, received many vexatious setbacks, mostly from the danger of explosions. The Inspectorate of Mines reports contain the following references to fatalities at Meiros:- 1896, one killed, 1911, two killed. There are also non fatal accidents at the colliery in 1899, 1902, 1903 and 1907. It must be pointed out that naked lights were in use at Meiros up until at least 1914. Also in this year, the company became known as Meiros Collieries Ltd.

We have already learned about the Thomas James Masters and Solomon Andrews ownership of Meiros in my "Forgotten Years" series. Their rare visits to the colliery always caused panic amongst the officials and men. The Colliery Manager under the Masters-Andrews ownership was a Mr. Thomas Hopkins. Hopkins was a mining engineer held in high repute. The colliery's peak period was during the early 1920s and in 1921 eight hundred were employed at the mine. The manager replacing Hopkins was another respected individual from Kenfig Hill in the form of James Lewis. James Lewis was a keen advocate of mines safety and encouraged far more stringent rules to the rescue team which was operating on his arrival. The company with the controlling interest in the mid twenties was Guest Keen and Nettlefolds, Cardiff, and remained so until 1931. The Meiros undertaking was acquired by Guest Keen to make available the large output of gas coal in the pit. But over the years as existing seams approached exhaustion, the quality deteriorated and economic operations became increasingly difficult. Finally, in the June of 1931, the Meiros Colliery closed.

Sources: Richard Hoare Jenkins by Trefor Rees M.B.E., Miskin, Pontyclun.
Mines Inspectorate Report 1896

MEIROS COLLIERY, OWNERS AND MEN FROM 1907

Meiros Colliery No. 2 and 3

Commenced 1888 Llanharan Welsh Estate & Property Co. Ltd.

Coal Company	Company/Managers	Mine Manager	Men Employed
Meiros Gas Coal Collieries Ltd.	W.E. Nance T.H. Hopkins 1 St Mary Street Cardiff		
1907	"	"	364
1908	"	"	364
1909/10	"	Ernest Brett	365
1911	"	"	365
1912	"	"	335
1913	H. Yorath 1 Stuart Square Cardiff.	S.R. Hopkins	300
1914	"	T.H. Hopkins	300
Meiros Collieries Ltd. 1915	W.E. Dash Marine Buildings Mount Stuart Square Cardiff.	"	200
1916	"	"	200
1917	"	D.M. Arbuckle (Agent)	500
1918	"	"	500
1919	"	"	500
1920	"	"	600
1921	Guest Keen and Nettlefolds Ltd Marine Buildings Mount Stuart Square Cardiff. (Subsidiary John Lysaght Ltd)	"	700
1922	"	"	700
1923	"	"	700
1924	"	"	700
1925	"	No Listed Manager	700
1926	"	James Lewis	450
1927	"	"	455
1928	G.K.N. National Provincial Bank Blds, Cardiff	"	450
1929	"	"	450
1930	"	"	450
Meiros Colliery Ltd. 1931	H. Glyn Roberts	"	451

Mine closed 16 June 1931. Company wound up by March Son & Co., Chartered Accountants, Baltic House, Mount Stuart Square, Cardiff.

Source: Colliery Managers Year Books 1907/8; South Wales Coal Annuals 1904 - 1937

Some of the staff of Meiros Colliery Carriage & Wagon Company Ltd.

The only people recognised on this photograph are Mr. George Allan (far right with painting stick in hand) and Mr. Pontin of Harold Street, Llanharan (fourth left, back row). The Carriage & Wagon Works was situated near the viaduct bridge on the Square, Llanharan. c. 1923.

THE 'YARD STICK' MAN

Jacob Woberton could be described as quite simply illiterate. He could not even write his name and after living on this earth for seventy six years went to his grave still unable to provide his signature. With such sad qualifications our story about this likable mining individual must be regarded as one of unique quality.

Jacob came to Llanharan from Cinderford in 1895. He found lodgings with a Mr. Charles Payne, who owned Rhiwperra Cottage which stood on the left hand side near the top of the old Hollands Lane (now demolished). Jacob, after settling in the old cottage found work in the nearby Meiros colliery. Being illiterate didn't stop our hero from making his mark at Meiros. His ability in supervising the driving of main headings was soon noted. His knowledge of facework supervision was also keenly scrutinised. But also recognised by management was his inability to read, write or perform easy mathematical problems. On paper that is. The colliery management was astounded because Jacob's ability to counteract working problems in the headings was astronomical. A logical enquiry was made to Jacob by the manager, Mr. Thomas Hopkins. Evidently Jacob had spent several years in the drift mines in the Forest of Dean. It seems that basic instinct and the interest and desire to do well had put him in good stead. It is a known fact that in those early pioneering days the Forest of Dean miners were regarded as some of the best in the country. Jacob had simply listened and learned from the older miners, picking their brains as he went along. But what confused the management at Meiros was the fact that with Jacob being unable to do the simplest of sums, how come his heading work was so mathematically correct. Mr. Hopkins was astounded when he learned the truth. Jacob produced a yard stick (old measuring system three feet in a yard). The yard stick was Jacob's main instrument of daily work underground. His work was unquestionable and soon Jacob was made an official of the colliery. Walking around the mining areas of Meiros with his stick in his hand soon had him branded the 'Yard Stick' man.

Jacob's way of measuring was unique to say the least. This is how he would describe a given measurement to the manager.

(Area 2'9") – "JUST UNDER A YARD SIR".

(Area 3'2") – "ONE YARD AND STANDING PROUD SIR".

(Area 6'4") – "TWO YARDS AND STANDING PROUD SIR".

(Area 5'10") – "TWO YARDS WITH A LITTLE LOSS SIR".

Some of the miners used to get him in the pub and try to teach him how to work in inches, but they failed miserably. Whatever, Jacob lived into his seventy sixth year while living his final days near Llandaff, Cardiff. For years after the colliery closed the name of Jacob Woberton lived on with local tales of the 'Yard Stick' man.

Source:
Interview with Mr. Harry Sheppard for "Forgotten Years" series November 1975.

Meiros Colliery Rescue Team, early 1920s.

Centre of picture, front row, is Mr. William John Harris who sadly died following an accident at Llanharan colliery in 1931.

Mr. Reg Hutchins

Mr. Jack Wintle

Meiros Colliery Rescue Team Practice.

Mr. Reg Hutchins was one of the early pioneers of the rescue section at Meiros Colliery. Our photograph shows Mr. Hutchins during a rescue practice at the pit. In charge of the rescue unit was Mr. James Lewis, Manager; it was a very efficient unit indeed. Mr. Jack Wintle was described as one of the most dedicated rescuers. During his period with the rescue unit he was known to design various tools for dealing with numerous situations underground. In his last years with the team he had worked his way up to Team Captain.

MR. JAMES LEWIS, MANAGER, MEIROS

Mr. Lewis came to Meiros colliery during the early 1900s. He was a strict advocate for safety at Meiros and encouraged continuous practice with the Mines Rescue Team which was a prominent feature at the pit. The Meiros, despite having a number of fatalities during its years of existence, had, on average, an excellent record. Mr. Lewis was manager of the colliery up until its closure in 1932.

THE ELECTRIC LIGHT MIRACLE

One of the quaintest stories to materialise during my researches came from Mr. Edgar Hole, during an interview in 1971. He tells of the first experiment of electric light in the village in 1897. Evidently, this miracle materialised through the generosity of the Meiros Coal Company. We learn that our Squire, Colonel John Blandy Jenkins, Llanharan House, approached the Meiros management inquiring whether it would be possible to conduct their electricity down from the

mine to the Square. He informed the owners that a large gathering was expected at a Hunt dinner and function in the High Corner House, pointing out that if the area around the Inn could be lit up it would prove an asset in organising the large contingent of pony and traps expected. The Meiros Company were only too pleased to oblige. They immediately set up their system of lights on the trees which were standing on the Square. Mr. Hole stated that on the night of the Hunt function the village was full with local people to witness the switching on of the new fangled 'electric light'. It must be remembered that in 1897 the only light available to the village folk was paraffin storm lamps.

The Meiros Company allowed the lights to remain on the Square for one month, being switched on every Friday night. On each occasion the crowds turned up to wonder at the scene. It is understood that the electricity was created through large generators which were installed at Meiros colliery. When the lights were eventually taken away from the village the inhabitants wrote to the Meiros Company by petition asking for them to be returned. The company declined, and only the passing of time saw the introduction of electric light in the village. Mr. Edgar Hole recalled one elderly gentleman named Dick Rees, who was in his mid eighties, making the following statement on seeing the lights for the first time:

"Duw, duw, I never thought that I would see 'lectric in my lifetime. What a wonder it is to look at indeed....."

With such a statement, the mind boggles to think what the old man would have said if he had witnessed the introduction of aeroplanes or television today. Mr. Edgar Hole himself was born in 1888, and saw the introduction of the above-mentioned. He categorically stated during my interview with him that he preferred the old way of life. The old cultures, friendships and tranquility of those early days meant a lot to him.

Welcome 1915, goodbye 1880. George Frederick Tasker, master sinker (left) poses for the camera with his stackbuilding crew. (November 1915). This is a unique print as it shows the old 1880 stack at the side of the modern 1915 structure. Immediately after this photograph was taken the old 1880 stack was demolished.

Meiros Colliery 1915

Glamorgan Education Committee.

An Authority recognised by the Secretary of State for the purpose of granting Certificates to Colliery Firemen, Examiners or Deputies.

COAL MINES ACT, 1911.

Certificate of Qualification of Fireman, Examiner, or Deputy under Section 15 (1) (b)

This is to Certify that

Richard Donovan

residing at 26 *Heathfield Crescent, Brynene, Llanharan*

has been duly examined and has satisfied the examiners

That he is able to make accurate tests (so far as practicable with a safety lamp) for inflammable gas:

That he is able to measure the quantity of air in an air current:

That his hearing is such as to enable him to carry out efficiently the duties of fireman, examiner, or deputy.

(Signature of person authorised in that behalf by the approved School, Institution or Authority.)

W. Jenkins
(Chairman).

Date

Name of approved School, Institution or Authority.

Glamorgan Education Committee.

Reg No. 364/37

Fireman's Qualification Certificate.
During the 1920s Llanharan Primary School was used by the Meiros Colliery as a Classes and Examination Centre. Evening classes enabled mining personnel to get their Classified Certificates for Qualified Firemen and Examiners or Deputy Permits.

EDGAR HOLE AND THE 1896 EXPLOSION

Mr. Edgar Hole was born in the 'Castle Cottage' which, before demolition, was situated above the Mill House, Llanharan. His father, John Limebeer Hole was a Devonshire man who came into the village with the opening of Meiros colliery. At Meiros, he was to become a deputy-fireman, a position which sadly was to end in tragic circumstances.

2 February 1896, Edgar was seven years old. At the Meiros pit that day his father was going about his duties on the east side of the workings. It was 7.00 a.m. when the explosion occurred. Edgar Hole takes up the story:

"My mother was one of the first people to know in the village of the accident underground. One of the officials from the colliery was sent down to tell her that my father had been caught in the explosion, but was out of the pit and would be fetched home shortly. About 8.00 a.m. my father arrived home, he had a towel around his face and shoulders and was led into the house by a Mr. David Evans, another official who lived in nearby Llanharry. We could see that dad was badly burned. Within the hour a doctor came to him. My father was then covered in what looked like very thin tissue paper. He was taken into the living room and put to sit upright in a chair where he stayed silent for three days before he died. My mother had sat up with him the whole time, I don't think she had any sleep for the whole three days and nights. I shall never forget my father sitting there, he was a terrible sight. I am sure that if it had been today he would have been rushed straight to Chepstow and possibly lived through the ordeal."

The explosion in which John Limebeer

Mr. Edgar Hole (left) while working at Llanbad Colliery, Brynna.

Hole died is recorded for 2 February 1896. The report states that one man died and eleven were injured. See Meiros colliery (file on explosions) in "Forgotten Years" Vol. III, page 89.

On a lighter note, Edgar Hole brings to mind a sharp and realistic look at Llanharan and its early village life. Generously, he recalls that in the year 1895 the only building between the Square and Dolau on the left hand side of the road was the Welsh Methodist Chapel. The Welsh Chapel played a small but significant part in Edgar's life. In 1918, after purchasing a violin and having only had ten lessons, he went along to the Welsh chapel and accompanied a service there. We learn that he was asked to return on several occasions after that.

Llanharan, during the days of Edgar Hole was a picture card scene. He tells of a large water pump situated on the Square, just outside the High Corner House. During the dark winter evenings you would see the people going about their business carrying hand lanterns, electric light a thing very much of the future. In 1893, Edgar was allowed to go to school with his sisters. Llanharan Primary had been opened for one year only, being built in 1892. The headmaster of the school was a Mr. John Smith who was a devout disciplinarian. We learn however, that he was also a caring headmaster. If he saw a child genuinely falling behind with schoolwork, he would take an interest and even go to the point of meeting the parents.

During the summer months after school, Edgar spent a lot of his time up at Whitehall Farm. The farmer there then was a Mr. David Davies. At Whitehall Edgar spent most of his time in the barn crushing up swedes for cows, a practice not often seen today. He was paid for his labours the princely sum of 1/-d. (5p) plus free supper. Later, he worked for a Mr. Ivor John who had a grocery shop on the Square. At Mr. John's he earned 2/6d a week (12$\frac{1}{2}$p) plus one meal a day. Edgar also remembers when his mother used to send him down to Bryncae Farm to see a Mr. Gwilym David. The farm sold fruit jams of a very high quality. A six pound jar of jam cost 1$\frac{1}{2}$d.

In those days travelling entertainers came to the village. They used to 'pitch up' in Sam Miles' field (now Llanharan R.F.C. Dairy Field Ground). He recalled wild animal shows coming to the village. You would pay at the gate and walk along a line of grilled cages which were stretched across the field. He told how the children of the village used to stare in awe at the unusual array of wild animals. He remembers vividly that during the animal show's two days stay, the field by night would be patrolled by the owners carrying shotguns.

On other occasions magic lantern shows were held in Sam Miles's barn. Later, the Studt family brought films into the village. These shows were put on in a shed in the field where Hillside Avenue now stands.

During the summer months water had to be carried from the pumps. Up in Meiros Lane (behind the Seymour Avenue houses) there was a well with ice cold clear water (still there today). Edgar tells a quaint story about the well. It is believed that the water source carried a religious significance concerning Baptism. The story was evidently talked about by the old folk of the day in the village. Edgar Hole himself believed that the old well should have been preserved for posterity. Described as 'Holy water' miners took bottles of it underground. Six months before his thirteenth birthday, Edgar went to Meiros colliery to seek work. Mr. Thomas Hopkins, the mine manager, told him that a new law had been introduced forbidding any lad under the age of thirteen working in the pit. Disappointed, he went back to the farm to scratch some money until his time was right. He remembers the railway station being built built in 1899; and he saw it close in 1965. He brings to mind the opening clearly because at the time all the religious denominations had banded together to stop the project. Their fears were that the thundering trains stopping at the station would destroy the peace of the village.

With his thirteenth birthday upon him, Edgar entered the mines. His first experience was at Llanbad, South Rhondda, Brynna. The colliery then was owned by W.W. Woods, Llwynypia. He recalls working in very bad conditions there. One foot ten inches and two foot seams were commonplace at Llanbad.

Not knowing how the price list for coal cutting was calculated, we can only quote from Edgar's tape:

"One shilling and five pence halfpenny a ton, plus thirty three and a third. One penny would be added for every four inches under two foot ten. If eight inches under two foot ten, then an extra two pence would be added to the one and five pence halfpenny a ton."

It was dangerous work and Edgar openly admits that he didn't like working in Llanbad colliery. He thoroughly believes that he worked through the years that fringed on the borders of slavery. But then - it was work in the pits or starve. After a period he left the mine and worked in the drifts at Brynna. There were three drifts in the area of Llanbad. They were the Ladysmith, the Klondyke and the Kimberley. He worked in all three before coming back over the mountain to work in the Meiros. Apart from better conditions in the pit, the Meiros wage structure was slightly better. They were paying one and eight pence a ton.

During his lifetime, Edgar Hole saw many changes in village life. He witnessed the demise of the miller, shoemaker, slaughterhouse and, of course, Meiros colliery.

When the first World War broke out he left Meiros and joined the Navy, sailing on HMS *GOSSAMER*. (see "Forgotten Years" Vol. III) After the War, Edgar and his lovely wife Gladys Vera opened a shop on Chapel Road, Llanharan. Throughout their working lives they were both highly respected citizens. They retired from the business in 1953 and built for themselves 'Brookdale Bungalow' on the site of the demolished Old Shop Farm at the foot of Hollands Lane. Here they were to spend the rest of their lives only yards from the ruin of 'Castle Cottage' where Edgar was born in 1889.

Author's wife Alecia Christine finds time to share a joke with Mr. Edgar Hole during the launch of Stewart Williams' "Glamorgan Historian" Vol. 10 on 1 October 1974 at the Bear Inn, Llanharry.

Source: These recollections of Mr. Edgar Hole are extracted from a taped interview which took place at his home in 1975. The author would like to point out that in "Forgotten Years" Vol. III, the date of Mr. Hole's birth is recorded as 1899; that date was, in fact, an error overlooked during the reading of the manuscript and the correct date should read 1889.

With special thanks to Mrs. Doreen Holland (née Hole) who gave me time and information over the years.

Meiros Colliery Dram Weighbridge.

This photograph shows a number of officials posing for the camera outside the weighbridge at the tram creeper. The gentleman second right (wearing lamp) is Mr. John Surridge known at the colliery as the horse vet. - 1919

MR. JOHN SURRIDGE

Mr. John Surridge came to Llanharan from Ogmore Vale and started work at Meiros colliery during the 1900s. We learn that John was an excellent horseman, with a very high knowledge of veterinary practice having studied books in the field. However, it must be pointed out that he never passed the required examinations to qualify as a fully trained veterinary surgeon. Nevertheless, his keen interest was noted by the Meiros management, and with a regular visit to the colliery by officers of the mines veterinary section, it was decided that John would be given the task of overseeing all the horses on the surface and underground at Meiros.

John Surridge had a free hand in his daily programme of work at Meiros. Regular examinations took place on all the animals working there. Underground, the pit hauliers learned to respect John and gave him all the help they could. After all, it was to their benefit to have a healthy animal working on the underground roadways.

One of John's most significant achievements at Meiros was the setting up of a 'horse hospital' near the colliery stores. A large building was utilised to take in all the sick and injured animals. On a visit to the colliery, one of the veterinary surgeons stated that the horses at Meiros were some of the healthiest that he had seen for some considerable time, and congratulated John on his competence and high standards. For many years after, everyone used to call John simply 'The Vet'.

John Surridge's ability and kindness to animals in general saw many local villagers taking their dogs and cats to his home for examination. Even though he was not trained he never turned anyone away, always giving sound advice and instruction to people right through into his late years. John was talked about for many years after his death, and is still talked about today by the very few surviving miners who worked at Meiros, with a deep appreciation and respect.

Source:
Interview with Mr. Francis Surridge (son) 1992.

Mr. Harry Sheppard with Bruce, one of the shire horses that worked the colliery yard at Meiros.

William Jones 'The Back' with Brittain

THE MEIROS SHIRE HORSES

All the facts concerning the shire horses at Meiros were provided by the late Mr. Harry Sheppard. Mr. Sheppard worked on the surface at Meiros with a horse named Bruce. There were five horses working on the surface at Meiros between 1915 and 1925, although some of the old miners still around will most probably bring to mind names not mentioned here. It must be pointed out that this information is about the period of Mr. Sheppard and also that horses injured and growing old were replaced from time to time.

During the time of Mr. Sheppard, Brittain, Bruce, Major, Windsor and Noble were the horses around the surface of the colliery. Their job was to move rails, obstructions, waste and any job which was applicable to surface work. In Mr. Sheppard's and Bruce's case they spent most of their time running drams of muck and waste up into the Argoed Edwin extension roads. Throughout the shift Bruce would trudge up and down the roadways with his two drams in harness. Mr. Sheppard would stand at the side of the shire giving encouragement throughout the shift.

"Bruce knew me like a book," said Mr. Sheppard during an interview with me on a walk amongst the Meiros ruins. "I would only have to whisper in Bruce's ear and the horse would do anything for me. I remember on one occasion the gaffer came from the stables to inform me that there was a problem down on the colliery yard. One of the shires had failed to move an old boiler which was wedged between two buildings. I went down to examine the situation. I could see that they were using Noble on the job and although the old horse was moving the boiler, it would not break away from between the buildings. They had given Noble too hard a task. I told the workmen to unhitch the horse and to take him away from the scene. The problem was that only one horse could go between the fine gap of the buildings. I put Bruce into the chain and hitch and when I was ready I took a tight rein close to his head. Whenever I was in a position where a job required a little more effort from Bruce I used to talk into his ear to encourage him. I know it may sound far fetched, but Bruce pulled that old steel boiler away from those buildings as if it was cardboard. Not only that, Bruce pulled the boiler for about twenty yards away from the buildings. I don't think I can ever bring to mind an occasion when Bruce ever let me down, or failed me. Often mind, we used to use two and sometimes three horses at a time to remove an obstruction. I remember one time when we had to go down to Church Terrace near the stone wall bridge to collect large wooden beams which used to be part of the bridge structure. It was our task to get these beams back to the colliery yard. To remove them we took Bruce, Major and Windsor. Although it was a slow and laborious task pulling up Seymour Hill, the horses never flinched and secured the job within two hours. Those shires were tremendous animals. When Bruce and I parted company, I found it very hard to adjust. After all, we had become very good friends. For months afterwards, I held a deep sense of loneliness. Whenever possible I would call at the stable after shifts and have a chat with the old fella. Later, some of the horses left the colliery. I don't know what happened to Bruce but I shall never forget him as long as I live. Thankfully, someone took a photograph of us together on the colliery yard, I look at it often. I will treasure Bruce's friendship forever...."

Mr. Harry Sheppard and Bruce were featured in the author's novel "Black Pyramids" published in 1980.

WHEN WATER BROKE INTO MEIROS

The day shift at Meiros on 18 November 1928 was just like any other shift. The colliery at that time was advancing new seams and headings at a fast rate in the new pit. The Six Foot seam was well into production and the two teams were working the Four Foot seam down to the Six Foot. Three men working in a section on that day were: John Smith, Wil Sedgebeer and Jack Hutchins. At about 8.45 a.m. that morning, the undermanager, Mr. Thomas Watkins was going about his regular inspection in the Pentre seam, West Level District. Mr. Hutchins takes up the story.

"It was about 9.00 a.m. when the undermanager, Mr. Tom Watkins, rushed into our area. We were experiencing a few minor problems which had set up a delay in our progress. Watkins was breathless when he came to us and told us to pack up and get from the area immediately. I sensed something was wrong because old Watkins was usually a quiet unassuming fellow. John Smith, our gaffer, turned to Watkins and told him there was a problem and we would soon get it right if he left us alone, but he again told us to pack up and get out, and to make our way to the pit bottom. We could now hear voices around our area and lamps were bobbing about. John Smith asked Watkins what was happening, but he refused to say anything only that we get out straight away. We then knew that something was

wrong. We picked up our things and followed the crowd of miners up the heading. It was a long haul from our district to pit bottom and I can remember to this day, while walking out, thinking of my father who was banksman on pit top. I couldn't wait to get to the surface to see him and find out what the problem was.

At pit bottom a full realisation hit us that something traumatic was in progress. It was obvious that the whole shift was being evacuated from the mine. I was amazed at the quietness and efficiency of the evacuation. The speed that the cages were going up and down also told us that urgency was the prime factor. When we got to the surface I could see the relief on my father's face as we hit bank. When he told me why we had been evacuated from the mine I broke out into a cold sweat. Evidently, Watkins, on his rounds in the West Level, had noticed that an unusual amount of water was building up underfoot. The further he entered the West Level the deeper the water became. By the time the water got knee-deep Watkins could see the problem, and his greatest fear had been realised. The 'pillar' between Llanbad, Brynna colliery and their own Meiros was deteriorating under the high water pressure allowing a dangerously high intake into the West Level. Watkins knew that if it did the area and lower levels would be drowned almost immediately. I often think back and say that God was on our side that morning. By ten thirty that morning every man and horse had been evacuated from the mine. We learned afterwards that Watkins was highly commended by the colliery owners for keeping so cool.

By keeping his find a secret and getting everyone to pit bottom, he saved a lot of panic and, no doubt, lives. One can imagine what the underground galleries would have been like if Watkins had just run in screaming that the water was breaking in, it's a scene not worth thinking about. Despite the fact that a massive inundation didn't occur, the new pit closed immediately and all future exploitation took place in the old pit. This worked until the official closure of the mine in 1931."

In the mid fifties the No. 3 Conway Main North Cross Measure was driven in the direction of Meiros to exploit the seams between the Meiros anticline and the Moel-Gilau fault. After lying for over 60 years it looked as if the Meiros was about to live again! Excessive cost however had the last word, and the project was abandoned. This was very disappointing because the Llanharan-Meiros link up would have been a remarkable achievement.

Source: Interview with Mr. Jack Hutchins, 13 June 1994.

Mr. Jack Hutchins had just finished the morning shift. Here he finds time to pose for the camera with Edie Hutchins and Mrs. Lettie Edwards outside No. 8 Coed Bychan, Llanharan. Note that Mr. Hutchins is still black from the pit. There were no pit-head baths at Llanharan Colliery in 1935 when this was taken.

The derrick stands above the old Meiros shaft awaiting the pumps in an effort to open up the old workings again in 1958.

Mr. H. Seymour Berry, Chairman, Meiros Collieries Ltd.

Mr. H. Seymour Berry, Bucklands, Brecon was a highly respected individual at the Meiros Colliery. It was said that whenever he was seen walking about the colliery there was trouble brewing.

It was during an interview with Mr. Edgar Hole, in the mid 1960s, that information came to light regarding this gentleman. Evidently, the Meiros owners thought Mr. Berry to be an excellent mediator when problems arose at the mine. He sat in on many meetings with the miners which were held at the High Corner House, and they eventually insisted he attended all meetings. After his death the colliery owners named the row of officials houses near the colliery 'Seymour Row' in his memory.

MEIROS COLLIERIES, Ltd.

Registered Office : 2, Dock Chambers, Cardiff.

Telegraphic Address : " Meiros, Cardiff."   *Telephone No. :* 4948/9 Cardiff.

Chairman : H. SEYMOUR BERRY, Bucklands, Brecon.

Directors : HOWELL R. JONES, Dowlais.
           SIR D. R. LLEWELLYN, Bart., St. Fagan's, n/r Cardiff.
           EDWARD STEER, Malpas, n/r Newport.
           T. J. CALLAGHAN, Penarth.

Secretary : H. G. ROBERTS, 2 Dock Chambers, Cardiff.

Agent : D. M. ARBUCKLE.

Name of Mine and Locality.	Managers.	Employees Under ground.	Above ground.		Railway and nearest Station.
Meiros, Llanharan	James Lewis	203	122	..	Llanharan
Pentre, Llanharan		425			
Cwm Ciwc, Pencoed	A. Barrie	—	—	·	,,
Wern Taw, Pencoed		306	88	..	,,
					G.W.

Seams Worked : No. 3 Rhondda and Pentre.

Class of Coal : Household, Manufacturing and Gas.

Annual Output : 300,000 tons.

Power Used : Electric.

Source: South Wales Coal Annuals 1904 - 37

The Filling of the Meiros Pentre shaft 27 September 1995.

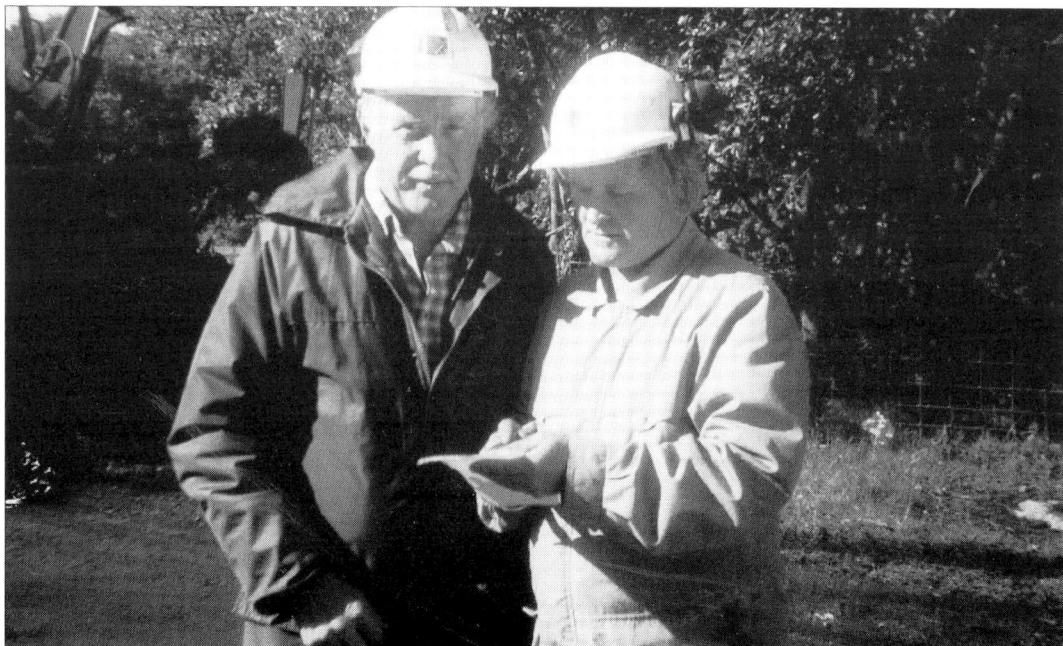

On Site Consultant Mining Engineer, Mr. Rees Holmes, discusses the filling implications of the Pentre Shaft at Meiros Colliery with T.J. Witts.

Mr. Mal Hughes, Drilling Engineer for Llettyshenkin Construction Co., (right) shows T.J. Witts (centre) how the shaft of the old Meiros Pentre pit would finally be filled. Photograph 27 September 1995.

Llanbad, South Rhondda Colliery, Brynna

The discovery of coal at South Rhondda, Llanbad Colliery in 1890 has already been comprehensively recorded in my trilogy "Forgotten Years". However, for those people who have not read my trilogy we recap briefly on the find of the Rhondda No. 3 seam at Brynna which was to change the whole way of life in the area.

We learn in the history books on coalmining that the foremost Industrial pioneer of the Rhondda Valleys was, Walter Coffin (1785-1867). It was Coffin who established the reputation of the lower seams of the Rhondda as the first bituminous coal of South Wales. He had earlier established the first deep mines. Coffin's biggest achievement was the discovery of the Rhondda No. 3 seam which was to bring fortunes to the Brynna area. Ironically, Walter Coffin was not unfamiliar with our district. He was the second son of Walter Coffin, founder of a lucrative tanning business in Bridgend. Young Walter was educated at Cowbridge Grammar School and the Nonconformist Academy at Exeter in 1804. He came into the family business but cared little for it. Soon he directed his own interests to the sales of South Wales coals. Young Walter's father had purchased land in nearby Llantrisant which included several farms. It was he who financed his son who, in 1809, was now a man of 24 years. Walter Coffin senior could see that his young offspring was determined to penetrate the world of coal, so succumbed to his son's wishes, giving his full financial backing. Young Walter's difficulties were considerable,

and with very little skilled labour in the Rhondda at that time he was forced to import his own skilled engineers. After a period of struggle, Coffin and his experts sunk a pit called Dinas Lower Colliery at a depth of forty yards. It was this seam of coal called Rhondda No. 3, first marketed as Dinas No. 3 that became famous as 'Coffin's celebrated coal'. This famous coal was to establish the reputation of lower Rhondda's bituminous coal, and later the rich find changed the historical face of our own locality.

Just imagine the situation, before the coal find at Brynna's Llanbad Colliery the community consisted of nothing more than several scattered farms. Brynna itself in the 1850s contained only an inn called the Eagle. The area was primarily Welsh speaking. Little did they know at the time that creeping up on their sleepy hamlet was an event which was to confound the realisations of top geologists of the day. Also, a partial destruction of the Welsh speaking way of life was only forty years away from being a reality.

In the 1860s attempts were made to sink a deep shaft at Brynna Wood and coalmining in the area actually began in 1820 where old maps show primitive explorations at Nant Ciwc to the west of Gelli Fedi, but that was nothing in comparison to the large scale mining which was to follow.

An attempt to start a deep mine at Llanbad, Brynna took place in 1885. A company was formed by a team of mining folk from the Garw Valley and Bridgend. Those early pioneers actually

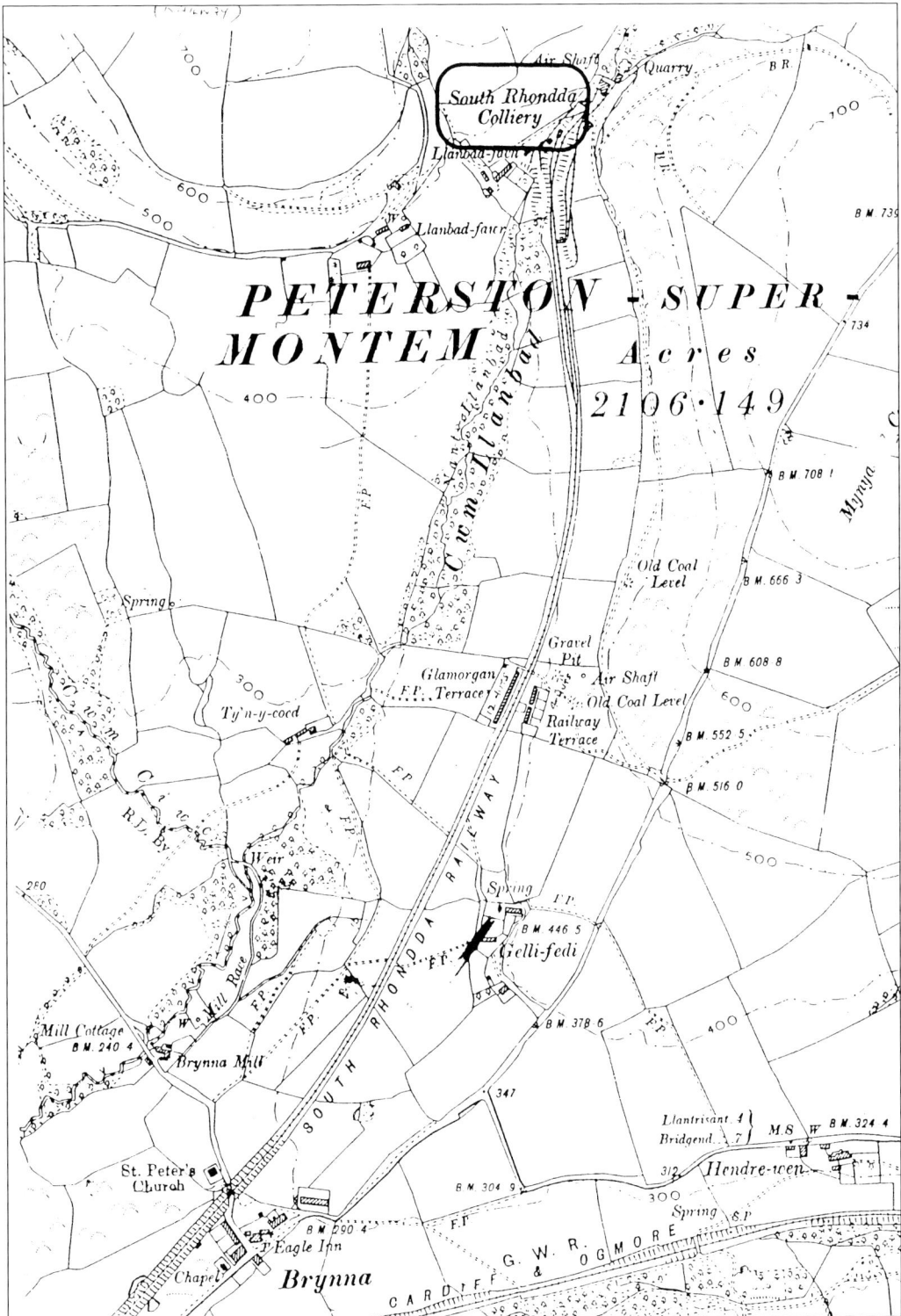

Early map of Llanbad Colliery and railways.

started their deep mine at Brynna but after several months through some cause or another, they became discouraged and abandoned the project.

The big find at Brynna is credited to Mr. Daniel Owen of Ash Hall, Cowbridge, who was at that time proprietor of the Western Mail newspaper. Mr. Owen was actually born in Trenos Farm, just outside Llanharan village. Daniel Owen formed a team of engineers and decided to go all out in an attempt to find coal. After eleven months the find was made. On the advice of his own geologists, Daniel Owen called in further experts to determine his find. Everyone agreed, Owen had struck the Rhondda No. 3 seam in 1886. It was a tremendous find. One wonders what those earlier pioneers must have thought when they heard the news. Yes, it was proved conclusively that the seam at Llanbad was the vein of coal discovered by the late Walter Coffin. What made the find so remarkable was that the Rhondda No. 3 was not only confined to the Rhondda Valleys. It was certainly an important event at Brynna, because before that actual find it was believed that the No. 3 was well nigh exhausted in Glamorgan. Full marks to Daniel Owen and his inner beliefs. As Llanbad Colliery progressed the works proved that the supply of this seam was inexhaustible.

The new colliery made astronomical changes to the area. New people came flooding in from the English border counties. Men, women and children from Coleford and Cinderford in the Forest of Dean and from Cornwall came in their droves. One can imagine what a nightmare it must have been for up until then it had been a Welsh speaking farming stronghold. The Llanbad Valley at Brynna soon became one huge throbbing mining bonanza. Other seams were soon found making the coals at Llanbad amongst the richest in the world, equal to those in Aberdare and Rhondda Valleys. Added to Daniel Owen's fortunes was the fact that all the early seams were easily workable.

The first manager appointed at Llanbad was Mr. David Davies, formerly of Cilely Pit, Tonyrefail. By 1893 the pit was well under way with the distribution of coal made possible with the setting down of a railroad from the colliery down through Brynna into the siding of the Great Western Railway at Brynna Gwynnion. The social environment changed alarmingly. At one time during the early bonanza, it was suggested that a new village be built on the mountainside surrounding the pit. Also, plans were even formulated by some of the religious followers working in the mine to rebuild the old Capel Llanbad church on top of the mountain. However, apart from Glamorgan and Railway Terraces, (16 huts) for officials of the colliery, nothing constructive materialised, with most of the families opting to settle in Brynna, Llanharan and Pencoed.

By 1900 the Llanbad Colliery was listed as owned by the South Rhondda Colliery Company Limited. In 1910, another rich find was to add to the fortunes with the discovery of fireclay lying in the Rhondda seam. This gave rise to the brickworks which, when established, became one of the most prominent works in the country. Like all good things, they must come to an end. By 1925, there was concern over established seams. The coal was readily available but geological conditions were creating far reaching difficulties which were beyond the engineering capabilities of the day. By 1927 problems got to disastrous levels and the pit was closed. The closure of Llanbad did not create immediate problems because Brynna

Wood at this time was operating three drifts and miners were in demand. The closure of Llanbad was a sad affair inasmuch as the Brickworks itself was dependent on the rich fireclay which came from the pit. The works closed down almost immediately and the bulk of the bricks were transferred to nearby Wern Tarw Colliery.

Today, Llanbad Colliery ruins are hidden away in the valley near Llanbad Fach Farm. In fact, the old stables and buildings are still in use as stock buildings for the farm. We can truthfully say that the people of the Brynna of today can thank the likes of Walter Coffin, Daniel Owen and those English families for the growth of their village.

Source: Mrs. Rebecca Thomas, formerly of Llanbad Fawr Farm.

Daniel Owen
His mine at Brynna was the cause of the growth of the new community.

Second left (front) Daniel Owen sits for the camera with his owner partners on the opening of the South Rhondda Colliery, Llanbad, Brynna. 1886.

Llanbad Valley during the halcyon days of the 1890s.

This print showing the Lewis (Fawr) and Thomas (Fach) families at Llanbad during harvest in the 1890s was given by Mrs. Rebecca Thomas (Bryncae) who once lived at Llanbad Fawr Farm. Her grandfather, Daniel Owen, was responsible for the opening of Llanbad Colliery in 1886. Not long after this photograph was taken the colliery took over most of the lower fields.

Llambad Colliery officials 1920s in front of the downcast pithead.

LLANBAD COLLIERY, OWNERS AND MEN

List of owners, managers, commercial managers and numbers employed at the mine from the earliest recorded documents (1908).

The classes of coal mined at South Rhondda were household, manufacturing and gas coals.

Seams worked, Rhondda No. 3, New Seam, No. 2 and Hafod Seam, Rhondda Rider, Pentre, 2'9", 4ft, 6ft.

Depth of shafts – 696ft.

South Rhondda Colliery Co. Ltd. Llanbad, Brynna	Com./Managers	Mine Managers	No. Employed
1908	A.W. Travis Exchange Blds Cardiff.	William Williams	300
1909/10	"	"	276
1911	"	"	240
1912	"	"	300
1913	"	Dan Evans	400
1914	"	"	600
1915	"	"	600
1916	"	"	600
1917	Baltic House Cardiff	D.R. Lloyd	600
1918	"	"	600
1919	"	"	600
1920	"	"	600
1921	"	R. Wall	600
1922	Merthyr House Cardiff	D.M. Arbuckle (Agent)	450
1923	"	"	450
1924	2 Dock Chambers Cardiff	Archibald Barrie	300
1925	"	"	300
1926	"	"	300
1927	"	"	200
1928	National Provincial Bank Buildings Cardiff Docks	"	200
1929	South Rhondda Colliery closed down.		

Most of the miners from the closed mine took employment in the nearby progressive pits at Llanharan.

Sources: Colliery Managers Handbooks 1904 – 1935
South Wales Coal Annuals 1905 – 1937

South Rhondda, Llanbad Colliery, Brynna 1917.

The scene shows the colliery tramroads and the building on the left is the upcast shaft steam engine house. The building at the top of the picture (right centre) is the offices of the coal company.

South Rhondda Miners 1919

Left to Right: Thomas John Jones, Dai 'Bwt' Llewellyn, Richard Donovan, Hopkin Llewellyn.
During the 1970s a prominent politician made the following statement: "Get on your bikes". This quote was made to push unemployed people to travel to outside districts to look for work. The above photograph shows that the M.P.'s statement was nothing new. The above miners were from Treoes, near Bridgend. We see them here preparing to travel to South Rhondda Colliery at Brynna. Many miners came into the Llanharan and Brynna areas to work in the pits, travelling from Bridgend, Nantymoel, Port Talbot, Cardiff and the Rhondda Valleys.

The South Rhondda Express – Llanbad Colliery Coal Train 1910.

Although the little South Rhondda train was used to take the men back and forth from Brynna to the pit, its main work was to bring the huge coal stocks down from the colliery to the sidings at Brynna Gwynion. Up until the last few years the railway bridge stood near the Brynna Church. The old branch line passed the front doors of the 'Huts', two rows of wooden dwellings named Railway amd Glamorgan Terraces. During hard times children of the huts used to wait for the train to pass and jump onto the wagons to throw off a few lumps of coal. It was a dangerous practice, but we learn that when passing the 'Huts' the drivers used to turn a blind eye.

TRADITION

During the early 1900s when a miner was killed at Llanbad Colliery, Brynna, it was traditional that following the accident, four of the poor miner's friends would be selected by the manager as escorts to take the body home. A reliable messenger would be sent ahead to break the sad news. Friends and relatives in the area would be informed and they in turn would gather at the house to console the widow. Any children at the home would be taken in by a relative until after the funeral.

Taking the victim to the house from the colliery was a ritual. The front room of the house would be made ready to receive the corpse on arrival. The chosen group of comrades would push the corpse on a trolley down from the mine into the village. The victim would have been cleaned and prepared by the colliery ambulance team. Passing through the village, those people who were at home would come to the front gate and stand to attention as the small cortege walked by. After releasing the body of their friend to the family, the escort would then move over to the Eagle Inn where the landlord would be waiting for them. The trolley would be left outside the Inn while the four bearer friends would participate in a pint of ale to say farewell to an absent friend. This farewell ritual drink was accepted by the colliery management.

Another tradition, which is remembered by 84 year old Mrs. Laura Pearce, was when an infant died in the village. On the death of a young soul, the school at Brynna would immediately be informed. The headmaster or headmistress, depending on the sex of the deceased, would select six pupils plus two in reserve in case of illness or distress. On the day of

Mrs. Laura Pearce

the funeral the junior pupil bearers would be dressed in grey with a white sash across the chest. These pupils would then proceed to the house and claim the tiny coffin which they would convey to the Church. Mrs. Pearce herself participated in one such funeral procession and stated that it was one of the most traumatic occasions of her life. Sometimes, one or two of the child bearers would burst into tears *en route* to the Church and would immediately be replaced by a reserve pupil.

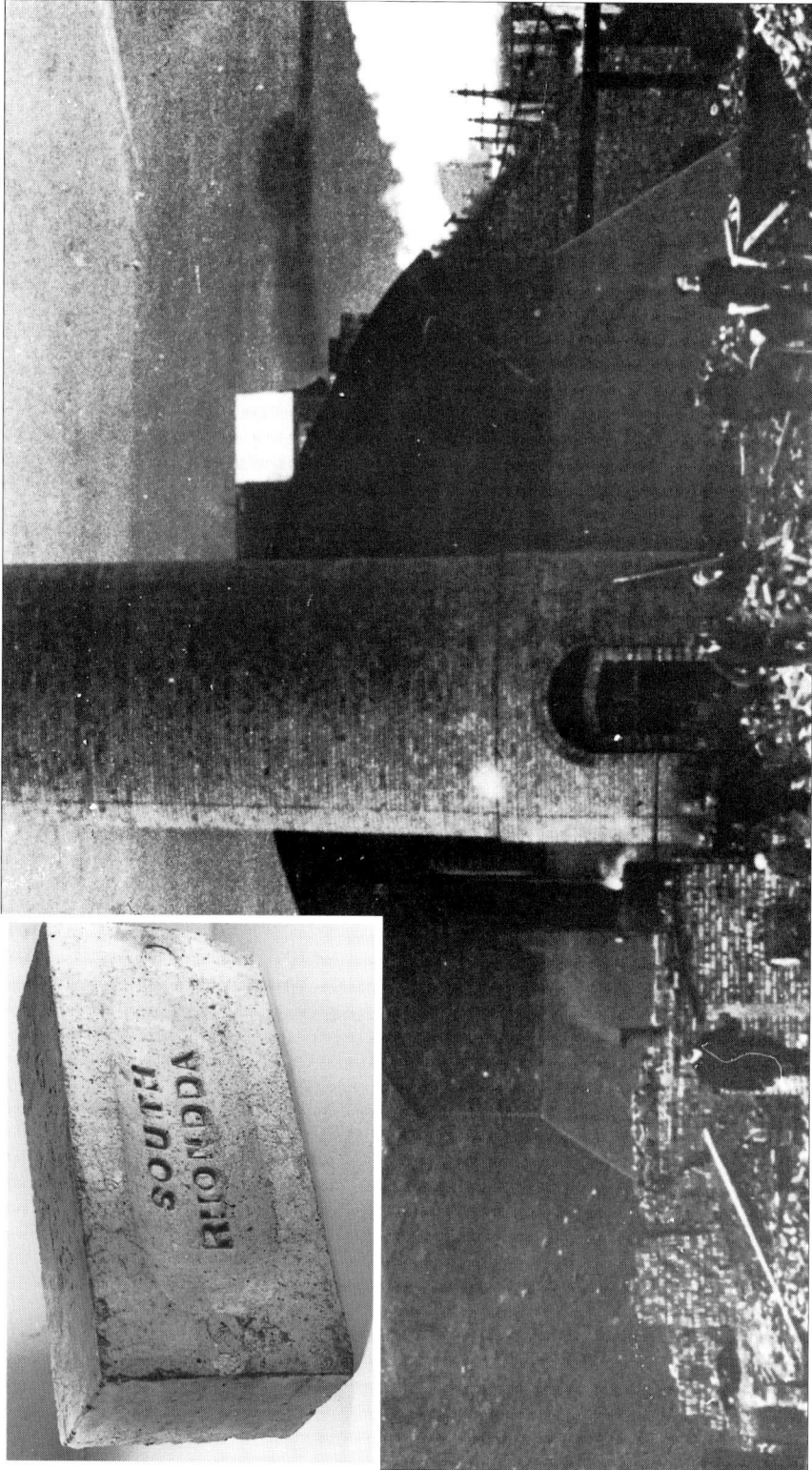

The South Rhondda Brickworks 1910 – 1927.

The No. 3 Rhondda seam was rich with fireclay. This led to the introduction of the brickworks in 1910. By 1919 the works became one of the most prominent and successful works in the country. It also went through modernisation in that year. Bricks from the Llanbad works were sold all over the country and lasted throughout the lifetime of South Rhondda Colliery. When the colliery closed in 1927 the Brickworks automatically closed with it and the bulk of the South Rhondda bricks were taken to Wern Tarw Colliery.

HEROES OF COAL

- Kenneth Clashm of Senghenydd, died 1938 at Windsor Colliery, Abertridwr.

- John Davies, of Trethomas, died January 4, 1933, at Bedwas Navigation Colliery.

- Evan Edwards, of Senghenydd, died October 14,1913, at Universal Colliery, Senghenydd.

- Richard Edwards, of Senghenydd, died October 14,1913, at Universal Colliery, Senghenydd.

- William Grubb, of Pontypridd, died ,June 26,1909, at Ty Mawr Colliery.

- Henry Heighway, of Brynhyfryd Colliery Offices, died May 8,1943, at Bettws Colliery, Ammanford.

- Lewis Jones, of Senghenydd, died 1955, at Windsor Colliery, Abertridwr.

- William Sparey, of Llanbradach, died November, 1932, at Llanbradach Colliery.

- Nimrod Witts, of Llanharan, died May 3, 1919, at South Rhondda Colliery, Llanbad, Brynna.

'The Forgotten Village'

THE HUTS

Early Brynna village records and church lists provide us with a substantial record of those early mining pioneers of the 1880s who established and lived in the now forgotten community of the colliery sinkers huts. Erected by the South Rhondda Coal Company in 1886, the 'Huts' straddled each side of the roadway leading to the Llanbad Pit. There were sixteen dwellings, four on the eastern side (Railway Terrace) and twelve on the west side (Glamorgan Terrace), situated above Tyn-y-Coed Farm.

Once the South Rhondda pit had become established the sinkers moved out and the small dwellings were taken over by colliery overmen and pit workers who could be on hand for any emergency. It must have been quite a traumatic place to live with the railway track running virtually outside the front doors. With quite a number of children within the families the parents would need to have had eyes in the backs of their heads, yet, during our research we found no evidence of accidents by train within the community. It must be pointed out that the coal train passed the huts three times a day.

The huts were certainly slap bang in the middle of a coal mining environment. Some sixty yards east of the dwellings worked the No. 2 Drift, while to the west the ill-fated Kitchener Drift was being exploited. The huts were certainly a well organised community. At No. 1 Railway Terrace, a shop was established by Mr. Walter Price, later, taken over by a Mrs. Kiff. Everything from soap to butter was sold there. The information gleaned from those now few individuals who lived there during the coalmining boom certainly paints a picture of character and warmth. I myself hold a personal interest because my grandfather Nimrod Witts worked with the early pitmen during the 1900s. Nimrod lived in No. 7 Glamorgan Terrace for two years before moving to William Street.

In volume III "Forgotten Years" I show a print of Mr. Lewis Gale outside No. 3 Railway Terrace. I was indeed fortunate in meeting Mr. Gale because after several visits to the now abandoned area I have been provided with a verbal history of how those settlers really lived within that small community. Mr. Gale pointed out that it would be impossible to give a true and accurate list of families who lived in each of the huts because they changed quite frequently. Just for our record we have compiled a list, collected purely from the memory of individuals, church records and community organisations over the years. There will obviously be discrepancies, but what we compile will at least show future generations that a small community once existed on this bleak mountain road.

It was certainly hard living in the huts. They relied on a pump near the old Llanbad railway line for their water. Each dwelling had a water butt (old barrel). The barrel would be situated under the gutter at the corner of the hut. The butt had to be kept filled at all times, because the woman of the house had to keep up her chores of washing clothes and cooking. Keeping the water butt full would generally be undertaken by the lads in the household. When the barrel became low, the lads would pray for rain because to fill the barrel would require many trips to the tap.

Facilities at the huts were virtually non-existent. There was no electricity, night light came in the form of oil lamps. The only luxury in the 1920s was the radio. This was operated by the use of accumulator batteries which were serviced weekly. Most families owned dogs, and at one time there were so many canines running around that the site became known as 'Dogstown'.

Mr. Gale pointed out that every dwelling had a small garden. The place was a carefree area to live. In the summer months the children played football and cricket on the side of the mountain, and a dam was made in the river down near Tyn-y-Coed Farm, where they would swim for hours on end. The women would carry out their chores chatting away over fences. On a Sunday the hill walks around the area would be full of banter from the men enjoying their rest day. From the huts, the walk to the old Capel Llanbad church on top of the mountain was a regular jaunt.

When the South Rhondda Colliery closed down in 1927 the huts changed hands even more, because many of the families left for other pits mainly in the Rhondda valleys.

During the 1950s, developments with regard to the local villages were moving forward in huge strides. The huts underwent stringent examination by the governing health authority and they decided that the dwellings were unfit for habitation owing to lack of facilities. It was decided that the new houses being developed in the surrounding villages would take the huts' tenants.

By the winter of 1954 many of the tenants had left. For the record, the last person to leave the huts was granny Gardener of No. 1 Glamorgan Terrace. The buildings themselves were soon to take on other useful roles in the community surrounding Brynna and Llanharan. Some were utilised as garden sheds, while others were converted into garages.

Today, only the red South Rhondda bricked steps and retaining walls remain to mark the small community's existence. Walking along the area where Glamorgan Terrace once stood one can still see part of the floor bases. Mr. Lewis Gale had the final words to say on that now gone and forgotten community......

"I will never forget the huts or the good people who lived there. My days in No. 3 Railway Terrace was a most rewarding experience. We have to be honest, we didn't have much money, any of us. But when I remember people like Charlie Peace, Mrs. Kiff, Granny Gardener and oh! so many many more, I realise how lucky I was to have known them. Their memory will always live with me. They will always stay fresh in my mind".

Source: Interview with Mr. Lewis Gale on the site of Llanbad 'huts' 3 November 1991.

Some of the individuals who lived at Railway and Glamorgan Terraces, Brynna 1904:	Sinkers		
	James Barnes	David Gough	Harry Sheldon
	John Coleman	George Hill	Fred Smith
	William Cooper	Joseph James	John Warren
	Charles Gale	Peter Morgan	Charles Williams
		Charles Reed	Evan Williams

Some family names from the 'Huts' taken from Old Club and Football Records.:				
Baker	Brown	Gibby	Jones	Ray
Bargery	Chard	Green	Kiff	Rodgers
Bratton	Davies	Hall	Lent	Simmonds
	Edwards	Houghton	Nash	Snookes
	Evans	James	Owens	Thomas
	Flower	Jenkins	Power	Wills
	Gardener	Johns	Preece	Witts

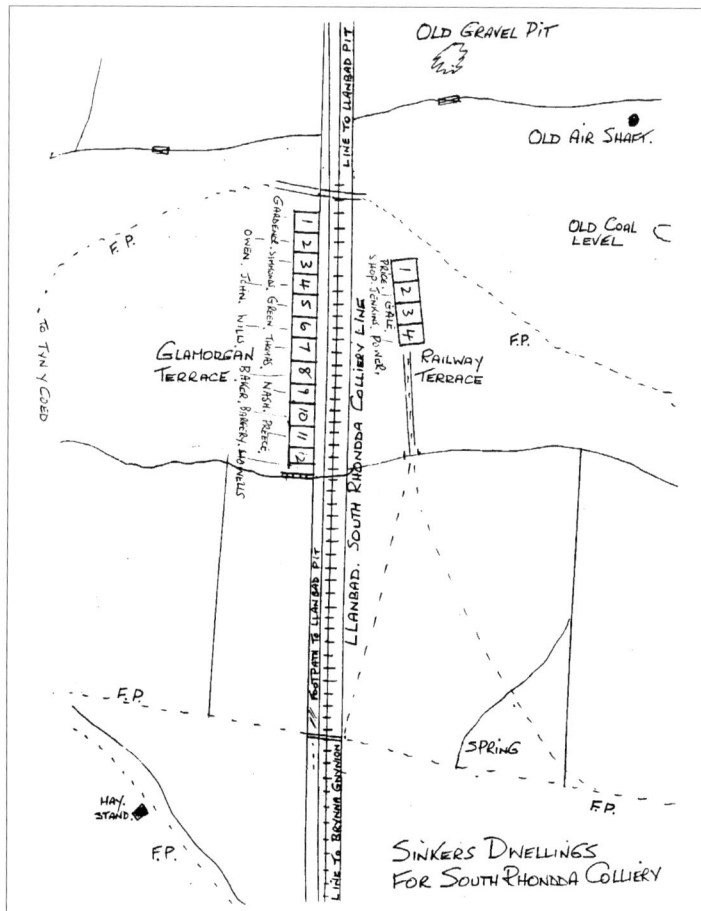

**Layout Plan of Glamorgan and Railway Terrace.
A small village 'The Huts'.**

Records are sparse with regard to the various families who, over the years, lived within this small mining community. However, the information gathered will give the reader an insight into an area which is quite simply described today as 'the lost village.'

Source: Modified from an NCB map, South Western area.

Photograph taken near 'The Huts' 1930s.
Back Row – Gwilym Lewis (Llanbad Fawr), Betty and Lyneth Hall.
Middle Row – Lewis Gale, George Hall and Edmund Lewis.
The identity of the young girl in front is unknown.

Taken at Llanbad Fawr Farm, Brynna.
Left to Right – Glenys Kiff, Eddie Lewis, Betty Hall,
Lyneth Hall and John Davy John.

Mrs. Nancy Gale

Mr. William Gale

The Gale family are a well known and established Brynna family. While living at the 'huts' they resided in No. 3 Railway Terrace.

In the field above their dwelling the Gales bred pigs. What a day 'pig killing' was. The animal would be slaughtered and taken down to No. 3 for dressing and carving. All the children from the surrounding 'huts' would gather around the Gales' house waiting for the pigs bladder which would be used as a football.

In his early days, William Gale worked at Llanbad Colliery. There he was employed as an underground haulier working with horses. On the closure of the Llanbad pit in 1927 he brought out the last two pit ponies from the mine. The two ponies were named Marble and Spider.

William, by all accounts, was one of the 'huts' real characters. We learn how he used to play the concertina and organ for the amusement of his family and friends. During the warm summer months he used to play his concertina while sitting on a stool in the garden. Within minutes of beginning his recital the garden would be surrounded with children singing at the top of their voices.

We have said it many times before, the likes of the 'Gales' and those early mining folk of yesteryear will never be seen again......

Mrs. Enid Thomas with her son Cyril outside their home No. 12 Glamorgan Terrace.

Children of the forgotten village.
Ivor, Bronwen and Trevor Thomas at No. 12 Glamorgan Terrace.

A Rare Print of Glamorgan Terrace.
Annie Merry Thomas poses in front of Glamorgan Terrace (1941).
The baby in arms is young Gilbert Nash.

Gilbert Nash poses on his pony in front of Railway Terrace 'Huts' 1952.

*Two local Brynna girls pose for the camera outside
No. 3 Railway Terrace, Llanbad.*

Owners of the Drift examine the damage.

THE KITCHENER DRIFT DISASTER.

The Kitchener Drift was situated under the marshland field known as Coed Cae. The actual site of the drift was at the foot of a field where Glamorgan Terrace stood, near Tyn-y-Coed Farm. The mine collapsed at about 2.30 p.m. on Saturday 4 November 1916. Killed at the drift were Mr. Tom Perkins and Mr. Caleb Tomlins. Mrs. Laura Pearce was an 8 year old at the time of the accident. She recalls the devastation and anguish of the Brynna people. "Brynna was a very quiet place for weeks after the funerals of the two miners, they were highly respected boys, well liked in the village." Stories are rife about the incident. One quaint story was about a young village maid named Alice. We learn that during the rescue operations at the drift she sat on a stool outside one of the Railway Terrace houses (huts) continuously staring down at the rescue attempt down below. On her lap Alice clasped a Bible tightly. This vigil continued from dawn till dusk until the two men were found and brought out of the mine. The young maid then left the area in tears. Today, only two spoil tips from the opening of the drift and an old engine haulage base remain as an epitaph to the sad occasion in 1916.

Mrs. Pearce died on Sunday 12 November 1995 aged 87 years. She served at Brynna Church (St. Peters) for 60 years, and was organist between Brynna and Llanharan Churches for over 40 years.

Source: Interview with Mr. Enoch Reed and Mr. Thomas Merry, Brynna. Photograph given by Mr. Harry Sheppard, Llanharan.

DAVID DAVIES OF LLANDINAM

The Ogmore Branch Line was constructed in the 1880s by David Davies, Llandinam, at a cost of around £133,000. Davies was a coal and railway entrepeneur who amassed a fortune with his companies. He owned at one time the Parc and Dare Pits in the Rhondda Valley and later the Ocean Colliery, Nantymoel. When the work on the branch line began, we learn that Davies made arrangements with the licencee of the Turberville Hotel for two of his engineers to board there. Also, meetings and wage payouts to the railway workers took place there. The pub must have certainly done quite well during that period satisfying the thirst of the workers.

We learn that the reason for the building of the Ogmore Branch was to carry the huge output of coal from the Nantymoel Colliery direct to Cardiff, instead of having to run it to Tondu via the main line. The line was also used by the South Rhondda, Brynna and Wern Tarw Pits. In the declining years (1960s) only Wern Tarw used the line extensively, coal, steel rings and pit props being the main traffic. The line closed down in 1963 when the J.O. Williams pit prop plant and the Wern Tarw Colliery closed.

Today house-building on the Llanharan section of the old line, opposite the Chapel Road houses, coupled with countryside growth through the Brynna Wood end has virtually seen the complete disappearance of a once prosperous branch line. The last bridge in the thickets of Brynna Wood is currently under demolition.

FAMILY RAILWAY LINKS -1847-

It was interesting to read the diary and notes recorded by Mr. Walter Richards, Hendreowen from 1847. This was the year when the South Wales Railway line was put down through the Hendreowen fields. Operations began in a field at Hendreowen called Cae Bont on 19 April 1847. Another point of interest from the record was the surnames of some of the workers: Davies, Humphries, Smith, Harris, Pyne, Stephens, Hassington and Lock only to name a few. Some family connections still in the village perhaps?

The name 'Pyne' comes up frequently with the mooting of the Ogmore Branch Line in 1885. There is a J. Pyne listed as 'Engineer' and is recorded as 'from Devon'. The present Mr. Douglas Pyne, one of two brothers who own Hendrewen Garage, west of Llanharan, confirmed that their family are of Devonshire origin, so there is a distinct possibility that the old railway engineer is one of his distant forebears.

Source: Family diaries of Thomas Richards, Hendreowen Farm, Llanharan 1951

Llanharan Railway Station, which was opened on 11 September 1899.
On the extreme bottom left corner can be seen the old Ogmore Branch Line mooted by David Davies of Llandinam in 1885.

The old Ogmore Branch Line railway cutting, situated on land below the Chapel Road houses. This line was put down in the 1880s by David Davies, Llandinam, at a cost of £133,000. It transported coal in the early days from the Ogmore Valleys as well as locally from the South Rhondda, Llanbad and Wern Tarw pits. The line was taken up in the late 1960s after the closure of Wern Tarw Colliery. The site in this photograph has now been developed by the Rhondda Housing Association.

The old Ogmore branch line bridge at Brynna Wood lies hidden in undergrowth. The only evidence left to show that the branch line existed.

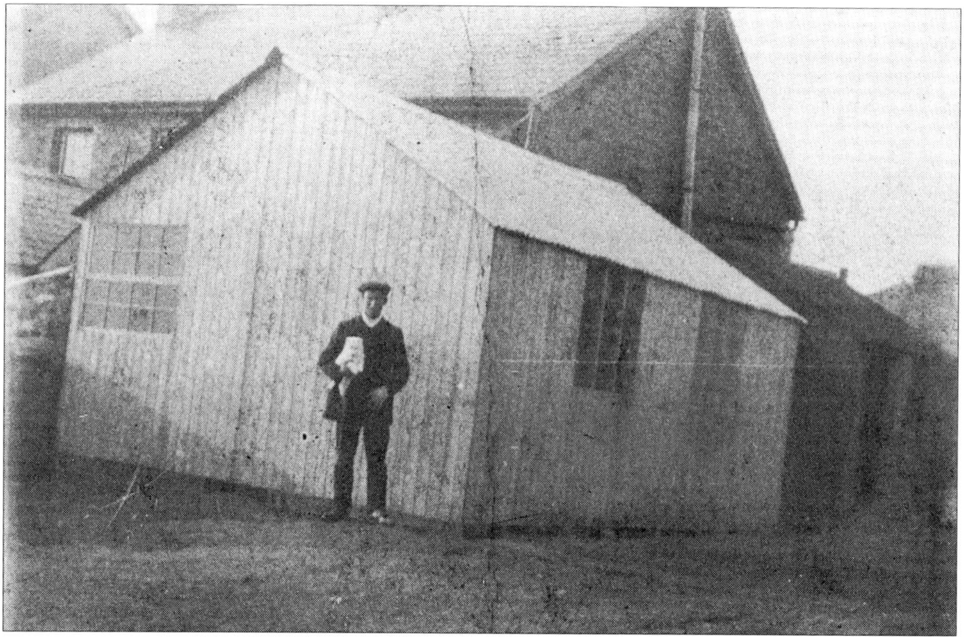

First Billiard Hall at Brynna

The old Billiard Hall at Brynna was certainly a thriving hive of activity during the early 1900s when Aaron David first set up the business to accommodate the leisure period of young miners working in the nearby South Rhondda Colliery.

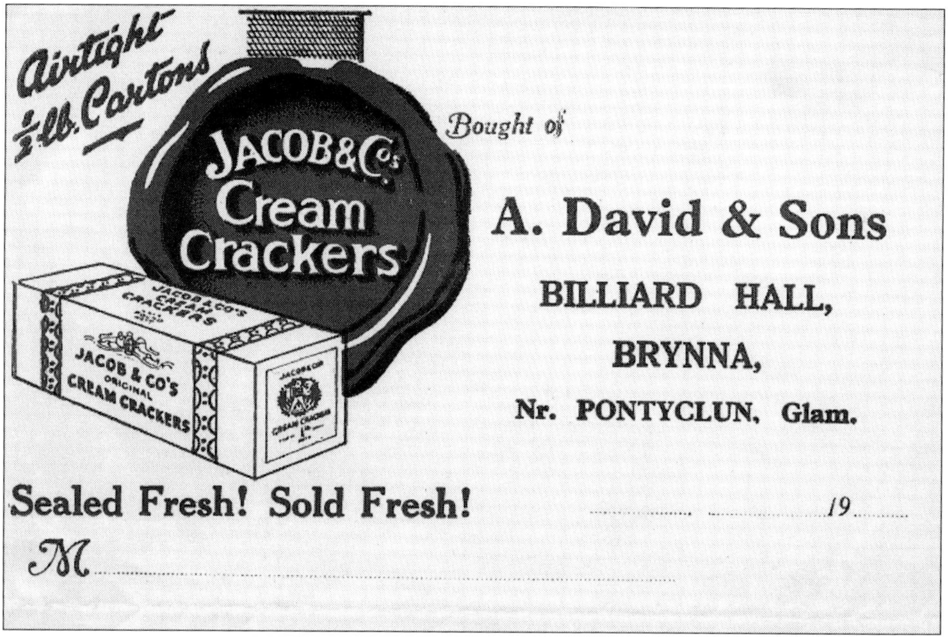

Airtight ½ lb. Cartons
JACOB & Co's Cream Crackers
JACOB & CO'S CREAM CRACKERS
JACOB & CO'S ORIGINAL CREAM CRACKERS
Bought of
A. David & Sons
BILLIARD HALL,
BRYNNA,
Nr. PONTYCLUN, Glam.
Sealed Fresh! Sold Fresh!
19
M

Apart from the Billiard Hall, the Davids' at Brynna ran a successful provisions business in the village.

Aaron David celebrates his 90th birthday with his family at Brynna.

One of the most influential families to settle in Brynna was the David family. They had established themselves at Brynna Mill since 1836.

Aaron himself was an influential contributor to semi national Eisteddfods and fought vigorously for the Bethlehem cause at Llanharan. His sons Joseph and Cyril were County Councillors.

1983 - T.J. Witts with his dogs Raq and Spot at the Llanbad Colliery Feeder.

The feeder walls held back the huge body of water which was used to supply the boilers for steam powered engines situated in the mine below. When the pit closed in 1927, the feeder was used by the local children as a swimming pool, the area on summer days resembled a holiday spa. Sadly, as the years passed, the pond filled with silt and became a dangerous hazard. Local farmers, fearing for the safety of the children, took drastic action and smashed away the centre of the dam, releasing the pond. Most of the dam wall stands today as a defiant epitaph to that bygone era.

Despite the fact that Llanbad Colliery closed down in 1927, the old power house and upcast engine house are still in remarkable condition.

The young girl in the picture is Emma Langford, the author's grand daughter. Only yards from where this little girl is standing is the old upcast shaft where her great, great grandfather worked in the early 1900s.

THE PHANTOM SPECTRE
- THE KIMBERLEY DRIFT, BRYNNA -

One of the quaintest stories linked to the Kimberley Drift Mine was narrated to me by the late Mr. David Reed, Brynna, during an interview when compiling my "Forgotten Years" series. Mr. Reed was in the rescue party who assisted in the ill-fated Kitchener Drift. See "Forgotten Years" Vol. I page 63.

The level known as Kimberley Drift at Brynna was just like any other level in the area during the 1890s. At least until work began driving a new measure north of the drift. After driving the new heading for about three weeks, the officials suddenly became very uneasy when going about their safety examinations. Especially alone! The new heading was a wet venture, and to add to their problems, various officials were coming out of the mine after safety checks complaining of an eerie light coming from the depths of the new heading. The colliery management immediately speculated that it was a rumour being spread about to try and stop the work. The manager of the mine issued warnings to his officials to dispel all this drivel about lights in the new heading. However, within three weeks the talk of sightings came to the fore again, much to the frustration and annoyance of the manager. Soon, all sorts of banter was linked to the mine which forced the manager to say that enough was enough and that at this stage a team of officials would enter the mine to try and seek out the mysterious sightings.

The manager with his top officials, seven in all, entered the drift mine together. On approaching the district the manager decided to go on into the heading alone! Entering the area he started his search vigorously. Suddenly, he jarred to a halt. His officials had been right all the time, for there, as clear as crystal, in front of him was a glowing light. Being a man of logic, and after a period of hesitation, he went on towards the eerie glow. Suddenly he burst out laughing, he turned and shouted out to the others who were waiting at the mouth of the new heading, they immediately ran down to him. He was still laughing as they approached and revealed the mystery of the phantom light. Evidently a piece of steel plating had been nailed to one of the prop collars by one of the earlier miners in the opening of the heading for marking purposes. With the conditions in the heading being wet, the reclining steel plate was creating a reflective mirror image. What the officials were actually seeing was a reflection of their own lamps. With the mystery solved work soon got back to normal. For a while the officials were subjected to further banter such as "Seen any good ghosts lately", or, if an official was going into the drift to do his rounds, "Watch the bogey man don't get you." For years the Phantom Spectre was the talk of Brynna.

We learn that many other pits in South Wales have been subjected to mysterious and phantom happenings, soon to be solved with logical answers. However, not all phantom and ghost stories are easily laid to rest. Many incidents unsolved now run through the waters of sealed galleries of flooded and forgotten mine workings....

The old Kimberley Drift left sealed and forgotten. This Llanbad mine caused much controversy with its legendary tale of a spectre carrying a lamp in the headings.

Horses still use the old Llanbad Colliery stables. These stables were in frequent use with the pit ponies right up to the closure of the colliery in 1927. The colliery area today is being successfully farmed by Mr. & Mrs. Howard Evans.

BRYNNA WOOD COLLIERY

Coalmining at Brynna commenced in 1861. The first exploration was through deep mining. The pit was called Bodwr Fach. However, sinking operations proved troublesome as the shafts were being sunk through loose and sandy ground. Vigorous effort was made on that first pit and the shafts did actually reach a depth of fifty one and seventy five yards. The pit was owned by the Brynnau Gwynion Coal Company, Swansea. After a very difficult period, deep mining at Brynna Wood was abandoned and coal operations continued with drift mining techniques (c.1879-80).

When in full flow the drifts at Brynna Wood were known as the No. 1 and No. 2 slants, and were in 1914 employing 409 men. In 1930 the drifts were working the following seams:

> Trydydd Seam
> South Fawr Seam
> North Fawr Seam
> Eskyrn Seam
> Six Foot Seam (Bodwr Fach)
> Six Foot Seam (Bituminous Coal)

Under the name of Brynna Collieries Ltd., most of the above seams were worked from the No. 1 slant. Throughout the early 1920s No. 1 and No. 3 were working flat out. The No. 2 was redirected as a ventilation shaft or return. When closed, the No. 1 was owned by Hendrewen Gas Coal Company Ltd.

Early maps show that Brynna Wood over the years has been heavily exploited. One early map shows seven drifts running through the area of Brynna. Apart from the above mentioned drifts, others were worked throughout the years, namely: Kimberley, Moder River, Hendrewen and Victory.

When talking of Brynna Wood, we must mention a very interesting personality in the form of John Benjamin Hawkins. Hawkins was manager of Brynna Wood during the 1920s until 1932 when ill health forced him to retire. He died on 30 March 1933. During his mining career at Brynna Wood he built for himself 'Brynna House' which is situated on the western edge of the wood. The story goes that after he completed the house he named it 'Llanharan House'. By doing so he upset the lady of Llanharan House, Mrs. Blandy Jenkins because the name clashed with her mansion. To save ill feeling J.B. changed the name to 'Brynna House'. Today, this fine building is owned by Mr. Raymond Slade and his family.

Sources:
South Wales Coal Annuals 1904 - 1937
Mines Survey Maps South Western area.

With special acknowledgement to Mr. Brian Donovan, former mining official of Llanharan Colliery for his kind assistance in the study of old maps and documents.

Brynna Gwynnion Colliery

This photograph shows the Brynna No. 1 drift mine in operation around the year 1922. The chief cashier of the mine was Mr. Edward Sabine, he is pictured here in the centre of the group with his daughter, Irene. The mine closed in November 1926. The No. 2 and No. 3 stayed open until 1935 when all operations were then concentrated at the Powell Duffryn mine, Llanharan.

FAMILY INVOLVEMENT WITH MINING IN BRYNNA

John Pelgrave
Born circa 1830

David Croft m. Hannah Pelgrave
1849 - 1903   1852 - 1941

George Croft m. Alma Young
1873 - 1945   1875 - 1956

Wilfred Croft   Harold Croft   Arthur Croft   Idris Croft
1898 - 1977   (only sons of George and Alma)

Hannah was born in the Channel Island of Alderney in 1852, the second child of John and Caroline Pelgrave. The family moved to "Hut Peterstone" in 1860 from Hirwaun (Aberdare) when John became an "overlooker" of the Bynea Mine which was being sunk at Brynna Wood. It was here that Hannah's brother George was born in January 1881. Hannah lived in Brynna for no more than three years, for by 1863 the family moved again - this time to Farnham in Surrey.

The Pelgrave family finally settled in Whitchurch in 1867 and it was here on Christmas Day 1870 that Hannah married David Croft, a native of Wiltshire. Their son George, born in 1873, was to return to Brynna.

In 1912 George, his wife and seven children, moved to 18 William Street following his transfer from the Phoenix Brickworks in Cardiff to the brickworks at Llanbad. Apparently he was sought for his knowledge of the blasting process. He

was later joined at Llanbad by his eldest son, Wilfred, who was screening coal at the South Rhondda Colliery.

By 1916, George, Wilfred and Harold were working in Brynna Wood Colliery, George as power-house attendant. Later they were joined by the remaining two sons, Arthur and Idris.

All sons were present during the sinking of the Powell Duffryn mine at Llanharan, Wilfred and Harold as banksmen.

Harold and Idris were still working at Llanharan Colliery when it closed in 1962. Wilfred, who had subsequently found employment at Coed Ely Brickworks, assisted with the dismantling of the colliery by straightening the underground support rings recovered for re-use elsewhere.

THE PIONEERS OF BRYNNA GWYNNION COLLIERY

1861 CENSUS

ABODE	NAME	REL.	AGE	JOB	BIRTHPLACE
Engine House	John Howells	Head	30	Collier	Llantillio, Pertholey, Mon.
	Elizabeth Howells	Wife	27		Abergavenny, Mon.
	Mary Howells	Daug.	6		Garw Fach, Nantyglo
	William Howells	Son	4		Garw Fach, Nantyglo
	John Vaughan	Lodger	14		Dorstone, Palgath Herefordshire.
Not given	William Evans	Lodger	23	Labourer	Kilkenny, Ireland.
Brynna Hut	John Pelgrave	Head		Excavator	Marton, Lincolnshire
	Caroline Pelgrave	Wife	27		Marton, Lincholshire
	Susannah Pelgrave	Daug.	9		Jersey
	Hannah Pelgrave	Daug.	7		Alderney
	Caroline Pelgrave	Daug.	3		Hirwaun, Aberdare
	John Pelgrave	Son	3		Hirwaun, Aberdare
	Sarah Pelgrave	Daug.	2		Hirwaun, Aberdare
	George Pelgrave	Son	2 mths		Peterstone-Super-Montem
Not given	John Hagaity	Lodger	32	Excavator	Cork, Ireland
Not given	Nicholas Stole	Lodger	43	Navvy	Bedminster, Somerset
Not given	Jerry Nugent	Lodger	29	Labourer	Waterford, Ireland
Not given	Thomas Carty	Lodger	28	Mason Clerk	Waterford, Ireland
Not given	Edward Ryan	Lodger	23	Excavator	Cork, Ireland.

Early seam pattern of workings at
Brynna Wood during the early 1920s.
William and Southall Streets shown.

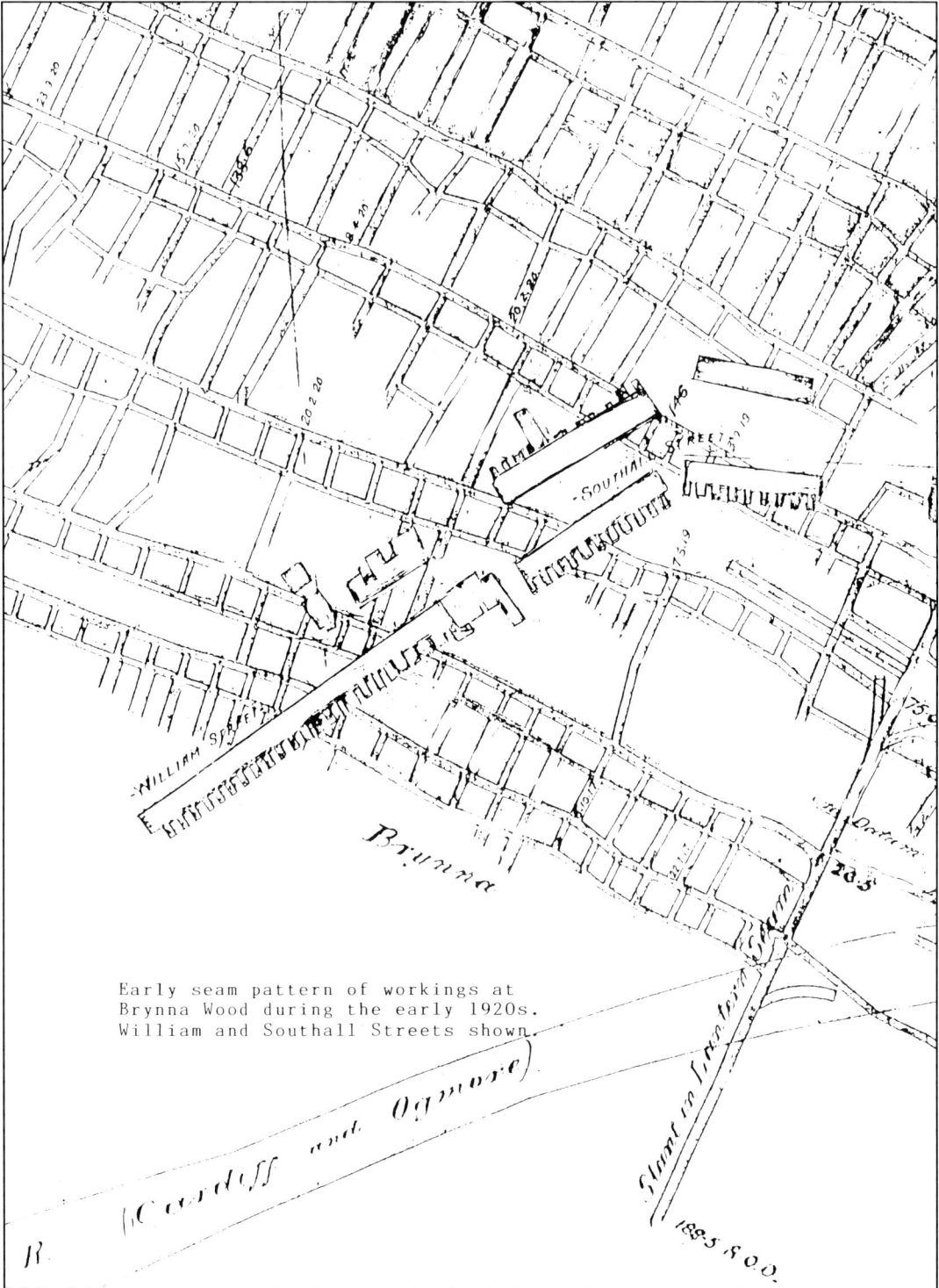

Brynna Wood Number One Slant.

Map shows seam working pattern under Brynna during 1920s.

Although the Brynna Wood mining ended in the mid 1930s and despite the fact that most of the woods' industrial scars have been demolished, this No. 2 Drift Return is in excellent condition. The bricks used in the construction of this building are a perfect example of the South Rhondda Brickworks.

The remains of the Brynna Wood No. 3 Drift. This mine holds a personal significance to the author because his late father, William Robert, worked there up to the time of its closure in the mid thirties.

1870 - 1962
Llanharan Colliery

Coal mining in the Llanharan South area is recorded back to the 1870s. During the early open-cast operations, old 'Bell Shafts' were unearthed in the district which indicates coal exploitation as far back as the 1860s. We already know that a shaft was sunk in 1870 and had only one seam. This colliery was called 'Bryncae' and was soon abandoned because the pit was wet and inclined.

It was in 1921 when the Powell Duffryn Company sunk the North Shaft. In my trilogy "Forgotten Years", I have already shown that the sinking of the new pit was to be a pilot project to help in the planning and success of the Llantrisant Colliery in nearby Ynysmaerdy. The Llantrisant pit had already proved the existence of the No. 2 and No. 3 Rhondda seams. We learn that the prospects in the lower seams were excellent and in 1939 the Powell Duffryn Company sent mining engineer, Jack Gregor to the continent to study a new method in coalmining called 'Horizon Mining'. When Jack Gregor returned, work commenced in earnest at the Llantrisant Colliery.

On 2 June 1941 an explosion at the Llantrisant pit wrecked the engine house, fan drift and mutilated the head gear installations. Tragically, Jack Gregor was killed along with three other workmen. So extensive was the damage that all operations at the colliery ceased, and a full effort was turned on at the Llanharan pit. Fortunately, the miners at the Llanharan project were quick in adapting themselves to new mining techniques. Speeds up to thirty yards a week were attained.

In 1952, work at Llanharan Colliery was going ahead with the driving of stone drifts at the rate of three thousand yards a year. First, the staple pit was brought into use, bringing coal down from the No. 2 to the No. 3 Horizon. The shaft was 116 yards deep and 12 feet in diameter. The pit being sunk in five months. It was hoped that the No. 2 and No. 3 Horizons would link up with the old Meiros Colliery workings. It would have proved a fantastic venture. However, nothing materialised and the project was abandoned after only a few months because of excessive cost. The major elements of the first Horizon mining reorganisation were taking shape.

Supplemented by the best in modern machinery, Llanharan Colliery would have brought about the conquest of the unpredictable seams of the South Crop. But sadly, geological conditions in the steeply contorted rock south of the Maesteg-Pontypridd anticline proved much more disturbed than expected. The colliery closed down in 1962.

Source: Coal Magazine 1953

A Showpiece Colliery - No. 2 Area -

POWELL DUFFRYN ASSOCIATED COLLIERIES, LTD.

Registered Office : 1, Great Tower Street, London, E.C.3.

Telegraphic Addresses : { "Coal, Hengoed." / "Carbonaceous, Bilgate, London." / "Powell, Cardiff."

Telephone Nos. { Hengoed 81 (4 lines). / London : Mansion House 3270 (13 lines). / Cardiff 7960 (6 lines).

Directors · E. L. HANN, Lanelay Hall, Pontyclun, Glam. (*Chairman*).
E. W. GANDERTON, Manor Close, Chislehurst, Kent.
LT. COL. HON. CHRISTIAN H. C. GUEST, 3, Queen Anne Street, Cavendish Square, London, W.1
D. A. HANN, Cascade House, Penpedairheol, Hengoed, Glam.
THE LORD HYNDLEY, 156, St. James's Court, Buckingham Gate, London, S.W.1.
J. H. JOLLY, Langdale, Barnt Green, near Birmingham.
SIR STEPHENSON H. KENT, K.C.B., Chapelwood Manor, Nutley, Sussex.
SIR DAVID R. LLEWELLYN, Bart., The Court, St. Fagans, Glam.
W. M. LLEWELLYN, Tynewydd, Hirwaun, Glam.
W. McGILVRAY, Silver Grange, Silver Lane, Purley, Surrey.
H. H. MERRETT, Brynhafod, Llandaff, Glam.
SIR EVAN WILLIAMS, Bart., D.L., "Glyn-Dwr," Pontardulais, Carm.

Secretary: ALFRED READ, M.B.E., F.C.I.S., 1 Great Tower Street, London, E.C.3
General Managers : D. A. HANN, F. P. HANN and H. McVICAR.
Engineers : IVOR WILLIAMS, IDRIS JONES, W. J. JONES, E. POWELL, P. LEWIS.
Agents : J. A. PRICE, A. TAIT, W. THOMAS, S. G. BASSETT, J. SHENTON, G. D. CORFIELD and T. POWELL.

Name of Mine and Locality.	Manager.	Employees Under ground.	Above ground.	Railway and nearest Station.
Aberaman, Aberaman	W. Moore ..	314	40 ..	Aberaman
Cwmneol, Cwmaman	C. L. Watson ..	450	50 ..	,,
Fforchaman, Cwmaman..	W. S. Jones ..	934	95 ..	,,
River Level, Abernant ..	J. B. Welbourne	580	68 ..	Aberdare
Lower Duffryn, Mountain Ash.	C. L. Watson ..	—	— ..	Mountain Ash
Penallta, Ystrad Mynach	A. T. Minhinnick	1,884	249 ..	Ystrad Mynach
New Tredegar	M. J. Davies	—	— ..	Tirphil and New Tredegar,
West Elliot, New Tredegar.	M. J. Davies {	625	115 ..	Brithdir
East Elliot, New Tredegar.		611	131 ..	,,
Bargoed, Bargoed	R. L. Lechmere {	942	135 ..	Bargoed
Bargoed Brithdir, Bargoed.	Oertel {	620	105 ..	,,
Britannia, Pengam ..	A. E. Hiscox	990	145 ..	Pengam
Ogilvie, Deri ..	W. H. Knibbs	877	170 ..	Deri
Llantrisant ..	J. Gregor {	—	— ..	Llantrisant
Llanharan ..		804	108 ..	Llanharan
Windsor ..	W. J. Badger ..	880	131 ..	Abertridwr
Nantgarw, Taffswell ..	..	—	— ..	Glanyllyn, Cardiff, G.W.
Albion, Cilfynydd	J. W. Jordon ..	858	155	

Seams Worked : Seven Feet, Bute, Four Feet, Gellideg, Six Feet, Rhas Las, Red, Big, Brithdir, Lower Four Feet, No. 1, No. 4, Upper 4, 5 Feet, No. 3 Rhondda, No. 2 Yard, Two Feet Nine.
Class of Coal : Steam, House, Manufacturing, Coking.
Annual Output : Over 5,000,000 tons.
Power Used : Electric, Steam and Compressed Air. Voltage 3,300 and 550.
Other Mineral Worked : Fireclay.
Other Information : Owners of Coke-Oven and By-Product Plant.

The 1936 Powell Duffryn list of mines. Note the Llantrisant–Llanharan Collieries linked to one manager, Mr. John Gregor. The Llantrisant mine was closed after an explosion in 1942 in which Mr. Gregor was killed. The Llanharan mine went on to become a major part of the South Crop Horizon Mining programme.

The tips and colliery scars stand out prominently in this photograph which was taken from Chapel Hill, Parkside, by Mr. Bryant Perkins MIBC, 1961

YNYSMAERDY EXPLOSION - 2 JUNE 1941

When Llanharan North Pit Shaft was sunk in 1921, it was to be a pilot project to help with the planning of Ynysmaerdy Colliery. However, on Whit Monday 2 June 1941, at 1.45 p.m., a massive explosion ripped the pithead gear off the No. 2 shaft and wrecked the fan house and power house at Ynysmaerdy. The manager Mr. Jack Gregor, Noah Fletcher the morning shift winding engineman, David Thomas the switchboard attendant and Ernest Evans, banksman were killed. Such was the ferocity of the explosion the mine at Ynysmaerdy never re-opened. All further mining operations took place at Llanharan.

Below, the modern power house in 1940.

Utter devastation and horror greeted the officials and rescuemen at the Ynysmaerdy pithead after the explosion.

Workmen under the guidance of the local police begin the arduous task of clearing up the huge masses of timber and twisted steel.

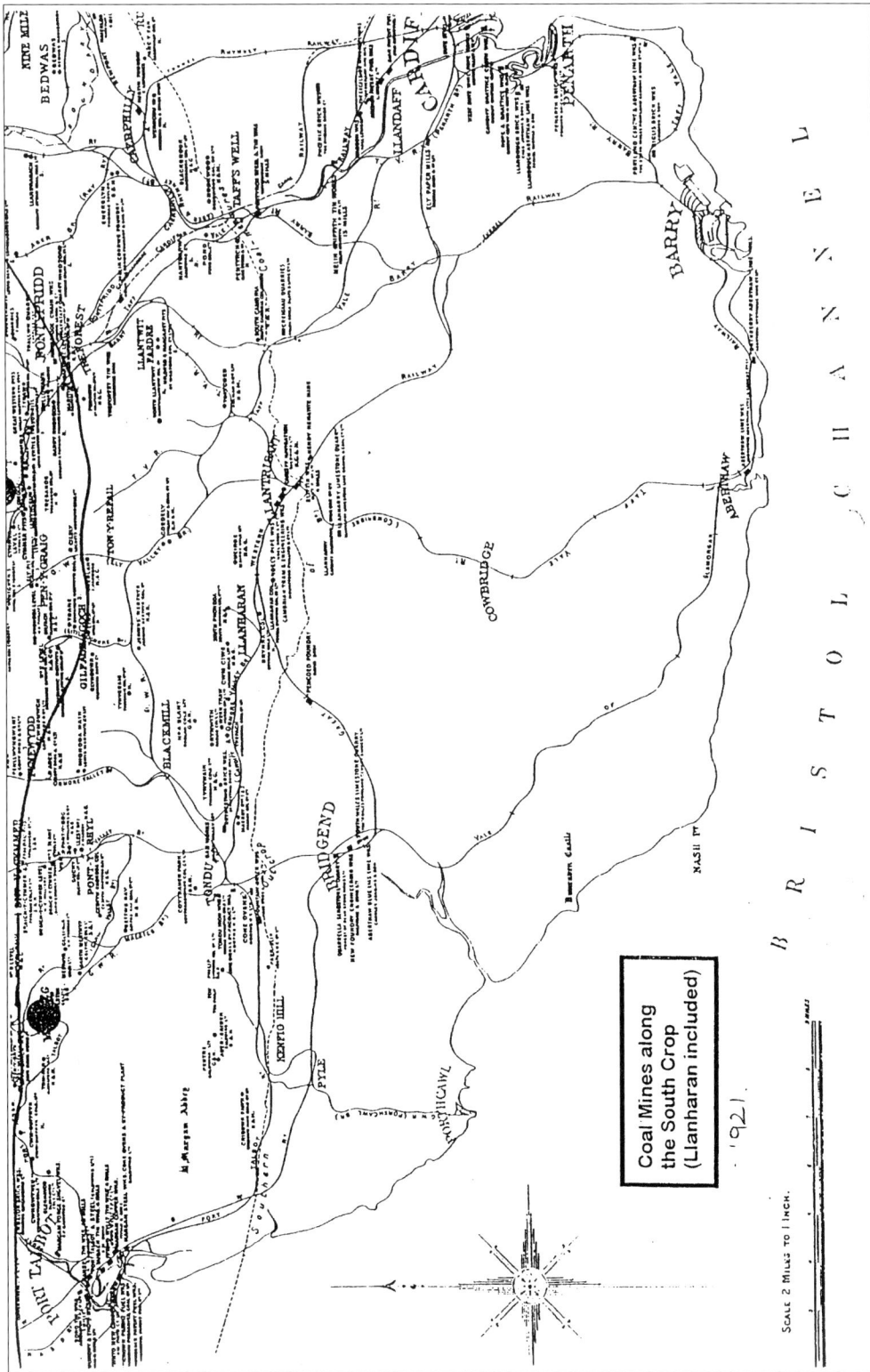

1921 Mines Survey Map

From Gordon's Map of South Wales, courtesy of Cefn Coed Mining Museum, Crynant.

Coal Mines along the South Crop (Llanharan included)

91

1958 Survey Map with South Crop mines

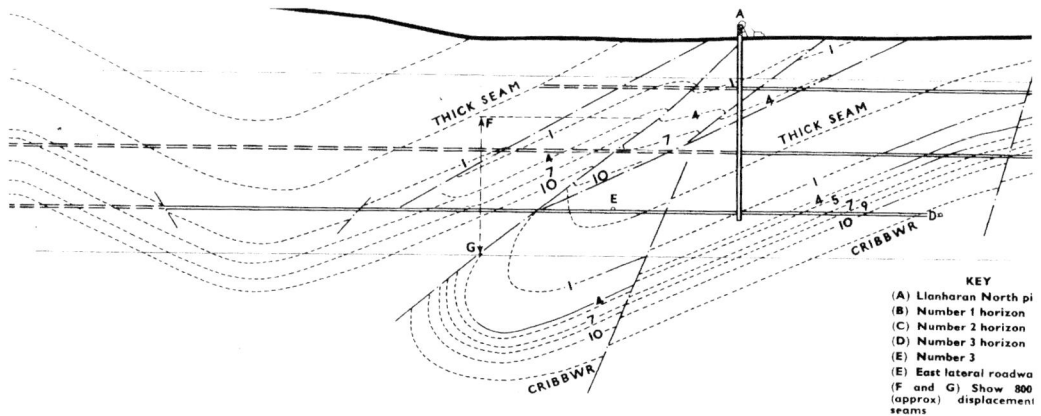

KEY
(A) Llanharan North pi
(B) Number 1 horizon
(C) Number 2 horizon
(D) Number 3 horizon
(E) Number 3
(E) East lateral roadwa
(F and G) Show 800
(approx) displacement
seams

Numbers show position of seams.

Section through the strata shows how the seams are folded and doubled back on each other by a major upthrow fault

In 1921 Powell Duffryn decided to put down the Llanharan North Pit. On its completion there was unresolved mystery - instead of eight seams as expected they found sixteen.

Fortunately they had sunk on the right spot. Had the new shaft been a quarter of a mile east or west they would have had to have gone through 150 feet of sand and gravel. Had it been a quarter of a mile north, the sinking would have been through an area affected by the major thrust which, years later, was found to be the cause of the disruption and duplication of seams.

After the Ynysmaerdy tragedy, all operations were centred at Llanharan, and Powell Duffryn's general manager, Mr. David Griffiths, believed that 'Horizon Mining' was the answer to the problems of the South Crop. The first major steps were taken at Llanharan. Progress was delayed by the war, but another important piece of work went ahead. This was the geological mapping of the area, in which Powell Duffryn and the Geological Survey co-operated. Geologist Mr. A.W. Woodland supervised and one of his assistants was a young apprentice surveyor, Roy Piggott (later at the age of 21 Roy was appointed surveyor at Llanharan and planned much of the re-organisation made possible by the extensive research).

PRICE TWOPENCE

October 15—21

RADIO TIMES

JOURNAL OF THE BRITISH BROADCASTING CORPORATION

(INCORPORATING WORLD-RADIO)

KEEPING THE HOME FIRES BURNING

In war as in peace, the work of miners, like those pictured here 'somewhere in Wales', remains of first importance to the well-being of the nation. A 'Home Front' programme on Wednesday will present a radio picture of the reaction in pits and homes to the new conditions.

Miners from Llanharan Colliery make their way home to Bryncae after a shift. Note the gas masks being carried at the outbreak of the Second World War, 1939.
Left to Right : Mr. L. Evans, Mr. Jack Trask, Mr. Wil Perriman, Mr. Tom Roberts, walking behind, right of photograph, Mr. Bill Owen.

94

Managers and officials of Llanharan Colliery

This is only a provisional list as records are sadly now not obtainable. I have relied in this list on help provided by former officials of Llanharan. For those names possibly left out from this list, I give my most sincere apologies.

Mr. J.S. Hughes, M.E., J.P., Llanharan Manager

Mr. Ivor James Prosser, Mechanical Engineer.

Mr. J.S. Hughes, the late manager of Llanharan Colliery, started in the village mine in 1924. He worked through the coalmining trade from shotsman to fireman, finally from overman to manager. Mr Hughes died in 1956. After his death two other managers took over concurrently, until in 1959 another Llanharan mining engineer in the form of Mr. Alan Reed took over the pit. In 1961 Mr. Reed left Llanharan to take over St. Johns Colliery, Maesteg. Up to the pit's closure at Llanharan in 1962, the mine was under the care of acting manager Mr. Bob Thomas.

Mr. Ivor Prosser came to Llanharan from New Tredegar when the North Pit was being sunk in 1921. He was to hold the position of mechanical engineer right up to the mine's closure. Mr. Prosser was shown in a film clip of the 'Blue Scar', a film which was partly made at Llanharan Colliery. Mr. Prosser died in 1965 aged 69 years.

The first names of some of the following officials are not known.

Managers
Mr. William Thomas
(opening of Mine 1921)
Mr. W. Bisp, Mr. Jack Gregor,
Mr. J. Veasey, Mr. D. Simpson,
Mr. Stan Hughes,
Mr. R.E. Jones, Mr. J. Jones,
Mr. Alan Reed.

Under Managers
Mr. Eddie Edwards, Mr. Bob Thomas.

Mechanical Engineers
Mr. I.J. Prosser,
Mr. Norman Thomas (Group)

Electrical Engineers
Mr. David Osbourne Evans,
Mr. Jack Ellis (Group)

Shop Foremen
Mr. Les Norman, Mr. Alan Hellings.

Surface Foremen
Mr. J. Davey, Mr. Harry Hughes

Assistant Managers	Mr. D.J. Sayward, Mr. Dennis Simmonds, Mr. Elvid Morgan, Mr. Tom Evans.
Head Surveyors	Mr. Hampson, Mr. R. Piggott, Mr. Meirion Lewis, Mr. Len Raymond, Mr. Gwyn Brooking, apprentice.
Overmen	Mr. R. Donovan, Mr. Ike Williams, Mr. E. Coulson, Mr. Haydn Davies, Mr. Em Matthews, Mr. W. Tibbott, Mr. A. Goldsworthy, Mr. W. Mote, Mr. Harry Hughes, Mr. Ron Bayliss, Mr. Wil Thomas, Mr. Evan Davies, Mr. David Davies.
Firemen	Mr. Gwillym Thomas, Mr. David Evans, Mr. Stan Welsh, Mr. Ted Thomas, Mr. Bert Piggott, Mr. Cliff Chance, Mr. Bob Powell, Mr. Glyn Thomas, Mr. Billy Griffin, Mr. Billy Thomas, Mr. Frank Coles, Mr. Mel James, Mr. Tom Thomas, Mr. Jack Jenkins, Mr. Harry Jones, Mr. Roy McAndrew, Mr. Glan Cater, Mr. Dil Davies, Mr. Len Clarke, Mr. Jim Powell, Mr. E. Harrison, Mr. Roy Farnham, Mr. Ted Thomas (Senior) Mr. Terry Williams, Mr. Tony Coulson, Mr. Fred (Maxie) Williams Mr. David (Ben) Jones.
Shotsmen	Mr. Dil Worth, Mr. David Ryan, Mr. M. Mote, Mr. Bill Pritchard, Mr. G. Gore, Mr. Gerald Morgan, Mr. Eynon Hawkins, Mr. Hubert Perkins, Mr. Mal Jones Mr. F. Summers, Mr. Wilf Powell, Mr. M. Price, Mr. Vince Witts, Mr. Dil North.
Head Cashier	Mr. E. James, Mr. Vince Saunders (assistant)
Training Officers	Mr. Cliff Chance, Mr. Stan Rees, Mr. Gerwyn Jones.
Timekeepers	Mr. Geoff Stephens, Mr. David Richards, Mr. Glyn Matthews.
Storekeepers	Mr. Griff Pearce, Mr. Ray Pick, Mr. Glyn Croft.

Officials make their way to the North Pit

Front three officials, left to right: Mr. Arthur Goldsworthy, Mr. Fred (Maxie) Williams, Mr. David Jones. The miner in the background is Mr. Sam (Ogmore) Davies.

Llanharan Colliery

Mr. T. Evans, Assistant.Manager and Mr. R. Thomas, Undermanager.

Mr. Herbie Powell, N.U.M. Chairman and Mr. Charlie Mace, Past Chairman.

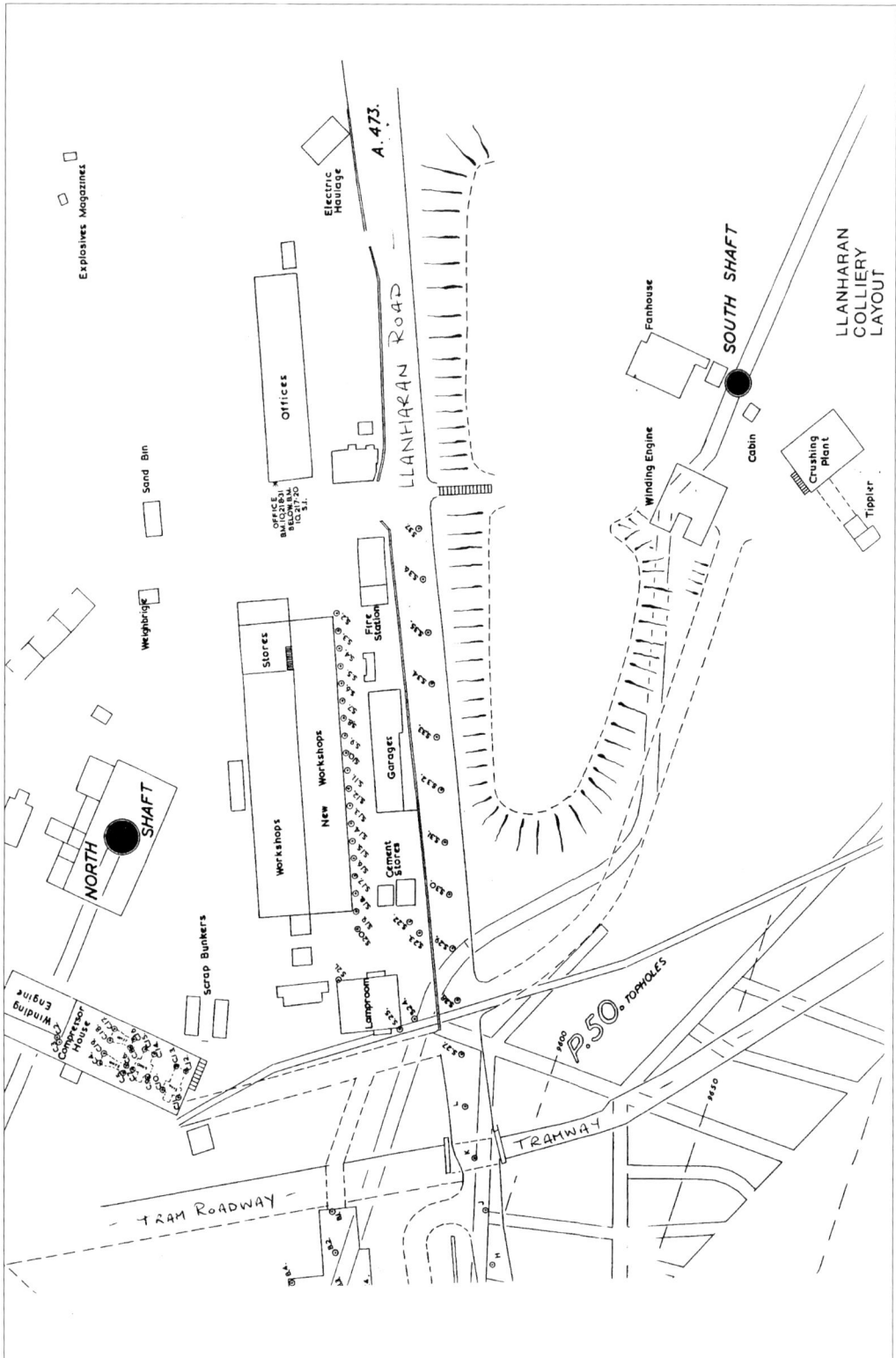

Llanharan Colliery Layout.

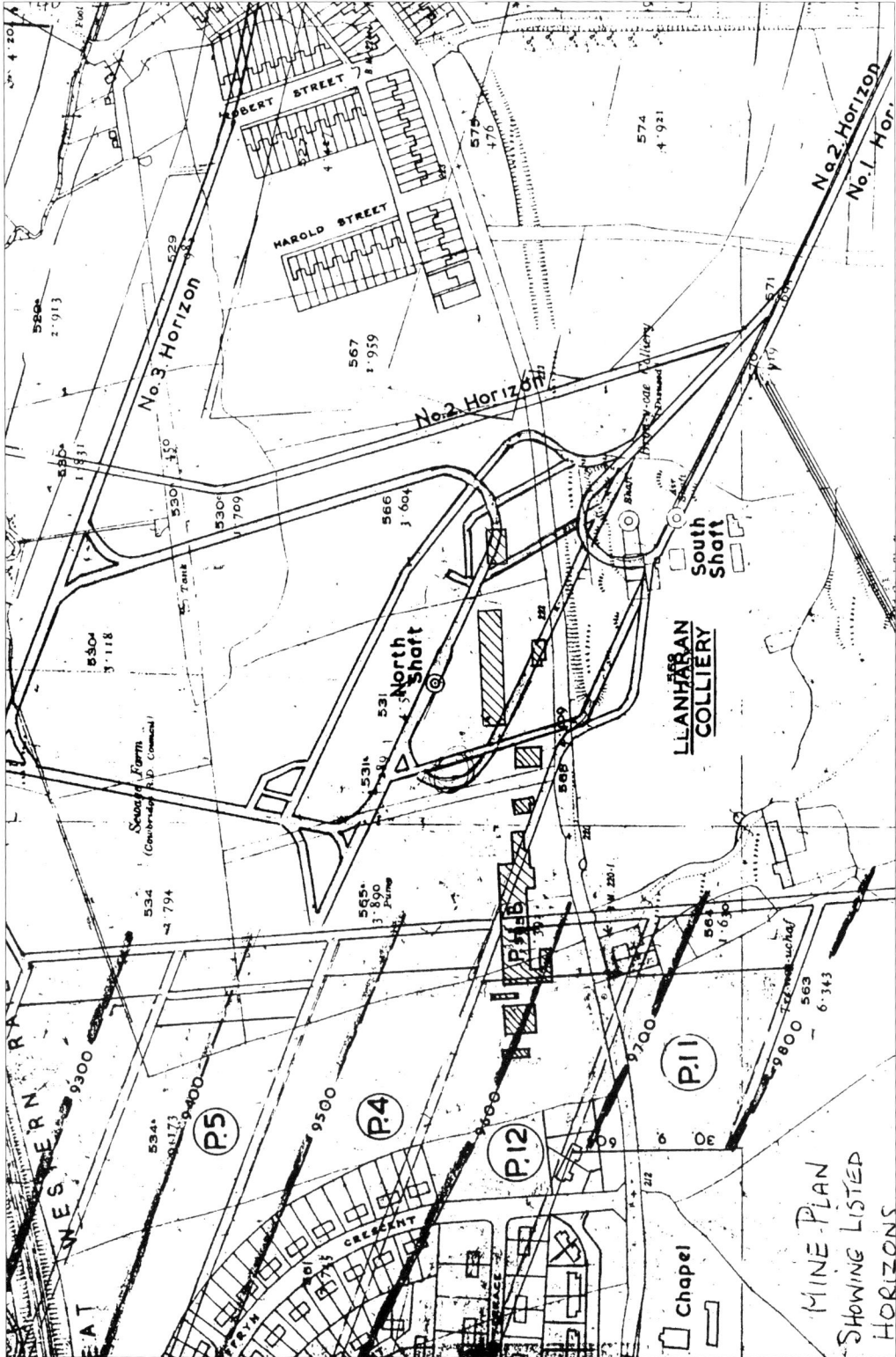

Mine Layout for Llanharan Colliery with Listed Horizons.

Llanharan Colliery

Stone from drift headings was crushed at the surface and returned underground for stowing. This work was done with a continuous shift of trams travelling up the South Shaft. Every week 1,500 tons of stone was sent out from the headings which penetrated the South Crop.

New installations at Llanharan Colliery meant increased engineering skills and extra technical work for engineer, Mr. Ivor Prosser and assistant Mr. Jim Davey.

Mr. Roy Piggott was appointed surveyor at Llanharan and planned much of the re-organisation.

At varying depths concrete lined level roadways like this were exploiting the South Crop. The Llanharan Mine was regarded as one of the most modern in the area and many new mechanical ideas were experimentally used here.

MRS. BETTY BAXTER NÉE TIBBOTT

After a period of studying at Clarkes College, Cardiff, Betty, at the age of sixteen, entered the employ of the Powell Duffryn Company, starting work at Llanharan Colliery, which was then during the 1940s fast becoming the showpiece mine in the No. 2 area (South Crop).

After serving in various departments, Betty eventually moved into the manager's office where she soon adapted and learned a considerable amount about mining principles and underground planning and mapping 'working through the plane of the upthrust faults' and 'cross measure drivages' within coal seam analysis became familiar jargon to the young Betty Tibbott. Later, she worked in the costing department and recalls the payment of wages to the miners on Friday afternoons. "It was hard work,"

Mrs. Betty Baxter (née Tibbott)

remembered Betty during an interview, "the pays would be made up in the morning. Remember, there were over a thousand men employed at the pit then." Betty told of the amusement in listening to the comments and banter by the men when collecting their wages. Some of the men would be arguing and quibbling with various officials over disputed payments of shifts. But all in all Betty concluded by stating that in general Friday was usually a good humoured period.

She soon became secretary to the manager, Mr. H. C. Bisp. "He was regarded as an excellent mining engineer, and highly respected by his officials." she stated categorically. "Mind you," she smiled, "he didn't always see eye to eye with some of the men in the mine, because he was a man who demanded results, and to be fair, he usually got them."

Betty learned to drive and explained how she used to travel weekly to

Mr. Wil Tibbott who was a well respected overman at Llanharan Colliery.

Cowbridge to collect forms for the miners to have their cheese rations, these were collected from the Cowbridge Food Office.

She was the daughter of Mr. Wil Tibbott a well respected overman at the colliery. Betty narrated how in 1947 the reputable London writer and film producer, Miss Jill Craigie, came with her film unit to the mine to shoot sequences for her production 'Blue Scar'. "She was a lovely lady." recalls Betty. "She used our office as a base and my father was given the task of escorting her and her film crew into safe districts in the mine to shoot their scenes. Many scenes were made at Llanharan and it caused quite a stir in the village at the time." When Miss Craigie left the colliery Betty recalls finding a beautiful silk handkerchief on the table of the office, obviously one which belonged to Miss Craigie. "I kept it in the draw of my desk for months but it was never claimed." she explained. When the film was shown at Llanharan Cinema, the whole village turned out to see it. Betty laughed, "I was thinking at the time how

John Phillips, the manager of the cinema, must have made a fortune the three days that the film was shown. There were indeed capacity audiences."

When Betty married, her husband, Mr. Glyn Baxter, came into the management of the mine and was a highly respected official. "It was really hard work on times" said Betty, "there were always technical problems at the pit. But there were fulfilling moments, especially when coal production targets were hit; during those times there would be great jubilation."

Betty ended her interview by quoting what many other former colliery workers have said during interviews. "I honestly believe that when the mine closed at Llanharan in 1962, the village died with it", but added "many of my fellow office staff have long passed on, but I will always remember them with a deep affection...."

Source: Interview Mrs. Baxter –
19 December 1995

WALTER WESTCOTT

Mr. Westcott's service to the mining industry spans a period of 44 years. It was in 1938 when he started at Llanharan Colliery which was then relatively humble beginnings as an assistant storekeeper and assistant timekeeper. However, his conscientious approach to his work saw him promoted to the Llanharan Colliery office after working only two years in the store. He eventually became the chief colliery clerk, responsible for the wages of approximately 1,000 men. In 1954 he was promoted to the No. 2 Area Office (Maesteg Area) in Tondu as the area statistician.

After a few years at Tondu he was promoted to a more senior post within the Area Cost Department. Owing to the contraction of the mining industry, and the closure of collieries in 1967, six areas in South Wales were contracted to two, one located in Tondu and the other in Ystrad Mynach. Mr. Westcott continued to work at the Tondu office in a senior position in the new area until 1972 when, due to further contraction, the two areas were reduced to one covering the whole of the South Wales Coalfield and located at Llanishen, Cardiff. He was then transferred to the new area as the deputy area cost accountant, a position he held for a number of years until his retirement in the June of 1982, at the age of 62. This was a senior position in the Finance Department, being responsible for the preparation and distribution of profit and loss accounts for each colliery and its associated activities. Mr. Westcott readily attributes his remarkable and successful climb up the ladder of promotion to the co-operation and support of his former colleagues, however one only has to look at other aspects of his life to understand

Walter (Wally) Westcott at Llanishen, Cardiff, while working as head of the Cost Accountancy Department of the National Coal Board.

why he is such a successful and likable individual. In addition to the onerous duties of full time occupation in the mining industry, he became clerk to the local council, a position he was to hold for 41 years from 1954 to 1995, when he retired at the age of 75. His council work and involvement with local affairs over such a long period of time makes him one of Llanharan's most respected people. His attitude to life in the community and his hard working efforts towards the upkeep of the Bethlehem Congregational Chapel cause has made him many friends over the years.

PICTORIAL VIEW

SHEWING THE DEVELOPMENT OF HORIZON MINING LLANHARAN COLLIERY.

WAGES IN THE SOUTH WALES COALFIELD.

The Minimum Percentage increased from 22¼ to 25, and the Subsistence Wage from 7/8 to 8/1 as and from January 1st, 1936.

UNDERGROUND.

GRADE	Minimum Standard Rate Per Shift.	Standard Plus 25 per cent.	Subsistence Allowance Per Shift.	Total Wage Per Shift.
Colliers and Timbermen—				
Pieceworkers	6/10½	8/7	—	8/7
Daywagemen	6/6	8/1.5	—	8/1.5
Coal Cuttermen	6/4½	7/11.62	1.38d.	8/1
Masons, Pitmen, Tonnage Hauliers ...	6/3	7/9.75	3.25d.	8/1
Rippers, Bottom Cutters	6/-	7/6	7d.	8/1
Hauliers* (over 18 years)	5/10½	7/4.12	8.88d.	8/1
Leading Hitchers, Ropesplicers, Timber Drawers, Airwaymen, Underground Winding Enginemen	5/9	7/2.25	10.75d.	8/1
Main Haulagemen	5/6 to 5/9	6/10.5 to 7/2.25	1/2.5 to 10.75d.	8/1
Ropechangers, Riders, Underground Banksmen	5/7½	7/0.37	1/0.63	8/1
Roadmen, Bottom Cutters (soft bottom)	5/4½	6/8.62	1/4.38	8/1
Hitchers (Ordinary), Sheafmen, Rollermen, Pulleymen, Jig Hitchers ...	5/3	6/6.75	1/6.25	8/1
Cog Cutters, Electricians	5/1½	6/4.87	1/8.13	8/1
Colliers' Helpers, Assistant Timbermen, Labourers, and other grades ...	5/-	6/3	1/10	8/1

*Hauliers between 18 and 21 years of age are only entitled to 4d. Subsistence Allowance equals 7/8.12.

Wage Structure (1)

BOYS UNDERGROUND.

Under 14 years of age	2/-	2/6	—	2/6
Under 15 years of age	2/3	2/9.75	—	2/9.75
Over 15 and under 16	2/7½	3/3.37	—	3/3.37
Over 16 and under 17	3/-	3/9	4d.	4/1
Over 17 and under 18	3/4½	4/2.62	4d.	4/6.62
Over 18 and under 19	3/9	4/8.25	4d.	5/0.25
Over 19 and under 20	4/1½	5/1.87	4d.	5/5.87
Over 20 and under 21	4/6	5/7.50	4d.	5/11.50

SURFACEMEN—MINIMUM RATES.

Fitters, Carpenters, Smiths, Leading Sawyers	5/3 to 5/10	6/6.75 to 7/3.5	1/6.25 to 9.5d.	8/1
Main Haulagemen	5/6 to 5/9	6/10.5 to 7/2.25	1/2.5 to 10.75d.	8/1
Banksmen	6/-	7/6	7d.	8/1
Stokers	5/6	6/10.5	1/2.5	8/1
Feeders	5/8	7/1	1/-	8/1
Other Grades	5/-	6/3	1/10	8/1

The figures given in these tables are Minimum Wages. At some Collieries the Standard Rates of the grades are higher, and where higher rates have been in operation they will continue.

Wage Structure (2)

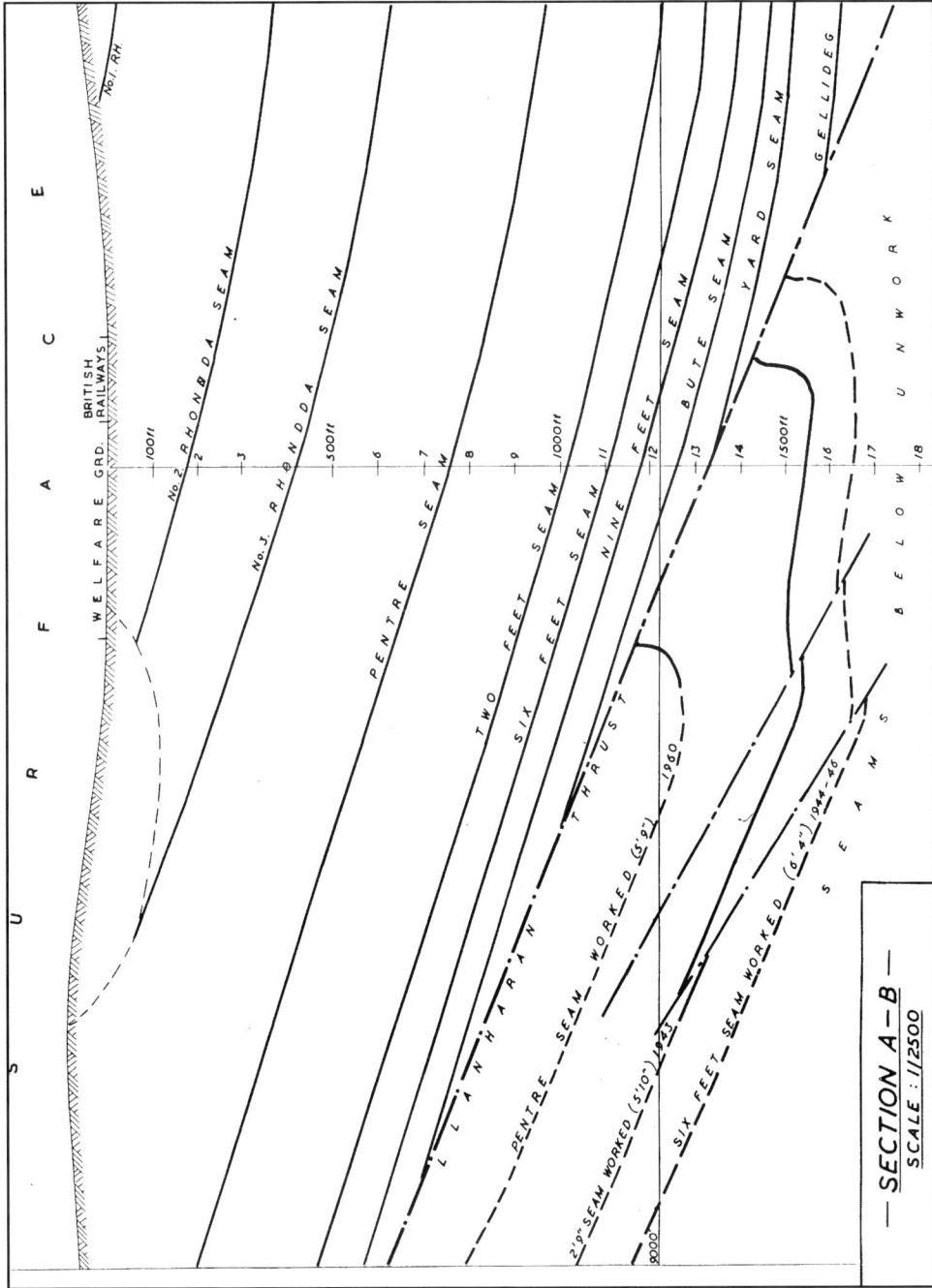

Seams worked at Llanharan Colliery during the 1950s.

No. 2 Rhondda Seam, No. 3 Rhondda Seam, Pentre Seam, Two Feet Seam, Six Feet Seam, Nine Feet Seam, Yard Seam and Gellideg Seam. (Seams below unworked).

11th January, 1951.

Dear Friend

Before Christmas the leaders of your National
Union called on you to make a special effort to
increase output and in particular to work on
Saturdays.   There was a fine response and I
want to thank you for what you did then.

But I want to ask you to carry on with your
effort right through the winter months.

We are still threatened with a serious
shortage of coal.   Apart from difficulties in
our homes there is a real danger that industry
may be slowed down.   You will realise that this
would mean unemployment for your fellow workers
in other industries and hardship for their wives
and families.   It would also be a blow to our
national recovery.

I am therefore asking you personally to do
your best to help to avoid this danger.

I ask you on behalf of the Government and of
the country to go to work on every regular working
day throughout the next four months, and to attend
all the Saturday shifts for which your pit is open,
or to work an extra half hour for five days,
whichever is the custom in your district.

One final word: knowing you as I do I am
sure that all of you will live up to the great
traditions of your calling and provide the coal
we need.   The nation looks to you;   I am sure
that you will not fail the nation.

May I wish you and your family a happy and
prosperous New Year.

Yours sincerely

C. R. Attlee

NATIONAL COAL BOARD
(SOUTH WESTERN DIVISION)

No. 2 Area

The Chairman (J. S. Hughes, Esq., M.E.) and the Organising Committee request the pleasure of the company of

G. Water, Esq.

at the

OFFICIAL OPENING OF LLANHARAN PITHEAD BATHS

On SATURDAY, 28th MARCH, 1953,

at 2.30 p.m.

The Opening Ceremony will be performed by :—

D. M. REES, Esq., M.I.M.E.

(Chairman—South-Western Division, National Coal Board)

R.S.V.P. to—
J. S. Hughes, Esq., M.E.,
Agent/Manager—Llanharan Colliery,
Llanharan, Glam.

Kindly bring this Programme with you

LLANHARAN PITHEAD BATHS (CON.)

ORDER OF PROCEEDINGS

1. J. S. HUGHES, Esq., M.E., Agent/Manager, Llanharan Colliery, will take the Chair at 2.30 p.m.

2. A. T. MINHINNICK, Esq., M.E., Area General Manager, will introduce D. M. REES, Esq., M.I.M.E., Chairman, South-Western Division.

3. Mr. D. M. REES'S ADDRESS.

4. TOUR OF INSPECTION OF BATHS.

5. REFRESHMENTS (by Invitation)
   SERVED IN CANTEEN.

6. SHORT ADDRESSES.

CHAIRMAN'S ADDRESS.

W. PAYNTER, Esq.   ...   President National Union of Mineworkers —South Wales.

F. MARCHANT, Esq.   ...   Area Labour Officer— National Coal Board.

Councillor HOLFORD MORGAN, J.P. }   Chairman —Cowbridge R.D.C.

W. SPERRIN, Esq., J.P.   ...   President, South Wales and Monmouthshire Colliery Examiners, Shotfirers and Overmen's Association.

A. PEARSON, Esq., M.P.   ...   Pontypridd Division.

A VOTE OF THANKS to D. M. REES, Esq., will be proposed by J. T. B. WELBOURN, Esq., Sub-Area Production Manager (N.C.B.)

Seconded by HERBERT POWELL, Esq., Chairman, Llanharan Lodge, National Union of Mineworkers.

CHAIRMAN'S CLOSING REMARKS.

HORIZON MINING

Throughout the changes that took place under the Horizon Mining programme over the years at Llanharan Colliery, output per manshift and total output was satisfactorily maintained at a very high level. This was due in large measure to the co-operation of both workmen and officials alike in what was termed a reconstruction experiment. The team work in driving stone headings was also a big factor in making possible the success of Horizon Mining.

Looking back, there are a number of individuals who deserve mention from that advanced programme set up during the late 1940s. Mr. Charles Mace, chairman of the N.U.M. Lodge and Mr. Tom Vivian, lodge secretary, did tremendous work to promote the new mining plan. Their willing co-operation made possible the speedy realisation of the scheme.

Yes, the ceremony of 8 October 1948 was a milestone in the progress of deep mining at Llanharan. It marked the beginning of a new phase in mining techniques in Great Britain, and was due largely to the initiative shown by Powell Duffryn Limited in the past and to the enterprise and persistence of Mr. David Griffiths, Powell Duffryn's general manager, who applied his skills to the task of reconstruction during the most critical years in the history of the South Crop.

Llanharan Colliery surface workers enjoy an evening out
at the Cambrian Hotel, Bridgend c.1952.

Llamharan and *Wern Tarw* Officials 1961

MR. H.C. BISP M.E.
LLANHARAN COLLIERY MANAGER

When Mr. Hubert Bisp died during the late 1960s, we saw the passing of one of the most notable mining engineers associated with the exploration of the South Crop.

Background on this most amiable gentleman is sparse, but we learn that he came to Llanharan Colliery as manager in 1941, after a period near Bargoed. Throughout his working period at Llanharan, he made a major contribution. His written work on the driving of hard headings, and seam programmes, which he compiled in 1948 and read before The South Wales Institute of Engineers, was enthusiastically recognised at a time when Llanharan Colliery was going through the modernisation stage of Horizon Mining.

Llanharan Colliery, which was situated on the South Crop of the South Wales coalfield was highly disturbed by severe folding, faulting and thrusting. Moreover, the seams had an average inclination of 12 inches per yard, but varied from 8 up to 24 inches per yard in different parts of the pit. These conditions made road formation in the plane of the seam and transport on such roads extremely complicated and costly. Consequently a decision was made to re-organise and Horizon Mining methods came into fruition. This, briefly, envisaged the driving of all main roadways (laterals and cross measures) in stone at pre-determined gradients to intersect and win the seams to be worked. The planning entailed the elimination of all secondary coal haulage to be replaced by gate and trunk conveying to a fixed tram loading point on the main haulage plane itself. The new plans, when fully operational, pleased Mr. Bisp because in the first two years it was a complete success. Under him Llanharan's districts were the first to be developed under these lines of operation. Modernisation in the form of suitable gradients for locomotive haulage was introduced. In his report, he indicated that his success depended on the team of officials and men who had quickly adapted to a new working structure. His report went as follows:

"I wish to thank all who have co-operated with me in both the driving of hard headings at the pit and in the compiling of my work in this document. This includes all workmen and officials engaged in the new operations. Special thanks to the following persons.

Messrs. David Griffiths and A. Tait, for their interest and encouragement at all times. Mr. I.J. Prosser, Mechanic, for his work and whole hearted co-operation on the mechanical side. Mr. W.J. Hampson, Surveyor, for his assistance in the work and preparation of diagrams for the paper."

Mr. Bisp eventually handed the manager's reins to Mr. J.S. Hughes, who vigorously fought to maintain successful planning at the mine. Sadly, Mr. Hughes died after a spell of ill health in 1956.

As stated, Mr. Bisp died during the late 1960s. Although time cast a shadow over coal mining, the legacy of H.C. Bisp's excellent work is held in a number of Welsh mining museum records.

Mr. Bisp's daughter, Sandra, who was at one time a reporter with the South Wales Echo, is alive and well and believed to be living abroad.

I would like to thank Mr. Bernard John Walters of Pencoed who kindly loaned the following underground prints showing examples of mining machinery installed in the Llanharan Colliery during the 1950s. Mr. Walters and his team at Llanharan were responsible for the introduction to the pit of two very important systems - the German scraper chain machinery and the Dowty Free Prop system.

Panzer Face, Llanharan Colliery, showing German scraper chain.

'Panzer' face, Llanharan Colliery
Photograph shows the German scraper chain in the Panzer face. This print was described as –
"German scraper chain in process of 'snaking'."

Mr. Bernard Walters examines some of his mining equipment which he introduced for Dowty Engineering into the Sripur Colliery owned by the Lodna Coal Company, near Asansol, West Bengal, India.

Left to Right - Mr. Bernard Walters, senior engineer, Mr. N.N. Kapur, mining rngineer and Mr. J. Jootla, manager.

During the 1950s five pits in the South Wales Coalfield were selected for a modernisation programme. For this action engineer Mr. Bernard Walters of Pencoed was given charge. His team was responsible for the introduction of the modern Dowty Hydraulic Prop system into the Llanharan mine. Mr. Walters, who still resides at Pencoed, spent over 36 years with the Dowty Company.

During the mid '60s he was sent to India to supervise the installation of hydraulic pitprops in a mine in Bengal and it was there that he noticed that the standard of living near the mines was higher than that elsewhere. He spent two months in India, his work taking him to a number of settlements throughout the West Bengal coalfield. He was amazed how little the Indian workers knew about mechanical mining when he arrived there. The workers had to have the simplest of tasks explained to them. But once they knew how to adapt to his newly introduced system they became polished teams of workers.

Returning to South Wales after his period in India, Mr. Walters continued as resident engineer for the Dowty Company.

Llanharan Colliery 'Panzer face' 1954
The above photograph shows the distinctive uses and positions which the Dowty Prop Free System could work. The new technology at Llanharan made the mine one of the most advanced in South Wales.

Workmen pose for the camera at Llanharan Colliery 1954.
Left to Right: David Lewis, Billy Rees (Gilfach). Charlie Bundy, unknown, Ianto Howells,
Front: Emrys Edmunds.

Wern Tarw Colliery officials 1953.
The gentleman sitting left of the table is Mr. David Miles, M.E., Werm Tarw manager. On his left is
retiring official, Mr. Stan Rees, to whom a presentation was made at the Kings Head, Pencoed.

Our photograph shows two Llanharan Colliery (house coal) delivery men during a moment of relaxation. Sadly we cannot put names to them. "Powell Duffryn House Coal Llanharan" can be clearly seen on the side of the lorry. c.1922.

Llanharan South Pit headgear - 1960

Pay day – Syd Worgan calls in the office to collect his pay. Syd was featherweight champion boxer of Wales in 1944.

JOSEPH PASCOE 1892 - 1961

Joseph Pascoe was born at Llanharan in one of the small cottages at Meiros Fach (now demolished). His parents came to Llanharan from Cornwall during the rich coal bonanza of the 1880s. After settling at Meiros Fach, William Pascoe took a job at Meiros Colliery and soon became an official there. In later years Joseph himself followed his father into the mine.

Talking about his life, Joseph explained that he began his mining career at the age of fourteen. He started work at Meiros for 2/-d. per day (10p) and only saw the light of day on Saturday after working a short shift! He recalled an occasion when he and four workmates were trapped in an underground fall. One of the men panicked after the roof caved in. Thinking that the end had truly come the poor soul began crying hysterically. Being an experienced miner, Joseph kept his cool, calming the upset miner. Within three hours the rescue team broke through to them. Joseph stated that the poor upset miner must have been frightened out of his skin because he went up the pit and was never seen again.

When Meiros closed down in 1931, Joseph went to work in Wern Tarw. His final move was to Llanharan Colliery, where he remained until he retired through ill-health in 1959 aged 68 years.

During his early days, Joseph was a playing member of Llanharan R.F.C. It must be pointed out that his brother Danny was capped for Wales in 1923. We should also recall that the Pascoes were part of those early pioneers who established Rugby Football in the village. The story of Llanharan's early rugby days are well documented through the collieries and the Meiros Cup, a competition held between local colliery teams. Collectors items of the Meiros Cup days, medals etc., are treasured by a number of families to this day. In later years Joseph became a prominent member of the Llanharan Constitutional Club serving on its committee, and was its president for a period of ten years.

People like Joseph Pascoe never die. They are part of a rich hardy age easily brought to mind. The demise of the collieries saw the passing of many of these outstanding characters and personalities. So much so, that it can be truthfully said that the Llanharan of today has sadly lost its true identity.

Sources: Extracts from the "Llantrisant Observer" 1959.
Interview with Mrs. Violet Witts (*née* Pascoe) daughter.

Mr. Joseph James Pascoe with his wife Florence Martina.

Mr. Pascoe worked for over fifty years in the local pits namely Meiros, South Rhondda, Wern Tarw, before working at the Llanharan Pit until he retired at the grand age of 68.

Mining officials honour Llanharan collier Mr. Joseph Pascoe

Surrounded by members of his family, friends and hospital staff, Mr. Joseph Pascoe received a watch from Mr. A. Coulson (overman, Llanharan Colliery) to mark fifty years service in the Llanharan District. Left to Right: Mr. Idris Pascoe, Mr. Alan Reed (manager), Mr. Ray Brimble (N.U.M. Lodge), Mr. Ivor Pascoe, Mrs. Elizabeth Butcher, Mr. Trevor Pascoe, Mrs. Florence Alford, Mrs. Elsie Neate, nurses unknown, Mrs. Vi Witts and Mr. A.E. Coulson (official, Llanharan Colliery), making the presentation to Mr. Pascoe.

Llanharan Colliery Carriage and Wagon Works 1955
Left to right: Mr. Bryn Matthews, Mr. Trevor Pascoe and Mr. Ivor Trotman

'OLD TOY'S BOYS'

'Old Toy' was the nickname bestowed upon Mr. Ivor Prosser the colliery surface engineer, who was frequently seen around the area chasing up the workers and in general keeping everyone on their toes. When seen about the colliery yard, the word would soon get around that "Old Toy was about". However, despite Mr. Prosser's hardline attitude, he was a well respected colliery engineer.

The photograph shows the south tip workers sitting on the 'tippler' during their break from work. 1951.
Left to Right: Back Row: T. Hardman, W. White, L. Wareham, T. Davies and H. Waters.
Front Row: W. Witts, B. Jones and J. Owen.

Llanharan Colliery Carriage and Wagon Works 1955.
Left to Right: Mr. Emrys Edmunds, Mr. Arthur Davey, Mr. Bryn Matthews and Mr. Ted Morris.
Front: Mr. Ray Pick.

Village will have silent mornings

Western Mail Reporter

PEOPLE of the mining village of Llanharan will regret the closure of the local colliery on August 25 in many ways.

But perhaps the least serious, although very significant, will be the end of the colliery hooter. Through the years, it has acted as a regular alarm clock for sleeping villagers.

Mr. Stan Dowler, who lives near the colliery, where he has worked for 33 years, said last night, "I am naturally very sorry to see the colliery closing because it will put the entire village out of joint.

Not the same

"We have relied so much on the hooter that Llanharan will not be the same with so much peace and quiet. It will alter the traditional colliery life of the village, although I suppose we will get used to the change in time."

With the exception of nine men, alternative employment has been found for the 450 men working at the colliery. They will have new jobs in other collieries in the No. 2 area.

Mr. Sid Worgan, landlord of the Bear Hotel, Llantrisant, has worked at Llanharan Colliery for 25 years. Like the others, he is sorry to see it close down. He has been offered alternative employment but has not yet decided whether he will accept.

Fortunate

Mr. Charley Bundy, a foreman, will take up a similar job at the Western Colliery, Ogmore Vale.

He said "I have been fortunate in having another job as foreman, but I shall not leave Llanharan village, where I have lived for the past 26 years.

"The Coal Board have done their best to fit the men into other collieries and have done a very good job under the circumstances."

The end of coalmining at Llanharan. The colliery closed on 25 August 1962.

The above report from the Western Mail carries a tone of sadness with the closure of Llanharan's last pit. The late Mr. Stan Dowler's words in the above statement, have, over the past thirty years, proved prophetic. "It will alter the traditional colliery life of the village."

The silent sentinel.
Photograph – Celtic Energy

Llanharan South pithead gear stands in silent isolation weeks before demolition. In the background, the old school, the council estate and the Bethleham Chapel, look down on the "silent sentinel". The cultural life of all three was centred around the pit.
The sites on the left of the photograph, Oakbrook and Chapel Hill Close are relatively modern.

Official Mr. Brian Donovan (centre) adapts to new surroundings.
Llanharan Colliery had closed and this photograph shows our ex Llanharan official at Garw Colliery, 1964.

The old washery ruins and railway sidings weeks before demolition.

Llanharan Colliery site 1977.
The opencast screens and washery stand awaiting demolition.

The colliery entrance and store buildings are shown in photograph (left) while the screens stand in excellent condition.

17 November 1993. The machinery moves in and the North Pit staging is about to be removed.

Standing near the pit mouth, author T.J. Witts looks for the last time into the shaft of the North Pit. The closure of Llanharan Colliery saw an effective end to deep mining at Llanharan.

Author with Mr. Jim Davies, site contractor. In the background the
Llanharan North Pit shaft is in its final stage of capping. 20 November 1993.

The capped North Pit shaft is marked denoting the end of deep mining at Llanharan, November 1993.

An obelisk on the site of the North Pit shaft gives the mine's historical details. November 1993.

The colliery has gone! Soon the scars of a once prominent mining era will be gone forever. Photograph 1994.

Filming 'Blue Scar' at Llanharan Colliery in 1947

Producer Jill Craigie (third left front) has just returned to the surface after shooting underground sequences for the film. Here our photographer shows a number of Llanharan colliers mingling with the actors. Jill Craigie made many friends while filming at Llanharan.

MISS JILL CRAIGIE - BRITAIN'S FIRST WOMAN FILM DIRECTOR

Jill Craigie caused a sensation in art and housing circles with her first two films 'Out of Chaos' and 'The Way We Live'. 'Out of Chaos' was widely received by art enthusiasts. Her attempt to explain how modern art "got that way" was, however, frowned on as a commercial proposition, but the critics had different ideas and came to her rescue forcing exhibitors to show Britain's first woman producer-director's work to the public.

'The Way We Live', a story of Plymouth's plan for reconstruction, was Miss Craigie's second venture. Again, box office minds tried to write off her work, but the press caught sight of it and praised the film enthusiastically so that it had to be shown.

Jill Craigie is described as a determined woman with a mind of her own, and when she was offered what she considered a lesser position, in spite of her achievements and praise bestowed on her two films, she decided, there and then, that she and the Rank Organisation should part company.

The documentary was a speciality of Miss Craigie's, and she wrote many "shorts" for the Ministry of Information during the war years.

She looked upon 'fiction' productions with deep caution, believing that to undertake such a venture one had to - "make sure you make a masterpiece of it, do it perfectly." She didn't, during those years after the war, have the money to undertake such a challenge, but even then deep down she secretly relished the idea. Her insistence on doing forthright and vital themes is one reason for her coming to South Wales, even though she still didn't have the financial resources of a big organisation behind her. Using her own independent capital she began writing and planning a script based on the Welsh mining communities, and in 1947 came to South Wales to make her film entitled 'Blue Scar'.

At the time Miss Craigie was asked why she chose mining as a theme for her film. "Well," she replied, "I wanted to do something important, and what is more important than coal today? When you think of coal, your thoughts go immediately to Wales - the singing, the valleys."

Abergwynfi and Llanharan were well featured in Miss Craigie's production. Abergwynfi was chosen because it was a compact village of 3,500 people and as she said at the time, "almost unbelievably photogenic." At Abergwynfi she set up her headquarters in the Western Hotel, which was an established haunt for the miners. She believed from the start that being amongst the miners and watching their daily routine was important to bring realism to her production. No stone was left unturned in her quest for reality. She knew that the Welshmen viewed 'picture people' with a jaundiced eye; so far the best efforts of Hollywood to depict Wales had gone down none too well. Miss Craigie endeared herself to the Welshmen of Abergwynfi, and one evening accepted the challenge of one cynic when asked - "How do you see the Welsh miner?" She was standing at the bar, dozens of eyes upon her, eyes that had seen through the years much misery and despair, here now scrutinising an 'outsider' who had come to study their way of life. "I see him," she began, "as a humorous sort of fellow, a

Left to Right: Mr. H.C. Bisp (Manager), Mr. David Davies, Mr. Benny Roberts, Mr. Jack Tomlins, Miss Jill Craigie, Mr. Stan Hughes (Under-Manager) and Mr. Wil Young at the Colliery Office.

man with humour in his make up, with music in his soul, with some heroism and plenty of grievances." Cries of "Hear, hear", convinced one and all that Miss Craigie would have all the co-operation she needed in her venture. One of her first moves was to offer a cash prize for the best short article on 'What I think about while working in the mines'. She wanted to know what went on in a collier's mind when working deep down in the coal face, whether they thought of supper that night, weekend sport or Betty Grable. The people there at Abergwynfi, she soon found out, were often bitter; bitter because they were frequently looked down upon. Phrases like "Oh, they're just from the valleys" or "She's only a collier's daughter", statements heard far too often, contributed substantially to the dissatisfaction of the men and women.

Fair enough, during those days of the 1940s, the colliery houses and settings never won first prize for eye appeal, but Miss Craigie noted that the interior of these small dwellings would have done justice to middle class homes anywhere. She was taken aback when she saw the cleanliness of the kitchens, in spite of all sorts of handicaps. The people amazed her, she was astounded that every village she encountered had its choir, and there was hardly a miner's cottage that she entered without a piano. Miss Craigie pointed out that the problems in Wales were comprehensive. You couldn't blame a young miner for being dispirited when his girl goes off with a white collar worker because he himself comes up from work black and must scrape away for half an hour to render himself recognisable. She learnt a lot about the family way of life at Abergwynfi. The girls of Wales had her profound sympathy. She pointed out that "Usually you found that the daughter of a

miner was brought up on the dole. She didn't want her husband to be a miner, to see him broken by silicosis. Visualising herself doing washing day after day, a chore without end. Often seeing a completely different way of life with the women of the towns, could you blame a young girl for opting for a collar and tie husband, in those circumstances."

In her film, Miss Craigie wanted to present the story of Wales truthfully and credibly to the public, also the miners' point of view and that of the pit manager and his officials. She had met a number of managers who ran the type of colliery dubbed by descriptive Welshmen as 'umbrella collieries', closed more often than open. But in one colliery manager she saw the depth of quality needed to bring true realism to her storyline.

Mr. H.C. Bisp, who ran the Llanharan pit, had in his hands one of the most progressive and modern mines on the South Crop. Up to date plant yielding fifteen tons of coal per man shift and using the most modern up to date machinery available. Mr. Bisp told Miss Craigie at the time, "I believe in planning as much as possible. We discuss all work with senior officials, then under-officials, and tell everyone what we propose doing."

Meeting the management at Llanharan was an inspirational time for her. She sat in on a number of manager/official meetings at the colliery office and made notes of all the refined details and facts spoken by the colliery team. During an interview with the late Mr. Stan Hughes, then under manager at Llanharan , he spoke of Miss Craigie's constant thirst for knowledge. "She was always writing things down, every detail, no matter how small. When the film came out I was amazed at the accuracy of the script. In the beginning of the film it showed officials talking to the manager in the office. That scene was typical of many that I had held on a daily basis with my officials. The mention of a broken sprocket on the Tredegar chain really made me smile and I would like to think that it was one of our meetings at Llanharan that inspired her script. The North Pit, the lamp room, stores, south tip, along with several scenes showing two of my officials, Mr. Ernie Coulson and Mr. Ivor Prosser, certainly opened a few eyes in Llanharan when the film was shown at the local cinema. The film certainly carried a lot of interest, because many of the villagers went to see it the three times it was shown, my wife and I included."

Jill Craigie's film was a great success when it hit the cinemas in the late forties. It had certainly achieved its intention. It really gave an intelligent representation of life in a typical mining village. As for Miss Craigie, she deservedly left her mark. Those people of Abergwynfi and Llanharan look back on her visit with a deep and lasting affection.

RACHEL THOMAS 1905 - 1995

Miss Rachel Thomas seen here in a scene from 'Blue Scar'. Many of the mining scenes in the film were produced at Llanharan Colliery, 1947.

When one talks of Welsh mining film productions, immediate memories of those heady days when mining was topical and sentiment glowed with a deep emotion come to mind. Two films which stand out are 'Proud Valley' and 'Blue Scar'. Ironically, Rachel Thomas played prominent roles in both. She earned a permanent place in Welsh screen history by portraying the typical mining 'Mam'. It was a role in which she shone like a bright star, reaching the hearts of all people living in such a deep mining atmosphere. In 1960, she took on the role again as Beth Morgan in the television adaptation of 'How Green Was My Valley', acting opposite Eynon Evans.

Born at Alltwen, Rachel lived most of her life in Rhiwbina, Cardiff. It was while appearing in novelist Jack Jones's 'Land Of My Fathers' that she was chosen to take the part in 'Proud Valley' (1939). 'Proud Valley' was a success and Rachel Thomas became a household name throughout the Welsh communities. It must be remembered that apart from several plays on radio, which she performed in the old Park Place studios in the early days, Rachel had had no professional acting experience, having spent a number of years as a Cardiff schoolteacher. She got the role in 'Proud Valley' on the recommendation of Jack Jones, who also took a role in the film. Rachel's performance drew tremendous praise from reviews which included one from the "Observer" film critic Caroline Lejeune.

On a personal note, visiting the home of Rachel Thomas was, for me, a memorable occasion. She was without doubt one of the warmest and most lovable people that I have ever had the privilege to meet. Our little chat which occurred only some weeks before her sad demise will live in my memory forever. She was such a wonderful lady.

While schoolteaching, Mrs. Thomas, then known as Rachel Roberts before her marriage, taught at Abercerdin Girls School, Gilfach Goch. In the valley she lodged with a family named Jones living at No. 3 Coronation Road. Rachel learnt much of the ways of a miner's life while at Gilfach, the experience obviously put to good use in her films. During our interview for this book she informed me that she was taken down the old Brittanic pit with other schoolteachers, an experience that she would never forget. Also while at Gilfach she became a member of the Bryn Seion Drama Society, recalling some wonderful memories with the group. Rachel Thomas's period in the valley is vividly recalled by Gilfach's established authoress Miss Katie Olwen Pritchard. In fact, during the time of interview both spoke of each other affectionately.

I take this opportunity to credit Miss Pritchard for her early encouragement during the compiling of my "Forgotten Years" Vol. I, giving me sound advice and basic ideas in the art of research. She was, without doubt, an influential person in my life which enabled me to go on and complete five more books on the history of my village, Llanharan.

Many scenes from 'Blue Scar' were filmed at Llanharan Colliery, and even today people of the village talk of the 1940s when the film people came. Rachel Thomas in her 'Mam' role comes quickly to the tongue, for those of us who experienced the rich mining family way of life will remember Rachel with a deep affection. One point is certain, because of the demise of mining, her role once synonymous with most valleys and villages in South Wales, will sadly never be seen again.....

Rachel Thomas passed away on Wednesday 8 February 1995. her stage, screen and radio career spanning almost sixty years.

Author T.J. Witts discusses the film 'Blue Scar' with one of the stars of the production. Miss Rachel Thomas is well known for her 'Mam' roles over the years, and earned instant fame when she starred in 'Proud Valley' opposite the late and great Paul Robeson in 1939.

'THE CITADEL DOCTOR'

Doctor Benjamin Samuel is remembered at Llanharan as a campaigning doctor. In fact, he was likened in those early mining days of the 1930s in South Wales to Doctor Andrew Manson – a doctor fictitiously immortalised by Scottish author A.J. Cronin in his best selling book 'The Citadel'.

Doctor Samuel was born in Tredegar after his Jewish parents had fled persecution in Russia. He qualified from the Welsh National School of Medicine when he was twenty one and worked as a locum in South Wales before coming to Llanharan and setting up a practice at No. 1 Bridgend Road (1936) to cover 4,000 people. He soon became very popular in the village. Understandably, because with Llanharan then being a thriving mining village, Doctor Samuel specialised in chest ailments. In fact, it soon spread around that - "Doctor Sam was good at chest complaints". He was an ardent campaigner at the Cardiff Pheumocomiosis Panel in the days before the National Health Service.

During the Second World War, Doctor Samuel was mobilised into the Army as a Military Doctor. However, his patients at Llanharan petitioned the War Office to allow him to stay in the village. The villagers' plea was accepted and the Military discharged our Doctor within weeks. It was said of him that he was devoted to his flock. At one time our practitioner made an appeal for blood, and two blood mobiles were brought into the village from Cardiff Royal Infirmary. The response was unbelievable with hundreds turning up to give blood. But what really got to Doctor Samuel was witnessing a long line of miners in the queue having taken time off from the day shift.

Our photograph shows Doctor Samuel with his wife Lisa at their home in Mahariya, Israel – 1983.

In leisure time, what there was, Doctor Samuel used to join the men and teach them how to play chess. His friend, a Doctor Monroe, from nearby Tonyrefail, did the same and soon chess competitions took place between the miners of both communities.

From 1948 to 1970 Doctor Samuel worked in America at the Los Angeles Health Department as a District Health Officer before moving, with his wife, to Israel near the Lebanese border where he worked as a village doctor until he died.

Lisa, his wife, is a niece to Professor Albert Einstein. During my research it was rumoured that the great man once visited the Samuel family at Llanharan. However, Mrs. Doreen Holland, formerly of Llanharan and now living in Talbot Green, is a lifelong friend of the family; she contacted Lisa who still lives in Israel, and she categorically states that no such visit occurred, but informed us that Albert Einstein did visit Britain in the September of 1933 and made an important speech at the Royal Albert Hall in London. Members of the government were there and Lisa herself was invited. Later, Professor Einstein contacted her and gave her the memorial brochure of the event which she treasures to this day. Shortly after his speech in London the Professor left for Princeton, New Jersey, where he had accepted a professorship for advanced studies. He remained in Princeton until his death which occurred in 1955.

Special acknowledgement to Mrs. Doreen Holland, who did so much on my behalf in retrieving information of the above.

WERN TARW COLLIERY

Wern Tarw came into prominence when the Meiros Colliery Ltd., who were working the No. 3 Rhondda Seam at Meiros and Cwm Ciwc, decided to further their activities in the same seam.

The new development began in 1912 and by 1917 the Wern Tarw Slant was working the No. 3 Rhondda Seam, employing 192 men, most from the Pencoed, Brynna and Llanharan areas.

The Rhondda No. 3 Seam was worked successfully by the pillar and stall method. This method was used because of disturbed ground which eventually limited work in most seams at Wern Tarw. In fact, it was because of heavy faulting that the No. 3 Seam was abandoned in 1951.

The shafts at Wern Tarw were sunk in 1917. They were 19 feet in diameter and sunk to a depth of 90 yards. In 1926, both shafts were sunk a further 130 yards into the Six Foot Seam.

It was in 1935 that the Low Temperature Carbonisation Company of Barnsley became interested in Wern Tarw as a Coalite investment. By 1939 an output of 5,000 tons of coal per week was attained at Wern Tarw, and a steady production was maintained for about a year. However, the output began decreasing steadily during the late war years. The contributory factor was the fade out of the Pentre Seam due to washout (disappearance of coal seam) on the west side, and the disturbed ground on the east.

In 1951 the NCB decided to transfer 87 men to Llanharan Colliery. This move was looked upon as the first steps to the closure of the Wern Tarw Pit. The incident brought much frustration between the NCB and NUM. The transfers went ahead nevertheless, and Llanharan Colliery closed in 1962, Wern Tarw outliving it by 3 years.

After continuing with difficulties for a number of years, fire broke out in the Wern Tarw in the 1960s. Despite vigorous effort and tremendous cost to save the mine, it was decided to abandon the project. The Wern Tarw Colliery closed down in 1964/5.

WERN TARW
WHERE NEXT ?

Last week, we the miners of Wern Tarw, came out on strike against the Policy of the National Coal Board in transferring 87 men to another colliery.   In fact they gave notices to 10 more than the Executive was informed of.

Rather than provide the pay and other conditions in the industry to attract sufficient Welsh lads, the Board is trying to solve its man-power problem by closing collieries (Cilely), by transferring miners, and by introducing Italian labour.

In our opinion Districts in our colliery have been systematically "murdered" in order to establish a case for the Board.

This is a threat to the whole of S. Wales

What is happening to us at Wern Tarw can be arranged in most pits.

Is this to continue ?   Who is NEXT on the list ? IT MAY BE YOU. We say that NOW is the time to PUT A STOP TO THIS PRACTICE OF THE BOARD.

This is what the miners of Coedely, Newlands, Pentre and Aberbaiden say, too, as they have come out on strike on Tuesday in our support. We miners of Wern Tarw are grateful for this support, and feel confident that other pits will follow.

Only a stand can halt the N.C.B. There can be no repitition of Cilely. We say NO Transference.

The 87 men can be, and want to be kept in the pit.

We ask for your FULL SUPPORT

Although resolutions to the E.C. are useful, our whole history shows that only ACTION can solve these problems.

UNITED WE STAND, DIVIDED TRANSFERENCE AND CLOSURE WILL CONTINUE

Published by Wern Tarw Lodge Committee 12 6 51

The girls from the canteen prepare to go underground at Wern Tarw Colliery.
Left to Right – Flossie Howe, Edith Ellis, Milly Hopkins and Iris Ellis.

Wern Tarw Colliery during dismantling operations.

THE WERN TARW COALITE WORKS

In 1935 the Low Temperature Carbonising Company, whose headquarters were in Barnsley, became interested in South Wales as a site for a new Coalite works. It was found that coal samples taken from Wern Tarw were suitable for making coalite.

Instead of buying coal from Wern Tarw, it was decided to buy the colliery outright, and to save expensive transportation costs the new plant was built alongside the G.W.R. branch line. Helped by a grant from the Nuffield Trust, the South Wales Coalite Company was formed in the April of 1937. The company set itself a target of 5,000 tons per week, 3,000 tons of coal came from the No. 3 Rhondda, Hafod and Pentre seams and were blended at the Coalite plant.

A considerable re-organisation at Wern Tarw was carried out. Electrification of the colliery became a priority. Also 350 h.p. haulages were installed. All the tramroads and colliery yard were concreted. The screens were modified and the washery extended. Underground, all horses were dispensed with and conveyors were introduced everywhere. In 1939 it was all systems go and the plant did actually produce 5,000 tons in one week. The Second World War broke out and in the latter part of that year the Coalite plant closed down after only running experimentally for a month.

During the War all movable equipment and machinery was taken away and used at Wern Tarw Pit, which, in 1945 employed 790 men. Two years after the War the colliery was nationalised and this resulted in a complete liquidation of the Coalite Company.

Source: The late Dr. W.G. Thomas. Department of Industry, National Museum of Wales, Cardiff.

Workmen during the dismantling of Wern Tarw Colliery and stack in 1965.
Back Row: Walter Redwood, Dai Lanyon and Tom Jones.
Front Row: Dai Morgan and Clayton Thomas.

1965. The demolition men pull down Wern Tarw stack brick by brick.

COEDCAE DRIFT MINE

Coedcae Drift Mine opened in the January of 1961. It was a 750 yard slant which worked the Rhondda No. 2 seam and employed approximately 150 men. A number of the officials at the new drift came from nearby Llanharan Colliery which was nearing closure at that time (1962).

The Coedcae was the last major project that the National Coal Board exploited in the area. Sadly, it was not a very successful one. The No. 2 was a bad seam which contained 28% ash in the coal band which could not be separated. This coal was used as 'mixing coal' by the steel company. Poor production soon caused the mine's downfall and in the July of 1973 it closed. Dismantling operations took six months. In charge of the supervision was Mr. Ted Thomas, Llanharan (Official).

For the record:

Manager   Mr. Nicholas

Overmen   Ted Thomas, Tom Oram,
           Arthur Goldsworthy,
           Ron Bayliss.

Deputies   Glan Goldsworthy,
           Dilwyn Davies, Bert Piggott,
           Frank Coles, Glan Bynyon,
           Joe Belcher, Glyn Oram.

I would like to thank Mr. Ted Thomas (overman) for facts appertaining to the Coedcae Drift Mine.

Source: Mr. Ted Thomas (overman) who worked at the drift.

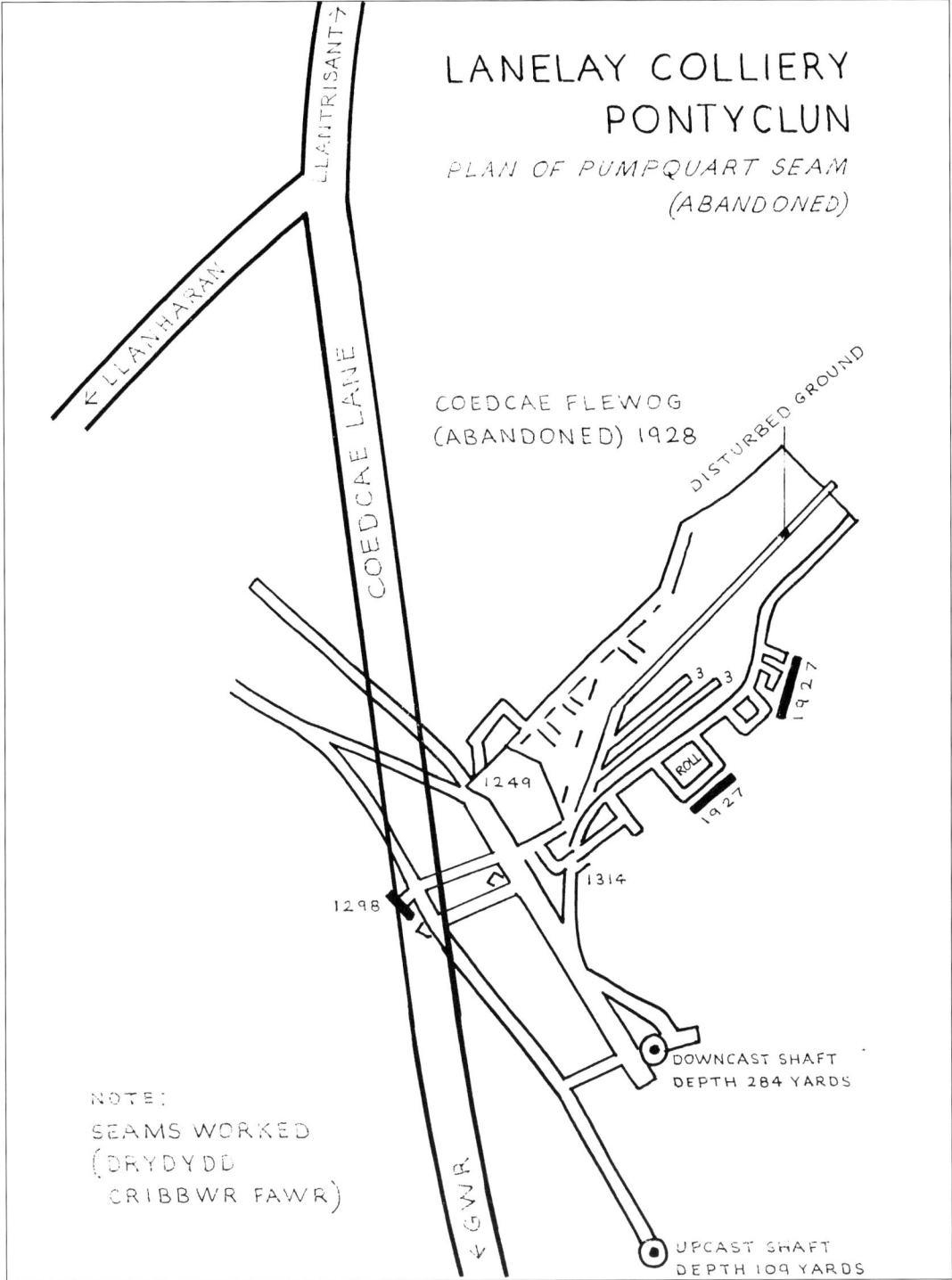

Lanelay Colliery, Pontyclun.

(Source: by kind permission of Mr. David Preece, Treharris from his private collection.)

COEDCAE FLEWOG COLLIERY, COEDCAE LANE, NR. PONTYCLUN.

Sinking operations 1878.

The Coedcae Flewog Colliery was owned by Thomas James Masters, the coal pioneer who also owned nearby Llanharan's Meiros Colliery. In fact, quite a number of miners from the Llanharan area worked in the 'Flewog'.

Loftus Terrace, Pontyclun, was owned by the Coedcae owners and the small dwellings accommodated many of their workers. (demolished 1967). The Coedcae Lane pitshafts were as follows:

Downcast Shaft   284 yards
Upcast Shaft   109 yards

It is believed that the pit closed down sometime in 1928. However, I have not been able to find documentary evidence.

Loftus Terrace.

Many of the miners at the 'Flewog' lived in Loftus Terrace. The late Mr. Harry Sheppard of Llanharan once informed me during interview in 1972 that often Mr. Masters had to visit the terrace to settle disputes and conflicts which had occurred amongst the families, most problems happened after weekend drinking sprees. In fact, so frequent were the disputes that the street's reputation heightened and it became known as 'Hellfire Row'. However, many 'characters' lived there over the years and when the street was demolished in 1967 it left many golden memories of personalities and customs.

LLANHARRY DEEP MINE - TORGELLI -

The nearby village of Llanharry is well recorded for its haematite iron ore mine. Opened in 1901 it gave employment to many district families. For many years Llanharry was the only working iron ore mine in Wales. Some 200,000 tons of ore was railed annually to Guest Keen Steel Works at East Moors, Cardiff, where the iron was used for high quality castings. It was a devastating blow for Llanharry when the mine closed down on 25 January 1976.

Coal mining did actually take a foothold at Llanharry as far back as 1602, when one Sir Robert Sidney leased a coal pit on Llanharry Meadow to Edward Davie at a yearly rent of ten shillings. We learn that other small drift mines were worked on Llanharry Common. A clearer picture about coal mining at Llanharry emerges around the year 1871 when a deep mine was set down at Torgelli. This mine was to be a major project and when work commenced it was called Llanharry Colliery. Old maps of 1874 show the seams worked as: Trydydd, Slatog, Six Feet, Nine Feet and Cribbwr. The mine went through a very difficult period. It was water prone and underwent geological difficulties. After its closure, all mining operations were concentrated at Llanharan and Brynna.

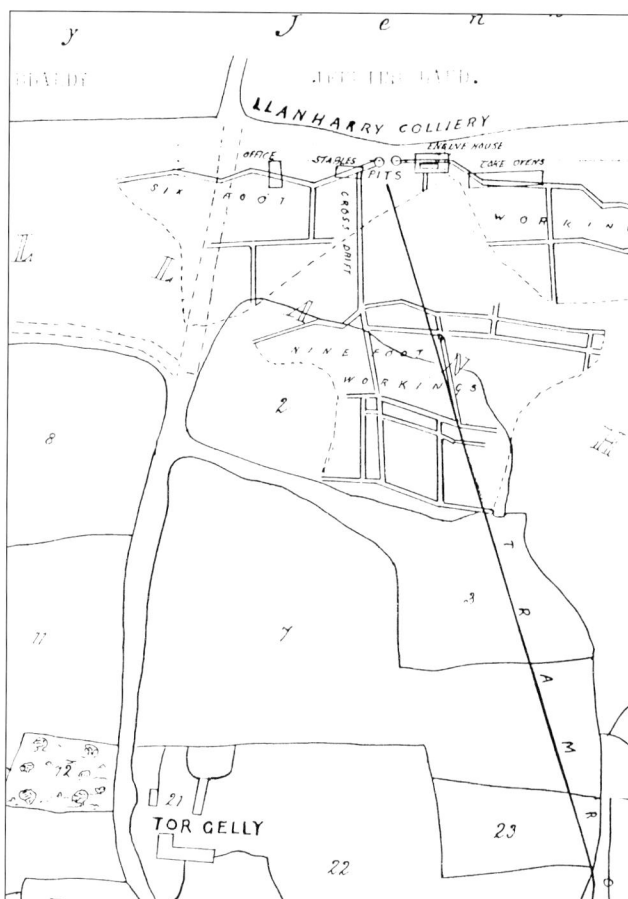

Map of the Llanharry Colliery 1871   *Source: Mr. David Preece, Treharris*

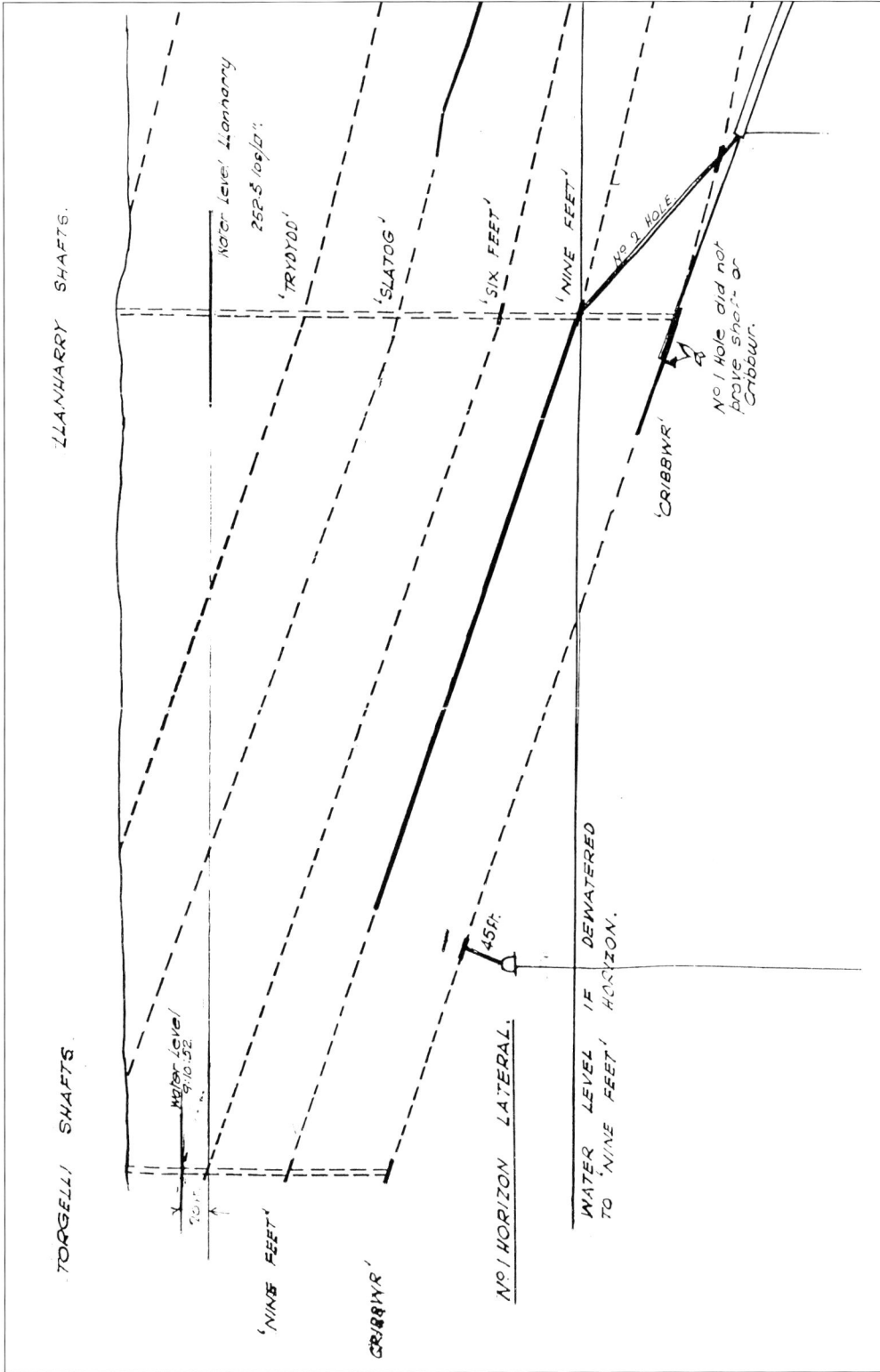

The map shows that the Llanharry mine worked the Trydydd, Six Feet, Nine Feet and Cribbwr seams.
(Source: Mr. David Preece, Treharris)

Women - their role in a mining community

We learn through records that women played a significant role in the mines during Victorian times. That early society was clearly alarmed at stories of harsh labour amongst the children at the time. But also they were shocked by what was described as wholesale immorality which was believed to have been taking place underground. Those early records tell of horrific practices of men and women working, practically naked, underground together. Also it was noted that there was an increase of illegitimate children during that period and blamed the cause on what went on amongst the half savage population below ground. Such was the fuss that the then Lord Ashley rushed a Bill into Parliament which banned all work by women underground and limited the hours that could be worked by children. This Bill became law in 1842, but records again tell us that women worked on colliery screens as coal sorters right up until as late as 1948.

Having taken a brief look into the female contribution in the mines, their role in Wales was primarily centred in the home, and what a role it was. We only have to study the local Church burial records of the period when the coal boom took a foothold in Llanharan and Brynna during the 1900s. Here, a picture is formed showing the price that women paid for coal. Many died in their twenties, thirties and forties. My own grandmother to whom this book is partly dedicated, was taken to her grave in her forty first year.

What must be considered is that many families consisted of six or seven sons, who along with their fathers, worked in the mine. Normally, the working family went out into three shifts, mornings, afternoons and nights. What also must be considered is the fact that during those early days there were no pit head baths. The woman of the house was expected to organise all the bathing arrangements. This task usually took place in the kitchen, where up to two tin baths would be made available, depending on how many boys were coming off shift. One tub would be used to wash off the thick black coal grime from the 'upper half' of the body, while the other was for washing the 'bottom half'. Normally the mother and daughters (if any) would work as a team to provide water. The fire would be roaring with buckets filled with water brought to the boil. When the miners arrived at the house their clothes would be removed and shaken to be hung in the outhouse. Later all wet clothes would be dried out over the fireplace, ready for the next shift. I can recall my mother filling several saucepans and boiling them over the fire in preparation for my father coming home after shift. I see him clearly on his knees leaning over the old tin bath as 'mam' washed his back. During the working day the women had their allotted tasks in the home. Outhouses had to be scrubbed, steps and back yards vigorously washed, and cleaning the house was a daily chore. The hardest task was scrubbing and washing the working clothes. Bedding was daily washed and miners clothing, which consisted of flannel shirts and underclothes which were called 'Long Johns', was woollen and very hard to handle when sodden with water. This washing task used to drain the strength from the women. By ten o'clock in the evening they would virtually be rendered exhausted. Food preparation was another arduous task. The most popular dish after shift would be soup which contained various vegetables, beef and dough balls which were added for 'filling'. On Sunday, the main dinner preparation began as early as seven in the morning, with the fire being lit to heat up the oven for the Sunday joint.

The saucepans for the vegetables usually took up the whole grate, and the house would be filled with steam with windows running with condensation. Yes, quite simply the women's work went on and on in one laborious chain of labour. One elderly lady from Llanharan informed me:

"A man worked hard for nine hours a day, our work in the home was endless. With the modern things the girls have today, they don't know they are born, and a good job too." - Good job indeed.

Source: Interview with Mrs. Amy Inglis and Mrs. Violet Witts.

SOME EARLY MEMORIES
- MRS. AMY INGLIS.

I was a youngster living in Chapel Road, Llanharan, when Powell Duffryn sank their pit on meadowland right in full view of my house. When I returned to the village recently, it upset me to see that the colliery had completely disappeared. I have many memories of coalmining within my own family life which I often recall with rich nostalgia. All that is left of the Llanharan pit is a steel obelisk

Mrs. Amy Inglis

indicating the place where the old North Shaft was - how sad!

I can remember standing on a wide window ledge of our house, No. 31 Chapel Road, Llanharan. My mother's arm was about me as we watched the lambs jumping about on 'Gronows' field (now School Terrace and Park Terrace). On the meadowland across the other side of the railway line, I remember watching the engineers sinking the Llanharan North Pit Shaft, also the new houses being built at Bryncae. The old school on Chapel Road was almost bursting at the seams with the influx of new pupils, as many as thirty two were in my class alone. In later years a new school was built at Bryncae and I was lucky enough to attend there for cookery classes once a week. We had lots of fun at those cookery sessions and made some ghastly looking dishes which my father always ate with relish declaring that my efforts were 'super stuff'.

Quite a few families kept pigs on Chapel Road and in most of the houses the cured pig meat would be hung on a beam in the outhouse along with black puddings and strings of onions. Old Rees the butcher commonly called 'Peggy Rees', would come along for the killing of the pigs. The killing took place in the back garden with the poor creature being firmly tied to a post and trestle. I never waited to see the pig being killed, I always fled down to the Dolau to my grandmother. I wouldn't go home for hours. My mother told me that I was born on a Friday. While I was being born in the house a Mr. Evan Lewis, the fruiterer, was hammering at our door. So later on I never forgot who Evan Lewis was. Mr. John Lobb senior came from Talbot Green selling all sorts of eatables off a cart every week. Also, a small family business called 'Hislopps' called on a weekly basis selling paraffin and candles and all sorts of household utensils.

Chapel Road in those days was the main road to Brynna, the council road and its houses were yet to be built. They came in the early 1920s, built on Gronows farm land at Coed Bychan. Mr. Gronow at that time used to mine his own coal from workings he had excavated himself. The entrance to a neatly propped drift appears in a hole in the small wood which was just at the edge of the field where Coed Bychan Crescent stands today. Some of the village boys used to crawl into the mine, but when the men of the village heard that their sons were entering the workings, they realised the danger and went into the drift with shovels and filled it in. Much to the disgust of Mr. Gronow. The old drift however was never reopened.

If my count is right the Gronows had six daughters and we knew them all very well because, in their turn, they would come to our house with their own butter and lovely crumbly foist-milk cheese which they carried in a wooden tub covered with a cloth. They were lovely people but were also an extremely unlucky family. Two of the daughters died in childbirth and Ted, one of the sons, lost an arm in an accident with farm machinery.

Life at Llanharan as a child was great during those early days. No need for money, and fields all around to play in. Brynna Wood was beautiful up at this end of the village. When you got past the second stile there were huge trees each side of the path, tall, so the branches met, keeping out the sun. A little further down an open space with a carpet of bluebells, when in season in the spring. Other meadow flowers made Brynna Wood a dream area for a child. However, below, further down in the wood, we were not allowed to play because there were a number of drift mines there. Quite a number of men in the village worked there.

At our house on Chapel Road our kitchen had a flagstone floor and a huge open grate where a large iron kettle was always kept on the boil. There was no bathroom, so when my father came home black with the coal dust from Meiros Colliery, we children were put in the front room, up came the mats and dad took his wash in a tin bath in front of the fire. There weren't many bathrooms in Llanharan at that time.

We were allowed to have sweets once a week when dad would stop at Alice Hole's shop on the Square, on his way home from work, he would fill his tommy box and share the sweets out to us when he got home, it was the highlight of the week having sweets. Occasionally we were taken to Alice Hole's shop. I loved the place. Alice was an invalid and liked company, but the great attraction was her parrot. It would whistle 'The Grenadiers March' perfectly and it used dreadful swear words, its cage often had to be covered to shut it up.

The road surface in front of our house was lovely and smooth, so I had great fun with a hook and hoop. One could tell the seasons of the year in those days by the games children played. There were marbles, hop scotch, skipping to name but a few and, of course, 'Rat Tat Ginger' if you wanted to endear yourself to the neighbours.

Chapel Road was really busy on a Sunday when people came from all round the district, some on foot and others on pony and trap to worship at the Bethlehem Chapel. I went occasionally with my cousin to sit up in the gallery and listen to the lovely old Welsh hymns. If it was a popular tune, the last verse would be repeated over and over; and of course, the annual Gymanfa Ganu was not to be missed.

Dr. Samuel Tucker lived and held his surgery at the end of our road, he took great care of accident victims at the pits as well as being a full time G.P. He made most of his remedies himself and pounded up the ingredients while you waited. Dr. James Patterson set up a practice in Llanharan and later when he married the daughter of Mr. Aitkins of Pencoed, they started their married life in the large house next to the Turberville Hotel and lived there for some time. By this time the village began to expand, the new road to Brynna and the council houses being part of it.

1926 saw the beginning of the coal strike which lasted six months, at the end of it everyone was up to their necks in debt. It was a very sad time when people who had been contented and law abiding were now fighting each other in hate and bitterness. Some were even tarred and feathered for not believing in the strike and attempting to go to work. It was a horrible time and I think the less said about the tragic implications of the period the better. A lot of extra police were drafted into the village to try and keep law and order. These police were billeted in the High Corner and Turberville. It was a bad time for all of us, I remember being fitted out with a pair of heavy boots, part of a government consignment, which were distributed at school. I was thrilled with the boots because my only pair of shoes were through in the soles. We had a soup kitchen in the village which I never went to, as my mother always seemed to manage with veg from my father's allotments. I felt cheated not being allowed to eat from the soup kitchen, in my mind it held a magical attraction to it.

We had several good carnivals during the strike and a 'Go As You Please' which was held in the cinema, admittance was free but you were given a ticket by the door, part of a draw, which, if you were lucky, won you a piece of beef. Mrs. Blandy Jenkins from Llanharan House gave the beef, she gave up one of her cattle which Mr. Reginald Smith, the butcher, killed and cut up into joints. I didn't have a winning ticket but another family had two and gave one to me. We were all very grateful to that Lady from the 'Ty Mawr'.

I don't think life was ever the same after the strike at Llanharan. The days of plenty and contentment were gone forever! But my happy days in the old Llanharan of yesteryear will remain a joyous memory with me throughout the rest of my days......"

Source:
Interview with Mrs. Amy Inglis
20 February 1994.

A MEMORY OF THE VILLAGE
- ZENA MONGER

My name is Zena Monger *née* Dare. Born 18 May 1914, I lived on the Square in Llanharan with my parents, one brother and two sisters. We lived in the house that was later sold to Mr. John Gower who was a chemist, and the house was turned into a shop.

In those early days, the village was so pretty and prosperous. We had two huge beech trees on the Square in front of the High Corner Hotel. One of the trees was later removed and the new War Memorial took its place. Later the second tree was removed to make way for road improvement which would serve the new council estate.

My father, Frank Dare, was head mechanic for three collieries, Meiros, Wern Tarw and South Rhondda. He travelled with a Welsh cob and a governess car to all three pits. When the collieries closed for the summer holidays, my father would take us with him on his colliery checks to make sure all was well. It was marvellous to stand in the engine room and feel the sparkling engines all throbbing and pulsating away. Later in my life I had the same sensation on a big ship.

At Llanharan in those days we had no mechanical traffic. Horses and horse drawn vehicles were the order of the day, so we could play on the roads with relative safety.

Meiros Colliery had a dram line which came down to the railway sidings, via the viaduct bridges. They are gone now, but the old bridge walls remain. The drams used to go down into the siding weighbridge before being transported to the railways. The noise of the drams coming down the viaduct was loud. They would creak and groan. The noise could be heard all over the village.

When the Wern Tarw mine was sunk a Mr. George Tasker came to live in the village of Brynna, he was over-seeing the sinking of the deep shaft itself. It was such a tragedy when he fell to his death at the shaft. Mrs. Vi David told me, a few years ago, how my father who was 6 feet 4 inches tall, and a big man, had climbed down on a rope and brought her father's body to the surface.

Of course the mines dominated our lives, the village depended on them for their livlihood. Each day we would hear the minersí hobnailed boots walking through the Square up the steep hill to Meiros Colliery, and again when they finished shift they would return, their faces black with only their eyes and mouth showing.

One of my earliest memories was of the Meiros hooter blasting away and all the people rushing outside their houses to witness what was to be a tragedy. On the Square by the trees an old corrugated shed stood, it housed an old field ambulance from the war. As my mother and I watched we heard boots marching slowly. It was a dreadful sound. My mother kept repeating "Oh diwedd" over and over again, as the stretchers covered in grey blankets appeared. I remember my mother picking me up, crying all the while, and making me play in the garden. All I remember is that it was a terrible accident. I was never told how many died that day. I suppose I was too small to understand. But to this day the sound of boots walking strikes dread into my heart.

We only had candles and oil lamps, but all the collieries had generators to make electricity which, to us in the village, was unheard of. One day my father told us to be on the Square that evening at dusk, to see the newly erected wooden pole with a green shade, shaped like a chinese coolieís hat, on the top. We all stood and watched as the light came on, our very first and only light in the village.

My father was a captain in the St. Johns Ambulance Brigade and all accidents on the Square were brought into our parlour. Every Sunday afternoon motor bikes would come to grief on the corner by the blacksmith's shop. So many accidents occurred near the wall that later it was removed and the road altered.

My father also led a team of men who were trained to rescue miners who were trapped. They were called the Bryncethin Rescue Service.

Came the day when the coal was slowly being worked out at Meiros and water breaking into the mine. So other coal areas were sought and the Brynna Wood Drift Mine was modernised - my father worked there. I often walked into the drift mine with my father to see the pit ponies. I can assure you that I did not like it, the smell of the coal, the darkness and the damp were horrible.

My father always brought his miner's lamp home with him because he could be called back at any time. One of my memories is of someone hammering on our front door requesting my father's immediate attention. Every day him lamp would be meticulously cleaned and prepared for such an occasion.

There was terrible poverty in those days and the miners were paid a disgustingly small wage. Miners did not have anyone to support them and they often went on strike. Those who broke the strike were called blacklegs and abused by striking colleagues; it was a fearful time. As the men who broke the strike returned to the village after shift others who did not work would pelt them with flour and rotten eggs. It was frightening to be caught up in it. When today I see mansions and splendid houses built by the coal owners I am appalled at the sheer cruelty of it all.

Llanharan then was such a close community, we knew every person who lived there. Powell Duffryn opened a colliery, built a village, called it Bryncae and peopled it with families from other valleys. A new school had to be built, as Llanharan Primary could not take the new influx. A few of us had lessons in the Church Hall, which up to then was our Sunday School premises.

One day we watched as Irish labourers arrived in lorries to start digging up the farm fields to make a road. Next came the foundations for houses. So the village had a crossroads. When I look back at all the work that was done, it was all shovel, picks and hard graft. No bulldozers and heavy machinery.

As time progressed, we moved from the Square up to Brook Terrace - in the new council houses. What a boon that was, especially as we now had electricity and an electric iron. Previously we used flat irons that were heated on the coal fire.

I can remember the first bus that came into the village; until then we had the charabancs which were quite an experience. We all had to have wooden cases to stand on before we could climb into the vehicle. The first bus was a single decker with a conductor on board. My mother and I stood on our doorway waiting to greet Mary Martin and Roy, who was a baby in a shawl. We thought it was marvellous to see a modern bus stopping to let off passengers.

Today I can hardly recognise the beautiful village that I once was a part of, but the mountain still remains.

I left the village to train as a nurse in London in 1933. I was courting Frank Evans, the eldest son of Sergeant and Mrs. Evans. They lived in the bungalow on the Square. Frank was in the Royal Navy and was going on a tour of duty that would last three years. He was stationed in Bermuda for two years. We both returned to the village and married in January 1937. Then we moved to Plymouth, Devon, where our first daughter was born.

In the summer of 1938 I went home to stay with my parents. They had moved to a village outside Crosskeys. My second daughter was born there. Frank volunteered for duty on a submarine. After staying at Barrow in Furness, where the submarines were being built, he was moved to Gosport where the submarines were being tested. Here the crew were taught how to escape in the event of an accident. He was called to serve on the Thetis but a friend on the Thistle asked him to change places. As you know the Thetis sank on her trial run. We were devastated.

War was being anticipated in Plymouth and we were all really frightened. I returned to my parents and took my home with me. I was lucky as poor Plymouth was bombed flat.

Frank had a lot of bitter experiences with the war at sea and had already sunk a few enemy ships. In April 1940 his ship was reported missing and it was only two years ago that I managed to discover where he died, and how. Frank was only 27, I was 25, my children $2\frac{1}{2}$ and $1\frac{1}{2}$ years.

I was still living with my parents when the war ended, so stayed on to keep house for my mother who was ill. I met my second husband, who was divorced with one son. We married in 1950 and had three more children. We all lived in Taffs Well.

I have six children, John, who like his father, is a doctor, Kay (née Evans) who is a sister in C.R.I. Kay is married to a Baptist minister and has a daughter and granddaughter. Diane (Evans) has retired as a Midwife and we live together. Jennifer (nee Monger) is married and she and her husband are in the civil service. They have two daughters, both teaching. The eldest daughter is married with one son. Christopher (Monger) the fifth child, is married and living in America and is an author, like his father. He is also a film director and travels all over the world. Anthony (Monger) my youngest son is married and has a stepson. He is a civil servant and also writes and has prizes for his poetry.

I am pleased to say that all my children have done well. As for me, I am now 81 years old. My second husband died in 1972 but I still live in the family home with Diane. The family visit often and keep in touch.

We all met recently for the premiere of Christopher's film 'The Englishman Who

Went Up a Hill and Came Down a Mountain'. We were quite a crowd that evening. A wonderful and proud moment for us all.

It is strange that no matter where I travel, my roots will always be in Llanharan. Whenever passing the village, we stop and walk up to the Church, but sadly we never see a familiar face. I suppose most have long gone. Never mind, they will live long in my memory. Just as the fields and mountain remain so does the war memorial at the foot of Hillside Avenue, with Frank's name carved on it. Sadly, my brother Felix and sister Mavis are now dead. This leaves my sister Beryl who is a widow, and myself.

When Terry Witts asked me to give him a little information on my life in the village, I found it difficult to choose from my memories. There is so much that

Mr. Frank Dare
(Zena's father)

comes to mind about that lovely village of yesterday. What I have chosen I hope will evoke some nostalgia to the reader. I wish Terry all the success in his endeavours to make Llanharan's past a permanent record to be carried into the future.

A MEMORY OF THE 1926 STRIKE BY VIOLET MAY WITTS.

Stories about the 1926 strike are spoken about by the older folk even to this present day. Some facts appertaining to the hardship of those days really go beyond the borders of sanity in people's aggravated attempt to survive a period of dangerous unrest. The strike itself was a powerful reflection of life, when men who previously were workmates and playmates were thrust into a nightmare situation. What is right, and what is wrong? A fact only the individual can ascertain. However, during the strike many stories materialised which deserved recognition. The fight for survival and the protection of their children became a priority during that period of adversity. One such story comes from the Pascoe family of Harold Street, Llanharan. We have earlier described the life in the pits of

Joseph Pascoe. Here we tell a story of the strike, of an incident regarding his good wife Florence, told through the generosity of his daughter Violet May, who was a child of eight at the time of the conflict.

"Not long after the strike started, mostly everyone was beginning to feel the pinch - my own family being no exception. At the time I was the eldest of six children. To survive then most of the men in the village turned to hunting rabbits as a part of that food chain of survival, but that soon wore thin with the animal in this area virtually becoming extinct. I remember a baker who my mother called at the time 'our saviour' coming into the village with his van and supplying the striking families with bread on tick. He was a Mr. Johns, whose bakery was in Bridgend, near to where the old Embassy Cinema stands today. Mr. Johns' van was a welcome sight twice a week. Despite being informed that he was making a rod for his own back by supplying strikers, and that he would have no hope of receiving payment after the strike, he kept up his delivery. When the strike was over many people in the village were in debt to him. Some heavily. The book keeping with regard to 'bread bills' was organised by a Mr. Coleman who lived in the village. He called weekly to pick up the owed money and to be fair most people who had appreciated their 'saviour' during the hard time, paid up every penny they owed. Some people in fact were paying their bills for years after the strike was over.

One incident of the strike will stick in my mind forever. With a house full of children in a strike, one of the main priorities was keeping a fire in the grate. A lot of the men picked coal off the tips. This practice was brought to the notice of the police by the colliery management which brought in a night-time patrol by police officers. If a collier was caught picking coal off the tips he could go to jail for two days - many did. On the other hand a hefty fine could be registered which would cause a setback to the family survival needs. However, great sympathy was seen to be shown when a youngster or mother was caught on the tips. In general their coal would be confiscated and they would be removed from the tip with a warning.

One evening I was with my mother on the tip which was only a few yards away from the bottom of our street, Harold Street. We had been picking coal for about an hour and were about to come from there when this police officer came around the side of the tip and caught us red handed. My mother couldn't run because at the time she was heavily pregnant. I stayed by her side as the police officer walked up to us. Looking at the bag of coal, then at my mother, he warned her that she could be prosecuted and should leave the area immediately. Also, she was to leave the bag of coal there with him. My mother looked him straight in the eye and bluntly told him that it had taken her an hour to fill the bag and that she had children in the house who needed a fire. The officer seeing that my mother was pregnant replied sharply, "Good Lord woman, you will go to prison if you don't go from here." My mother again refused to leave the coal there and told the policeman that if he would kindly put the bag of coal on her shoulder she would leave immediately. The officer was now in a state of near panic shouting "Heaven above woman, you will have me hauled before the authorities if you don't go from here." He then looked about sharply, snatched up the bag of coal and placed it on my mother's back. "Now go quickly", he shouted again. He then left us in a hurry to get on with it. We slowly made our way home. Two days after the incident my mother gave birth to Henry, our youngest brother.

I shall never forget those days or the people that I grew up with. Never mind what they say about the bad old days, the people then were different somehow. They were closer together, more like one big family. For a start you knew everyone in the village then and you shared each others values. When the colliery closed I think this village lost most of its identity - yes I am sure of that...."

Special Note:
Mrs. Pascoe's son Henry was sadly on the ill-fated Tudor airliner which crashed in March 1950 while bringing Rugby supporters home from Ireland. He was killed.

Like father like son!

1938 – The young lad in the picture proudly takes the role of miner from his father. Sons followed fathers into the pits during those hardy days when coal was King in the area. For the record the young boy in the picture is Mr. Brian Witts the author's brother, whose father, William Robert, worked in the South Rhondda, Brynna Wood and Llanharan Collieries.

My late brother was tragically taken from us on the 22nd July 1999. During my early research he accompanied me on a number of important interviews, taking and preparing selected photographs which are used in this publication. – He is sadly missed.

Even the dog joins in!

Our photograph shows the author's daughter Helen posing with her pet dog 'Pen' in 1972. Mining was coming to a close in the area when this picture was taken, however, Helen accompanied her father to see a number of the drift mines that were still prominent on the local mountainsides at that time.

Helpers in the Miners Hall soup kitchen during 1926.

1926 saw the beginning of the coal strike which lasted six months, at the end of it everyone was up to their necks in debt. Police were drafted into the area to maintain law and order. They were billeted at the High Corner and Turberville Hotels.

Police at the Turberville Hotel - 1926.

- OPENCAST -
THE LAST FRONTIER

Since the closure of Llanharan Colliery in 1962, the area has developed into one of the most important and modern opencast sites in the country. The first project began in 1969/70, the site employing, at that time, approximately 260 men. British Coal brought in a number of specialist engineers from different aspects of mining, but in general most of the work force came mainly from the locality. Around half a million tons of coal was produced yearly for use at the Port Talbot steel works. Also developed at that time were the railway sidings near the old Llanharan mine leading onto the main Western Region transport system. The first phase of opencast mining ended in 1986.

Now known as Celtic Energy Ltd., the present development, Llanilid West Revised, began in the March of 1993. The contract date was signed on 15 March and coaling work began on 21 May 1993. At that time advanced planning estimated that the site would reach completion in 1996, work was then to begin in reclaiming the land for agriculture and woodlands.

The contractual tonnage of coal in 1995 stood at 4,000 tons per week with a manpower force of around 70 men. The market for this product is in cement manufacture and British Steel.

On 19 January 1995 I was privileged to be in the company of Mr. Lewis Hands, the site manager, who gave me an insight into the opencast coal industry and its operations. The visit certainly opened my eyes and what really influenced me was the company's highly responsible attitude, not only towards their own working conditions, but their constructive and harmonious planning around the environment. Many memories came flooding back to me on the visit. The manager took me into the old South Pit building. Having already recently witnessed the filling of the North Shaft, it was a strange feeling being surrounded by the half derrick of the upcast shaft. A silent sentinel - still standing thirty three years after the closure of its pit. Having worked on the surface of Llanharan Colliery in the 1950s, my visit brought many faces to mind, some sadly long gone into history. One person who stood out however was my late father. He spent over thirty years in the mines only to die on the year of his retirement. Over the years I learnt that he, in his early mining days, worked in the driving of headings, a task which apart from being highly dangerous was a job ravaged with stone dust. This was proved in his sixty fifth year with a very high cost.

Looking back at horizon mining, it all now seems so inept and primitive. We know that in the latter stages of Llanharan Colliery's productive years, the management were experiencing tremendous difficulties, basically, fighting for survival. Those mining engineers and officials went about their tasks with full confidence, but many obstacles stood in their way; driving through the upthrust fault and geological conditions in the steeply contorted rock south of the Maesteg-Pontypridd anticline proved too much as the ground was badly disturbed. But for the opencast of today, this is irrelevant. Opencast in Llanilid worked through the Two Feet Nine, Upper Four Feet, Six Feet, Caerau, Red Vein, Nine Feet, Bute, Amman Rider, Yard, Upper Seven Feet, and Gellideg. They were highly volatile seams and worked all in the light of day.

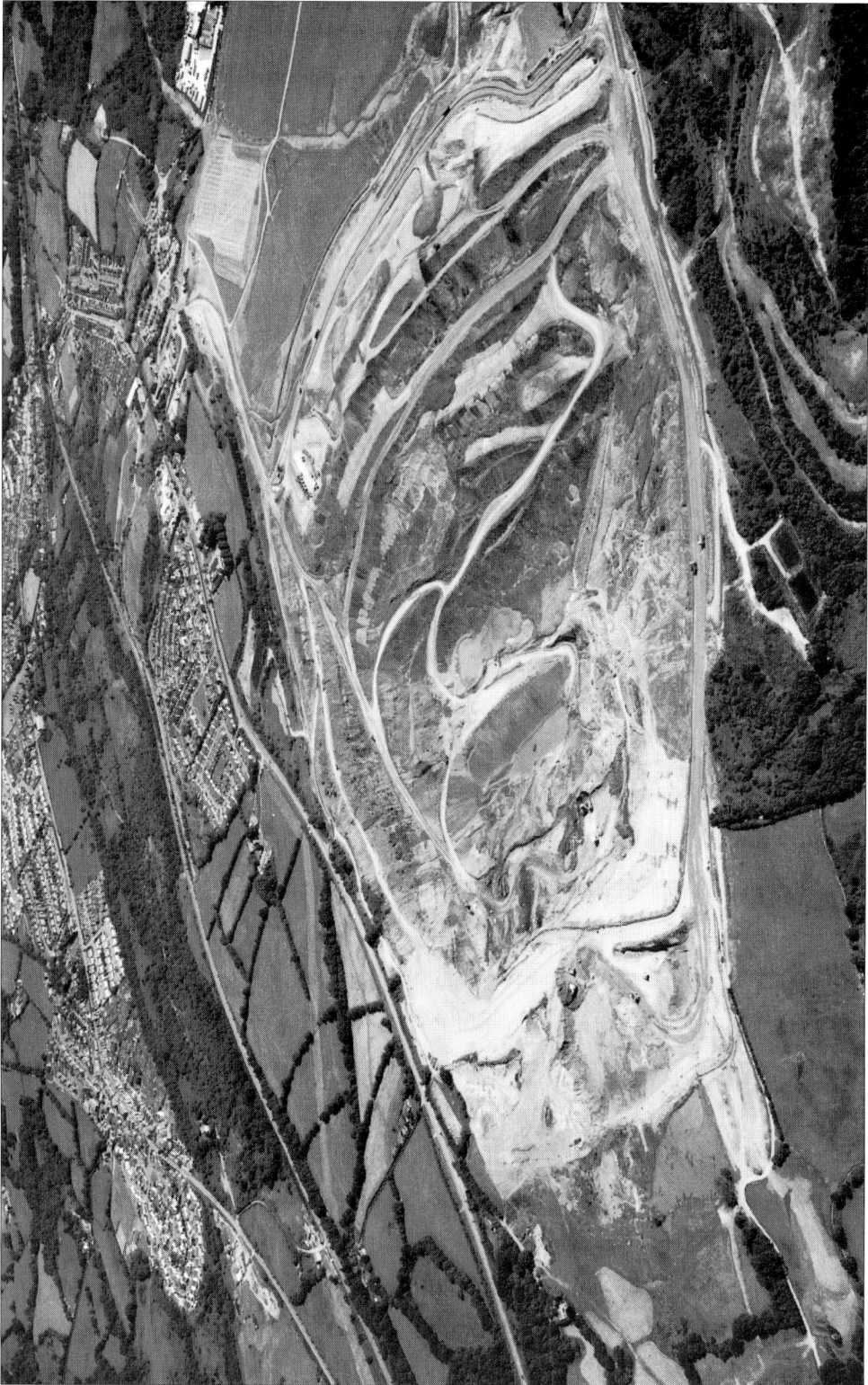

Llamilid West Revised Site.

Celtic Energy Ltd., began this second phase in their opencast planning in the March of 1983. Contractual coal tonnage was 4,000 tons per week by February 1995.

In some ways I wish that my father had been part of the opencast era. This modern technology would have at least given him and his fellow mining friends a richer and longer passage into their twilight years. However, many miners today still have confidence in deep mining production. Tower Pit being a prime example. Their fight for ownership of their mine was exemplary, they deserve all the luck in the world.

The rewards for Llanharan after the eventual demise of coal looks promising. As Mr. Bryan Riddleston, the Chief Executive for South Wales said:

"Celtic Energy Ltd., has a strong commitment to the protection of the environment and constructive restoration of its sites. It aims to search for the highest standards whilst undertaking the recovery of vital energy supplies........"

COMPLETE SEAM SEQUENCE - LLANILID & LLANILID WEST REVISED SITES

Llanilid (Coaling 20/7/1970 – 26/7/1986).
No.6 Rider, No.5 Rider, No.4 Rider, No.3 Rider, No.2 Rider, No.1 Rider, Top Abergorki, Bottom Abergorki, Pentre, Upper Gorllwyn, Lower Gorllwyn, Two Feet Nine, Upper Four Feet, Six Feet, Caerau, Red Vein Nine Feet, Bute, Amman Rider, Yard, Gellideg.

Llanilid West Revised (Coaling 21/5/1993 – 5/9/1996).
Two Feet Nine, Upper Four Feet, Six Feet, Caerau, Red Vein, Nine Feet, Bute, Amman Rider, Yard, Upper Seven Feet, Gellideg.

Celtic Energy Ltd., Site Staff.
Site Manager   Ioan Jenkins
Surveyor   Brian Lloyd
O.S.G.   Dewi Jenkins

Apart from unearthing old pillar and stall workings during their mining operations, Celtic Energy sometimes discover the earliest primitive methods of coalmining. When Llanharan opencast began their exploration in 1969/70, they recovered old 'bell pits' near Bryncae. The above is a perfect example of 'bell shafts' workings discovered.

Sources: Mr. Alan G. Powell, Pontypridd. Celtic Energy Fact Sheet by kind permission of Mr. Lewis Hands, Site Manager, 1990.

The seventh locomotive of a class which eventually numbered 484 was Hunslet Engineering, Leeds 1855, of 1943, seen here with its WD number 75006 at Llanharan NCBOE, Glamorgan, on 14 August 1965.

Llanilid West Site - March 1995.

The Old Llanharan Road Bungalows are gone! Note the road extreme right of print. The Llanilid West project is fast approaching its productive boundaries.

Since the closure of Llanharan Colliery in 1962, the area has developed into one of the most prominent opencast sites in the country. The first phase was completed several years ago, and this new phase known as 'Llanilid West Development' took up to five years to complete. Sadly, as always in development on this scale, a number of dwellings fall to the engineers' axe. Approximately 100 yards west from where the old Llanilid Lane ran (old Llanharan Road) is a perfect example of a small community being 'wiped out' in the quest for coal, but in this example through amicable agreement with the occupiers. Among the four dwellings demolished was 'Surrey Bungalow'; this building held many memories for the author because it was once the home of his late mother Nancy Evelyn. Although in recent years the bungalow underwent

Family link severed – 'Surrey Bungalow' demolished October 1993

modernisation after the Priddle family left the area, the author still brings to mind some memorable childhood days in and around the bungalow.

159

Other mines on the South Crop

In the compass of this book, it is difficult to cover in detail the full industrial background to every mine which played its part in the development of the South Crop. It would indeed require massive research to give a full picture. This volume is set out to provide the reader with Llanharan's coal mining contribution to the Crop, and of its way of life in the village at that time. However, I feel that a brief report on other mines running along the Crop will give an insight into the importance of the South Crop itself.

Nantgarw Colliery just like Llanharan was given a new lease of life with the introduction of horizon mining.

The sinking of Nantgarw pit was completed by 1915, to the unprecedented depth for South Wales at that time of 856 yards. The owners - Taylors Navigation Steam Coal Co. Ltd., employed 366 men in 1923, but later sold out to Taff Thondda Navigation Steam Coal Co. Ltd., in 1924. Later geological conditions caused problems at the mine and in 1927 the mine was again sold, this time to the Powell Duffryn Co. Ltd.

Nantgarw actually stayed in mothballs for a number of years until like Llanharan, 'horizon mining' plans were put forward for its imminent revival. The plans were approved in 1946 by the Ministry of Fuel and Power. The plan was made more practicable by the advent of Nationalisation in 1947 which permitted areas of coal to be worked from the shafts not previously owned by Powell Duffryn. The new scheme came under the newly formed South Western Division of the National Coal Board. From the end of 1952 coal was worked successfully until 1974. At this point, the N.C.B. decided to link Nantgarw and Windsor, to develop a single streamlined unit concentrating mining in the more orthodox Windsor seams and bringing the coal production out at Nantgarw, where a modern washery unit would prepare it for its intended markets.

The combined Nantgarw/Windsor mine employed around 650 men, producing over 4,000 tons of high quality coking coal per week, most of which was used in the manufacturing of special foundry cokes. Working the six feet and nine feet seams the Windsor/Nantgarw unit contained more than 15 miles of underground roadways and over three miles of conveyors. Geological difficulties, like many mines on the Crop, saw its demise in the November of 1986.

Source:
Staff - Cefn Coed Mining Museum Records.

COAL SEAMS WORKED IN SOUTH CROP MINES.

Nantgarw/Windsor
Two Feet Nine
Upper Four Feet
Four Feet
Six Feet
Upper Nine Feet
Lower Nine Feet
Bute
Amman Rider/Yard/Seven Feet

Bryn Colliery
Two Feet Nine
Four Feet
Six Feet
Nos. 1, 2, 3, 4, 5, 6 seams
Little
Middle
Lower.

Cribbwr Fawr
Caegarw
North Fawr
South Fawr
Trydydd
Six Feet
Slatog
Nine Feet
Danllyd
Five Quarters
Cribbwr

Aberbaiden
Rock Fawr
Pentre
Aberbaiden

Ton Phillip
Rock Fawr
Tytalwen
Tynewydd

Coytrahen
Malthouse
Rock Fawr

Information on Llanharan and Brynna seams are recorded through individual reports within this volume. Seams include opencast production.
Source: National Coal Board 1908 - 1962 records, South Wales Coal Annuals 1904 – 1937. Mr. David Preece, Treharris, from his private collection 1997.

Local collieries in and around the Llanharan area have played a significant role in discovering and developing seams which were later exploited along the line of the South Crop belt. For example Llanharry, Coed Cae Lane, Wern Tarw, Brynna Wood, Tyn-y-Waun, South Rhondda, Brynwith, Cwm Ciwc and Meiros, all carried the main seams of the South Crop. The 1921 Gordons Map of the South Wales Coalfield, provides evidence of the successful working which went on during the early period. Our 1958 map shows most of the mines that became very successful under the new programme. Aberbaiden, Ton Phillip, Cribbwr Fawr, Newlands, Coytrahen Park and Bryn being the major collieries.

BRYN NAVIGATION COLLIERY
Bryn Navigation produced the best steam quality coal which was in great demand for household purpose. The colliery was situated near Port Talbot and the coal was available for shipping from Swansea, Cardiff and Penarth.

ABERBAIDEN
One of the largest gas coal group collieries was this Aberbaiden mine. The colliery was situated near the village of Kenfig Hill which had sprung up as a result of the mines introduction, and through nearby mining development. Aberbaiden was served by the Port Talbot Branch of the Great Western Railway Company. It was

another mine favourable for coal shipment. The colliery consisted of two slants, Aberbaiden and Pentre, these being driven in 1,500 yards and 1,900 yards respectively on the Rock Fawr Seam.

TON PHILLIP

The Ton Phillip mine was situated between Aberbaiden on the west and Coytrahen Park Colliery on the east, and was another valuable gas coal proposition. The mine comprised two slants – Tynewydd and Tytalwyn driven on the Rock Fawr seam.

CRIBBWR FAWR

Cribbwr Fawr was situated near Pyle, about six miles from Port Talbot. It consisted of what was known as the old slants Nos. 1 and 3, and Newlands Slant some distance away nearer Port Talbot. The total taking covered about 1,200 acres very rich in available coal seams of which the South Fawr, Slatog, Nine Feet, Five Quarter and Cribbwr were worked.

Source: South Wales Coal Annuals 1904 – 1937. Mr. David Preece, Edwardsville, Treharris National Coal Board Records 1908 – 1962

MARGAM MINE PROPOSAL

In the April of 1998 Celtic Energy Ltd. applied to the Neath Port Talbot and Bridgend County Borough Councils for planning permission to mine coal by opencast and underground methods from Margam Mine, the surface of which would be approximately one kilometre north of Cefn Cribbwr, near Bridgend.

The prospect of the new mine to access the extensive reserve of deep coal beneath Margam has been examined several times before, culminating with the former British Coal's application in 1984 to develop a drift mine on land west of Aberbaiden tips. For reasons of economics, however, the mine was never developed.

During 1997/98 Celtic Energy Ltd. evaluated the available geological information and formulated a proposal to access the deeper reserves by a preliminary opencast phase, thereby reducing the required amount of tunnelling.

Initially it is proposed to extend the current Park Slip West site some 500 metres to the west. This will provide a further four years of coaling and would be completed by the year 2004.

The creation of the opencast void would enable two access drifts to be driven north west, the locations already some 70 metres below ground level, to intersect the Nine Feet Seam. Production would commence in this seam, and eventually progress to the Gellideg Seam, at depths varying between 350 and 1,100 metres, with a minimum 20 years' reserves. The drifts would be connected to the mine surface, which would be built below the surrounding ground level, by tunnels constructed on compacted backfill.

Output from the opencast phase and deep mine would continue at the current level of 400,000 tonnes per annum, the great majority of which would be dispatched via the existing rail facilities.

When the application comes into fruition we will eventually witness the complete conquest of the South Crop from Nantgarw to Margam.

Source: Celtic Energy Report – by kind permission of Mr. Lewis Hands, Site Manager.

Life in the Village during the Mining Years

Mining in and around the Llanharan area during the 1930s brought significant inroads with regard to shops and businesses. It was said that in 1930, Llanharan village supported more shops than any other in Glamorgan. The list is certainly an impressive one and gives a good indication as to how mining contributed admirably to the employment status at that time.

SHOPS AT LLANHARAN 1930

Grocers
Bessants
Co-operative
Jenkins
Harris
Johnstons
John
D.H. Hopkins
Hole
Preece

Cycle Shop

Mrs. Sheene

Bakehouses

E. Richardson
A. Richardson
(2 Pasty Shops)

Fish & Chips

Morgan
Gilbert
Drapers

W. Price
Powell
Co-operative
London House
Bon Marche
Lee (Bridgend)
Manchester House
Watkins

Electric Shops

A. John
A. Martin

Hairdressers
Anglin
Bates
Spencer
Hancock

Newsagents

Post Office
A. John
Russell

Chemists

Gower

Fruiterers

Roberts   Morgan
Lobb
Davies
Dutton

Drug Stores

Thomas

Shoe Shops
Co-operative
H. Evans
Evans

Italian Shops

Lusardi
Basso
Sidoli
Oddi

Police Station

3 Constables and
a Sergeant

Billiard Halls
Miners Institute
Arcadia
Turberville Hall

Banks

Nat. West
Midland
Lloyds
Barclays

Small Shops
Rees
Sullivan, P.D's
Russell Co-operative

Ball
Harrison

Tailors

M.L. Phillips Evans
Thomas
Co-operative
All Bestear Tailors

Ironmongers

Davies

Butchers

Francis Pascoe
March (2)
M. Williams
Co-operative
Cooper
Smith (2)
Phipps

Llanharan Square and High Corner House during the mining years of the 1930s.

Note the early vehicles in the picture, also the High Corner yard was intact showing the old building which was used by our three Llanharan boxers for training

❖ THE COTTAGE, LLANHARAN, ❖

Sepr 27th 1924

Mr Dd. John

❦ Dr. to MORGAN & SONS, ❦

CARPENTERS, UNDERTAKERS, &c.

R. H. Dyer, Printer, Bridgend.

John Aaron Morgan was born at Llandinam, mid Wales in 1862. (See "Forgotten Years" series). At 'The Cottage', Llanharan, John established his undertaking business in the community and became affectionately known as 'Morgan the Undertaker'.

Central Stores. Family link spans 71 years.
William Hopkin at his store weeks before closure (July 1994).
The local shop ceased trading as a store as recently as 1994 when William Edward Hopkin retired. The business had been in the Hopkin family for 71 years. The use of this building as a store is still evident due to the 'Kardov flour' sign which is still clearly visible above the existing doorway, despite 50 years of weathering.

Rose Terrace, Llanharan

Rose Terrace 1924 This photograph gives a good indication of the shops in the village which provided the mining families with their daily needs. From the Gospel Hall – Bessants Ironmongery, Co-operative (drapery attached), food shop, Mrs. Sheene (clothes, toys, etc.) fish shop, London House Draper, Gilberts, Daniels sweet shop and Roberts fruit shop.

WILLIAM HARRIS STORES

Left to Right: Windsor Lewis, Dick Cowmeadow, Godfrey Farnham (manager), Reginald Hodgkinson, John Welsh - 1937.
The staff of William Harris Stores proudly pose in front of the store on Bridgend Road, Llanharan. Note that the window is dressed to commemorate the coronation of King George VI. May 1937.

Before the shop on Bridgend Road was taken over, it was known as 'Lewis's fruit shop'. Harris of Merthyr Tydfil purchased the building in the September of 1923.

When the shop opened, Mr. Godfrey Farnham started there as an errand boy. By 1930 he had worked his way into the shop with the counter staff assistants. By 1935 he became the store manager and by 1943 had worked himself right through to district manager, covering all the area stores.

As a shop, Harris's was indeed a successful one. During the 1930s the store employed eight assistants plus a delivery boy. Then, the bacon counter was selling six sides of bacon a week, another tribute to the coal mining community who bought their provisions within the village (no supermarkets in those days).

When Mr. Farnham retired from the store he opened his own business on the Dolau which he kept as a successful venture until retiring from the trade in 1963. Although Mr. Farnham and his good wife are now living in Pencoed, they are frequently seen in the village because they are staunch and faithful members of the Carmel Baptist Chapel.

Some of the delivery boys who worked at Harris's Stores:
Douglas Ware, Bernard Pascoe, Warnford Baker, Brian Witts. (Not a full list)

Source of photographs: Jacobsen, Photographer, Llanharan.

COUNCIL HOUSES

LLANHARAN

After the building of the Llanharan council houses in the 1920s. Note from this picture that the dairy had not yet been built and in the field hay stacks were a prominent feature.

Milk Factory, Llanharan.

Llanharan Dairy, 1932. This picture is well and truly history in itself. The dairy plant no longer produces milk. The railway station and bridge have been demolished. The branch railway line has long gone, and sadly, the Llanharan police station, situated on the left in the background has also been demolished.

Llanharan Co-operative Stores, Rose Terrace, Llanharan. Some of the staff pose for the camera. Left to Right – Dilys Trotman, Mr. Howell Rees (manager), Miss Vera Perryman.

Staff at the Co-operative Stores prepare for their annual outing in 1936. Back: P. Lewis, V. Cogbill. (middle) Miss R. Roberts, Miss A. Davies, Miss V. Perryman, Miss C. Rees, Miss D. Trotman. (Front) T. Edwards J. Evans (manager), R. Lloyd.

Mr. Tom Jenkins and Mr. Jim Pugh (mechanics) pose for the camera in the transport section of the Llanharan Dairy. We learn that quite a number of ex-miners worked in the new dairy when it opened in 1936.

Mr. Jim Pugh (chief mechanic) with Mr. Dick Martin (dairy foreman) pose for the camera at the dairy workshops 1936. The gentleman on the left is believed to be a Mr. Bill Brown of Tonyrefail.

Llanharan Co-operative Carnival participants gather outside the Workmen's Public Institute, before moving on to the football ground for judging - 1936.

Llanharan and District Co-operative Carnival, 1936. Here we see the carnival participants meeting outside the Miners and Workmen's Public Institute (later British Restaurant) now Llanharan R.F.C.

The day the circus came to the village

The elephant circus parade marches past the Gospel Hall, Dolau. The house top seen on the right of the picture is Prices' Drapery and Milliners (now Welsh Breakers shop). Photograph 1933.

Miners holiday at home week

*Meg Russell, Eluira Williams, Dilys Adams and Peggy Jervis **née** Shilabeer play up to the camera before joining the holiday week carnival 1951. (right)*

Residents of Trenos Place. Llanharan pose for the camera during the 1951 carnival week. (below)

Festival of Britain Day, 3 May 1951. The children of the Dolau and Bridgend Road families enjoy a tea party to celebrate the festive occasion.

After the party the children of Bridgend Road hold their sports events at the Welfare Ground. Festival of Britain Day, 3 May 1951.

THE LEGENDARY FREEMAN FUNFAIR

Freeman showpeople at Llanharan
*Left to Right: Mrs. Helen Freeman, Mrs. Amelia Phillips (**née** Freeman) and Mr. William Arthur*
Freeman pose for the camera while on a visit to Llanharan, possibly during the 1940s. Mrs. Amelia
Phillips was a respected lady at Llanharan. Many people will remember when she lived in a caravan
at the side of Llanharan Cinema. Amelia was the mother of John and Phil Phillips. Both brothers
were in the cinema business, John at Llanharan and Phil at Pontyclun. (See "Forgotten Years" Vol. I).

It is strange how nothing photo-graphically ever came to light about the Freeman's Funfair while I was compiling the "Forgotten Years" series. Yet these legendary showpeople made frequent visits to Llanharan, in fact they have held a link with the village going back to the early 1900s.

Harry Freeman first brought his fair to the village during the mid 1900s. This early funfair consisted of small rides, swing boats and side shows, with the main attraction being a large and colourful 'Galloping Horses' spectacle ride with a large loud organ powering away in the centre of the show. During an interview with a member of the Freeman family I was informed that the 'Galloping Horses' ride was, up until the end of the 1993 season, operating at full capacity at Coney Beach Funfair, Porthcawl. We were informed recently that this spectacular showpiece has now left Porthcawl and is under renovation before going out on exhibition throughout the country. Going back to those early days at Llanharan, the first fair during the early 1900s was sited on Sam Miles' field. This field today is now the new rugby ground for Llanharan R.F.C. The early Freeman's Funfair was illuminated with naphtha flares until the arrival of electricity. During those early days the fair was driven by two ornate steam driven traction engines, the

"Admiral Beresford" and "Cymro". Each with dynamos mounted on their smokeboxes, they could be heard clicking away every evening generating power for the rides. The "Admiral Beresford", which was a Fowler showman's engine, was also used to pull trailers from place to place. I was also informed that on occasions the engine was called upon to help out on local farms in the district. Sadly this engine ended its days in a breakers yard in Newport, sold for a mere forty pounds.

When Harry Freeman retired he lived for a while in Llanharan in a caravan at the bottom of Robert Street. Later, he moved to the side of the old cinema. The Phillips family, who owned the cinema, were cousins of the Freemans. After a period near the cinema, Harry moved to Pontyclun where he spent most of his days. The fair continued with his son William Arthur. From this time onward the Freeman family became even more popular, making friends throughout the principality. Their visit on 'miners fortnight' at Llanharan was always eagerly awaited by the children of the village. During the late forties the arrival of the fair would see at least fifty children watching at the gates of the Welfare Ground in anticipation as the showmen entered the field. Erecting the fair was sweat rending work. The showpeople were expected to build the rides in one day, work undertaken in all weathers.

At Llanharan it didn't take William Arthur and his wife Helen long to gain the same high respect from the village folk as was afforded Harry in his early days. Helen Freeman will be remembered by the latter day children of the 1960s as the lady who supervised the dodgems. Helen put a lot of effort into the fair and was noted as a no-nonsense person who took the business seriously.

If anyone was seen fooling around on the rides she would immediately stop the machine and remove the offending individual. Safety always came first with the Freemans. This precaution was upheld throughout their careers on the road, and still is today. Helen was a remarkable person. One evening, during the March of 1936, the fair was in Nelson, near Aberfan. She had just completed her duties on the 'Noah's Ark' at seven o'clock. By ten o'clock she gave birth to a son in her caravan. The family suggested the child be called 'Nelson' but Donald was the name chosen.

The 'Noah's Ark' ride was extremely popular with the children, me included. The Freeman's sons all worked the 'Ark' in their turn during its operational service with the fair. Teddy, Donald, Phillip and Billy are members of the family easily brought to mind. After handing your ride money (three pence) to any of the above-mentioned brothers, it was sheer magic to watch them walking up and down the fast ride while it was in full flight. Sometimes a child or sometimes an adult would become distressed, the showman on the ride would casually walk to the individual and hold them on until it stopped. They could walk on the ride as if they were on the main road. We youngsters would be hanging on for grim death as the ride spun around, staring in anticipation that one of the showmen would surely slip and be thrown about, but they were always surefooted and no such disaster ever occurred. During an interview with Mr. Teddy Freeman, I asked him if any of his brothers ever fell while doing the 'Ark Walk'. His answer was, "When you are walking the ride a hundred times a day, every day, it becomes a natural procedure, you don't even think about it, mind you, if someone tried to do it off the cuff so to speak, they would be thrown right off the ride." Despite Mr. Freeman's statement I still marvel at their balancing feat. Having mentioned the Freeman brothers, we should at this point mention their sister, Florence, who worked on the side shows of the fair for many years.

Sadly, William Arthur died in the mid seventies, aged 75 years, and Helen died in 1985 aged 91 years. The fair continued for a few years, but in 1988 Teddy Freeman decided to call it a day and retired. Today, the fair continues with William Henry Freeman and his family with the rides now consisting of Dodgems, The Twist and Octopus. The old 'Noah's Ark' now a far off memory. However, the 'Ark' is still in operation today up country but now known as 'Jungle Speedway'. Teddy's daughters, Eleanor, May and Victoria still travel the show working various side stalls. We could, in fact, write a full book on the Freeman family, they are without doubt a credit to the entertainment business. Today some of the older members of the family live in the Nelson area. Donald and Phillip still live in their caravans. On a personal note I will never forget when the Freemans came to the village, and the memories of those breathtaking rides on the 'Ark' will live with me forever....

Special Note: Many people know Helen Freeman as 'Nellie', a name put on her by the family. Mrs. Maria Freeman is formerly of the Scarrott family, another highly respected team in the world of fairground entertainment.

Source: Interview with Mr. Teddy Freeman and his wife Maria, 5 January 1994.

"Freeman's Noah's Ark"
The Ark was the most popular ride with the Llanharan children during the 1940s and early 1950s. The week leading up to the Miners' Fortnight, in July, would see the arrival of the funfair. Freemans were well respected showpeople at Llanharan and visited Llanharan up until 1972, spanning a period of 74 years.

Left: Donald Freeman with Florence on the platform of the Chair Planes. The planes were very popular during the forties and fifties. Photograph 1940.

The Freeman Brothers Erect The 'Noah's Ark'.
The erecting of the 'Noah's Ark' was always eagerly watched over by the children of the village. The 'Ark' was the most popular showride in its day during the late forties and early fifties. Our photograph shows (left to right) Phillip, Donald, Teddy and Billy Freeman.

Mrs. Helen Freeman was highly respected throughout the funfair circuit. At Llanharan she was known as 'Nellie' and affectionately called 'The Lady of the Fair.'
William Arthur Freeman finds time to relax outside his caravan with one of his grandchildren. Just like his father before him, William gained the highest respect during his annual visits over the years to Llanharan.

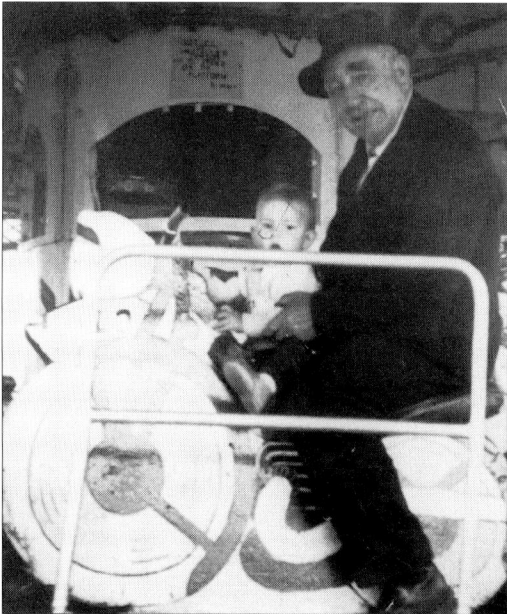

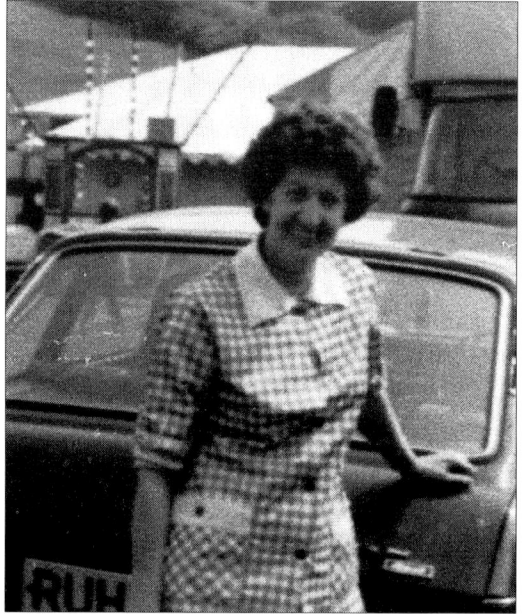

Mr. William Arthur Freeman with one of his grandchildren when the fair was at nearby Llanharry in 1965. (left) Mrs. Maria Freeman when the fair was at Llanharan in 1972. Maria, Teddy Freeman's wife, is formerly of the famous Scarrott family, another highly respected band of showpeople. The Scarrott Fair used to be regular attenders at the famous St. Mary Hill Fair during the early 1920s.

Kay Danter stands in front of the 'Ark' with Teddy Freeman's daughter, Victoria Ann. The Danter family were another well known show family who travelled with the Freemans.

Mr. Teddy Freeman (left) with other members of the fair family.

THE ITALIAN FAMILIES IN OUR COMMUNITY.

The Italian link at Llanharan goes back many years, to 1908 in fact, when Charles Basso came to Llanharan from Ebbw Vale and took work at Llanharan Colliery before purchasing a premises on Bridgend Road, Llanharan and opening an ice cream shop. The Bassos were to establish themselves in the village maintaining their business activities for over seventy years. (See "Forgotten Years" Vol. III).

During the early 1930s the Oddi family of Italians opened a shop on the Square, Llanharan, also the Sidoli family opened a business on Bridgend Road. One of the best remembered in the Italian Connection was the Lusardi family. Their 'Flora Cafe' on Bridgend Road was, during the 1940s and 1950s, a thriving business. Every evening the establishment would be full to capacity with the youngsters of the village. It was indeed a favourite meeting place. Who will ever forget the lovely Gloria who made the delicious coffee during warm summer evenings. Gloria always had a smile on her face and never ever had a bad word to say about anyone. We learnt as kids that Mr. Lusardi was killed on the 'Arandora Star' which was sunk in 1940 during the war. The sinking of that ship was much talked about in the village then because many Italians lost their lives. Gloria, Dante, Gilio and Dorio were a family highly respected at Llanharan and it was with great sadness when Gloria passed away during 1994. The shop is long gone, but memories of this lovely family leave a deep and lasting affection.

During the 1940s a number of Italians came and settled in the village, some to work in the local mines. They settled well and became an integral part of our community. One of the most established Italian successes in the locality is the Llanharan Concrete Works on Llanharry Road. Gino and Giovanni Coco opened the business together and today it is one of the most successful businesses in the area. Gino takes a keen interest in the cultural life of the village and is well known for his support and sponsorship of sporting organisations in the district. Understandably, for his daughter Tina was up until recent times a competitive member of the mid Glamorgan Riding Club at nearby Heol-y-Cyw.

On a personal note I bring to mind the Basini family whose cafe on the Square, Llanharan during the 1950s and 1960s was a most popular meeting place for the young folk on the council estates, which included yours truly. Mrs. Basini (Anna) as I recall was a real personality. Her daughter Mary and son John I look upon as personal friends. Ray Dyer, Stuart Wetherall, Ken Coombes, Ken Brown, David Wallace and so many more were a part of those heady days when Basini's Cafe was the carefree meeting place for all.

Yes, the Basini family will always find an affectionate place in my memories.

It gives me great pleasure to mention the last link of the Italian connection at Llanharan. Mr. Les Servini is without doubt one of the most interesting individuals ever to adopt our community.

In 1950 Mr. Les Servini took over the old 'Swallow Cafe' on Bridgend Road, but the changing times and traffic increase threw the business into failure. Not deterred, this most gentlemanly individual gained admittance to Caerleon Training College and forwarded his career at Llwynderw, Heolgam and Bryntirion Schools before retiring at the age of 66 years. Despite retirement, Mr. Servini took classes in languages, teaching Italian, French and Spanish. Recently (1994) he wrote his memoirs in a book entitled 'A Boy from Bardi' a highly interesting and colourful account of his life and activities. He wrote his memoirs through encouragement from his Italian and Welsh friends.

We learn that quite recently he was awarded the title of Cavaliere by Italy in recognition of his services to language and the community.

THE LUSARDI FAMILY

Left to Right: Doria Lusardi, Colin Freeman and Gilio Lusardi outside the 'Flora Cafe' which was situated on Bridgend Road, Llanharan.

Vittorio in the 'Bracchi' which was situated on Bridgend Road, Llanharan. Three Italian shops were operating on Bridgend Road at the same time. Lucardi, Basso and the Swallow Cafe.

The Lusardi Family in 1932. Left to right: Antonia, Gilio (baby), Dante, Vittorio, Dorio (baby), and Gloria.

In 1939, there were many villages in South Wales with a cafe or shop owned by Italian families. These shops were known as 'Bracchis'. Most of the families originally came from Northern Italy, many from the twin towns of Bardi and Bedonia. These families, in general, sold ice cream, drinks, sweets and cigarettes etc. The name 'Bracchi' originated when the first established business was set up in Merthyr.

Vittorio originally came from Bedonia, coming to South Wales in 1919. He fought with the British Army in World War 1, was captured in Turkey and escaped, only to be caught later by the Austrians and imprisoned.

Many of the older inhabitants of Llanharan will remember the generosity of Vittorio Lusardi, especially during the miners' strike of 1926. It was Vittorio's practice to provide, on chosen days, free ice cream for the children. Many a miner was allowed to run up a bill on cigarettes and various items, which was paid back after the strike. Along with his wife, Antonia, he was held in high esteem in the village and many people were angry when Vittorio was arrested in 1940, when the Government arrested all people holding Italian or German passports. This plan was put into effect to make sure that any spies were caught. It led to great distress for many families, and sadly death for others.

When the vessel 'Arandora Star' carrying 1,500 German and Italian internees was sunk while conveying them to Canada, Llanharan was stunned. Not only were there many losses from the sinking, but a number of people in the village stated their disgust at Vittorio's passing, saying that the Lusardi family at Llanharan were as Welsh in heart as anyone living here.

After the war Vittoroi's wife continued with the shop on Bridgend Road. But in fairness, Antonia never really recovered from her ordeals and the loss of her husband. She died after a short illness at the age of 42 years. After their mother's death, the young Lusardi family took over the shop.

It is ironic that all three of Vittorio's sons served in the British armed forces. The eldest was in the battles of Nymegen and Arnem, while the others served after the war in the far east, Kenya and on the Suez Canal.

Mr. & Mrs. Eddie Frost at the Mountain Hare Inn, Brynna.
Both were highly respected while 'mine hosts'.

One of the most popular and easily brought to mind licensees at the Mountain Hare was Mr. Eddie Frost. Eddie, formerly of Pontypridd, and a former miner who worked in the Albion Colliery Cilfynydd for many years, came to Brynna and took over the 'Mount' in 1953. Along with his wife Beatrice, they became a very popular couple indeed.

When the Frosts took over the inn there was no running water behind the bar to wash the glasses and all cleansing water had to be carried in pails. However, after a short time trade at the inn improved vastly; so much so that the Brewery decided to modernise the place which brought in all mod cons including piped water behind the bars. During alterations a room which had been bricked up for over 35 years was found. It was believed that the old room was a 'brewing room' which, during the early part of the century, was common-place. The High Corner House at Llanharan being a fine example.

Setting their standard at the inn, the Frosts soon made friends. They encouraged local lads to the pub and formed a darts section. During the late 1950s a number of individuals from the local Llangeinor Hounds started meeting at the inn, and were so impressed by the character of the place that they introduced a number of 'Hunt Meetings' there. In 1958 a triple Meet took place with the Pentyrch, Glamorgan and Llangeinor Hunts.

Eddie and Beatrice were licensees at the 'Mount' from 1953 until the September of 1965 when ill health forced them to retire. Their reign was certainly a memorable one, and they are affectionately remembered even to this day. When they retired their daughter Valerie and son-in-law took over. They themselves left in 1977 to take over the Fountain Inn at Aberkenfig, also the now well known Foresters Restaurant where their son Stephen is chef.

TURBERVILLE HOTEL DARTS TEAM AND FOLLOWERS - 1948

The team as follows:
Left to Right: Back Row: Bob Jones, Simon Silcox, Ruffy Woodland, Jack Goodman, Bob Gardner, Tom Davies, Joe Basso, Bill Pascoe, Trevor Edwards, unknown, Glyn Pascoe, Tom Jones.
Front Row: Arthur Morgan, J. Reed, Tom Evans, Bill (Slogger) Williams, Bill Perkins, Evan Roberts and Bill Gallacher.

The 'A' team was very popular and encouraged friendly games with teams from outlying districts. Many friendlies were played in the Rhondda valleys because a number of the lads from the valleys worked in Llanharan Colliery – thus genuine friendships materialised between local and district club and pub teams.

The 'Turb' entered the 'People' newspaper tournament in 1948 and although they didn't get far in the competition, they made many friends on the way. As a local team in the late 1940s the 'Turb' was a reasonably successful side, with a number of talented players in the team. It must also be pointed out that a women's team was introduced there in the early 1950s which had its fair share of achievements. During those early days the Turberville was a hive of character and personality.

LLANHARAN CONSTITUTIONAL CLUB DARTS TEAM 1949

Darts was certainly one of the major sporting pastimes in the village during the reign of the collieries. Over 28 teams were run in the Pencoed and District League in the 1950s creating A and B sections in every public house and club.   As we mentioned in the "Forgotten Years" series, quite a number of 'stars' came to the front during those enthusiastic darting years. Our team below is a typical example of the mining influence within the darts fraternity.

Left to Right:
Back Row: J. McAndrew, Bill (Slogger) Williams, Glyn Pascoe, Syd Worgan, Bill Pascoe, Bill Perkins, Ly Wareham, Ken Shillabeer.
Front Row: W.R.D. Morgan, J. Gore, Trevor Edwards, Tom Padget.

LLANHARAN BARNSTORMERS

The Llanharan Barnstormers Comic Band was made up primarily from local miners. Although, throughout its prominence an outstanding array of individual personalities from the outside villages did form a part of this exceptionally talented carnival band. The band's leader, Mr. Vincent Witts, was an outstanding individual and is well recorded in the "Forgotten Years" series of books.

The Llanharan Barnstormers were, without doubt, one of the most colourful groups of entertainers ever to emerge in the cultural life of Llanharan. Within twelve months of formation, they became a wanted item throughout the Rhondda Valleys, and even as far afield as Swansea. It was in 1948 when the band reached its talented heights. At Aberavon, with a competitive field of six other comic bands, they emerged winners and champion band of Wales. As author of this book, I can say that it was a very proud moment for all the members of the band. Aged nine years, I was the youngest member of the band, being a part of the drummers section. It was certainly an occasion that I will never forget.

The old outfit had disbanded by 1953, but in 1965 it reformed again. However, despite the fact that the band continued up until 1967, the enthusiasm was not strong enough to put it anywhere near the class of the old unit. The mining era had ended and the talent which the pits had generated had gone forever.

Our photograph shows the old 1948 band during a concert at the Old Llanharan Schoolroom. Their showtime performance at the room held capacity audiences for two sell-out weeks. Such was the talent of that well liked and reputable band of the 1940s.

The famous Llanharan Barnstormers during their concert in the old Church Room 1948.
Back (Left to Right) T. Thomas, B. Edwards, T. Worgan, J. Watkins, G. Worgan, C. Bundy. A. Worgan and G. Stallard.
Middle (L to R) T. Morgan, R. Pick, R. Witts, R. Woodland, E. Roberts, T. Evans, J. Pyne, J. Powell, B. Perkins, D. Wooloff, Baldwin, D. Richards, unknown.
Front (L to R) W. Witts, V. Witts (Buster), L. Jones, Mrs. S. Jones, R. Ashton and W.R.D. Morgan.

JOHN HENRY HUTCHINS – BANDMASTER 1844 – 1928

John Henry Hutchins was a Berkshire man, son of a warrant officer serving with the Berkshire Regiment. However, John Henry himself was born in Cork, Ireland, when his father, like many serving soldiers in those days, took their wives and families with them during activities in other countries. On this particular occasion helping to maintain law and order during the potato famine in 1846. Later John Henry's father fought in the Crimean War and was reported killed, but turned up while the family were wearing black arm bands.

John Henry himself had military ambitions, and as soon as he came of age enlisted into the Berkshire Regiment, gaining a place in the Military Academy at Knellor Hall. Eventually he came to Wales and joined the Welch Regiment as Bandmaster. He later married a young lady named Mary Ann Evans, first cousin to Clara Novello Davies, Ivor Novello's mother. With his young wife, John Henry went to live for a while in Richmond Road, Cardiff, before going into married quarters of the then new Maindy Barracks where some of his children were born. Part of the Regimental Colours at Llandaff Cathedral were played in by the Regiment Band under the leadership of John Henry. Also, one of his duties was to trumpet in the High Court Judges when they were in circuit. It is interesting to note that one time Police Chief Colonel Lindsey of Cardiff was in his early days a cadet under John Henry in the Regimental Band.

An interesting episode took place in our hero's life when 'Blondell', who was a wizard on the tightrope, came to Cardiff and gave a breathtaking show on Sophia Gardens fields. John Henry went across on the high wire sitting on Blondell's shoulders while playing Yankee Doodle Dandy on his trumpet. We learn from the family that John Henry's high wire exploit was the most frightening experience throughout his lifetime.

John Henry Hutchins served thirty years in the Army, the same amount of time as his father. Ironically, his brother Luke served thirty years, giving the family ninety years military service between them. On leaving the forces he did several years as a warden in Cardiff Prison before moving to Llanharan, eventually settling in No. 31 Chapel Road. He was to make full use of his musical ability at Llanharan. The management of the thriving Meiros Colliery gave him a light job in the lamproom with the idea of giving our musician the opportunity to plan his musical motivation. The management itself was enthusiastic and came forward with financial assistance. Colonel John Blandy Jenkins of Llanharan House also took a keen interest, especially as John Henry was from the Berkshire Country. From the first meeting the Colonel took to John Henry immediately. Both were seen often as the months went by drinking together in the High Corner House. From that time a successful band was formed in the village and several concerts were given on the Llanharan Estate Parkland.

Under the leadership of John Henry, the band went from success to success. We have already in the "Forgotten years" series an excellent photographic record of the band. Later, Mr. Frederick Pick came into the village from Cinderford to assist in the band's fortunes. He was another musician with an excellent pedigree and gained high respect from the Llanharan House family. Today a number of local inhabitants tell numerous stories about those golden years when the brass band played at Llanharan Parklands during the hot summer months, many wishing they could see those magic scenes again.

Sadly, a thing of the past. They can thank the likes of John Henry and Frederick Pick for their memories. One point is almost certain, the likes of both characters will never be seen in the village again.

Source: Mrs. Amy Hutchins during an interview.

Special Note:
It must be pointed out that another well known character in the form of Mr. Tom Sheppard also played a large part in the band's success.

John Henry Hutchins - 1844 - 1928

Former Bandmaster with the Welch Regiment at Maindy, Cardiff. While living at Llanharan he played a significant part in the formation of the Llanharan Brass Band. This unit was first formed under the financial support of the Meiros Colliery Management.

GRANNY – MARY ANN (POLLY) HUTCHINS 1859 – 1955

Mary Ann Hutchins (nee Evans) was born on a farm in Llanishen, Cardiff in 1859. She was a first cousin to Clara Novello Davies (Ivor Novello's mother). Mary Ann married John Henry Hutchins who was a bandmaster at the new Maindy Barracks, Cardiff. They were married at St. John's Parish Church, Cardiff, and lived for a while on Richmond Road before moving into married quarters in the Barracks.

After thirty years service in the Army, John Henry left the forces and the family settled down for a while in Cardiff where he took up a post in Cardiff Prison. In later years he picked up his family again and came to Llanharan, where after a

while they settled in their new home on Chapel Road. Meiros Colliery was beginning to establish itself at this time during the late 1880s and John went into the colliery to seek employment.

I remember Granny Hutchins with a deep affection, living next door to her while at 26 Hillside Avenue. As a child I ran many errands for Granny. She was a well liked person and also well known. During her lifetime she was an active participant of a number of women's organisations. When she died in 1955 aged 96 years, I carried a feeling of great loss. Granny had been such a rich influence in my life during those early years. When I pass the house, even today, I give a thought to those halcyon days when I ran errands for a dear old friend.....

MRS. CATHERINE RAYMOND REED. J.P.

Mrs. Reed came to Llanharan from Tredegar in 1929 when her husband Joe took up a position at Llanharan Colliery. At Llanharan they set up home in the new Powell Duffryn houses at Bryncae. In 1931 their son Alan was born and it was ironic that, in later years, he was to become manager of the Llanharan pit.

In the village, Mrs. Reed immediately took a keen interest in the social and cultural life of the community. Many of the older folk will remember her untiring work as manageress of the old 'British Restaurant'. Her interest became so emphatic that she soon entered the world of local politics, and it was during the war years that she became a councillor on Cowbridge Rural District Council. The old Council then encouraged closely knit communities. Families were given the opportunity to remain in the village, keeping up that tradition of their parents and grandparents before them. The village of Llanharan under Cowbridge was like one huge family where local values remained firm and steadfast. Everyone knew each other and helped each others causes. Unlike the modern approach where 'people movement' is induced. Sadly, villages today seem to be run by unseen faces, completely out of touch with the people and their views.

The Cowbridge Council was a caring Council in which people like Mrs. Reed thrived. In 1958, she served on the Llanharan Commonwealth Games Committee. As many will remember, our own Hywel Williams was given the opportunity to compete for Wales. The Games opened the gate for Hywel as he went on to compete against Holland and Belgium and also for Great Britain against France.

Mrs. Reed was a person of determined nature. Along with Councillor Joseph Aaron David, she was awarded with a certificate for endeavour in getting the War Memorial moved back to the Square - its place of origin. For a number of years it had stood in isolation on the far side of the Welfare Ground, much to the disgust of many local war veterans. The monument is now situated at the foot of Hillside Avenue.

After approximately thirty years service on the Council, Mrs. Reed retired from office in 1962. She left Llanharan and went to Maesteg where her son Alan was now manager of St. Johns Colliery there. She died in 1974 and is today remembered as a hard working and dedicated servant of the community.

Left of picture stands the Royal British Legion club house. The local branch was first formed around 1923 when they met at the rear of the Square where the present Mid Glamorgan Construction Company now reside. This early building above was built on its present site by volunteers in 1933 out of old railway sleepers and any other timbers available at the time. How the scene has changed, below we see the present club which was modernised in 1963.

Sadly, on Tuesday 28 August 1996, after a long spell of uncertainty, the village was rocked by the news that the Royal British Legion Club had closed. Anyone who was part of, or a member of the club during its progressive years of the 1950s and 1960s must regard the news as heart rending. Yet another blow to our proud village, underlining the sad times in which we live.

To the Fallen at Dunkirk

God bless the men who's bodies lie
On sands across the sea,
They died that we may fight again,
To keep our country free.
They left their homes, when duty called
Their freedom to uphold,
They knew how hard the fight would be
Without them being told.
They held no fear, those men who fought
To keep the foe at bay,
They only knew that they were right,
In staying there that day.

In hell they lived for three whole days
To give their comrades time,
To reach the boats –
That waiting there
Would take them oe'r the Brine.
They rest in peace, now they are gone
Their faces seen no more,
But their names live deep within the years
Those men upon the shore......

Clifford Jacobsen
(While serving at Aldershot in 1940.)

Royal British Legion Standard Bearers during a Civic Function (c.1961)

*Left to Right: Mr. Fred Wooloff, Mrs. Mansfield, Mr. Ken Bailey and
Mr. Roger Ennis.*

Reg Hutchins and Bert Sheppard stand guard in the 'wooden hut' which was situated near the Llanharan Colliery. They were a part of the Home Guard unit active in the village on the outbreak of the Second World War. This photograph was taken in 1940.

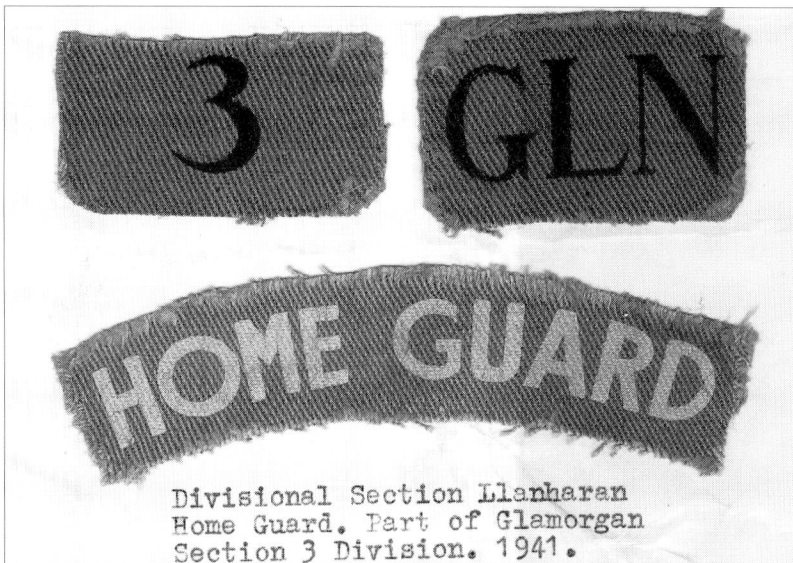

Divisional Section Llanharan Home Guard part of the Glamorgan Section 3 Division. 1941.

FIRE DRILL BUILDING.

The old fire drill hut was situated between the Chapel Road fish and chip shop and the Ewenny Fach river. This small brick building was erected before the Second World War to accommodate the local A.F.S. (Auxiliary Fire Service). A small band of individuals trained vigorously to create an effective fire fighting force. During the war, they were fully mobilised against any imminent German air raids. Manned simply with a mobile water pump unit, their main objective would be to save lives from attacks from incendiary bombs or building damage. Most of the team members were working in the local collieries. It was purely a voluntary unit. Fortunately, unlike Brynna, the Llanharan unit did not have to put their hard training into conflict operations.

Up until the 1940s, two tall pipes with a cross bar stood between the rear of their fire-hut and the main Hillside Avenue road. The pipes resembled rugby posts – used as hose drying out hangers after fire drill. At the tail end of the war, villagers witnessed an effigy of Adolf Hitler being 'strung up' and burned on the cross bar of the pipes. After the war the little brick hut was used as a meeting place for various village organisations. Today, the building is still in full use by the local Pigeon Club.

Also in the above photograph can be seen the pipeline running along the base of the river bank. This pipe was laid down by Powell Duffryn as a compressed air link between Llanharan and Ynysmaerdy, near Llantrisant. It was a costly venture. When completed, the pipeline ran from Llanharan Colliery through the village, over the mountain at Garth Maelwg, down into the Ynysmaerdy pit. Sadly, Ynysmaerdy as you have already read in this book, fell victim to a horrendous and tragic explosion. The Ynysmaerdy mine was closed immediately, and all operations concentrated at Llanharan. The mountain pipeline was removed during the 1950s, leaving today only small remnants of pipeline in our village to remind us of those far off mining days.

Auxiliary Fire Service, Llanharan.
John Phillips (Cinema) - Leading Fireman
J. Riddler - Leading Fireman.
Henry Witts - Officer in Charge - Section Leader.

National Fire Service Section, Llanharan.

A. Bates	N. Huckeridge
S. Bowden	E. Malpas
G. Cater.	W. Ockwell
C. Chilvers	S. Preece
G. Dean	R. Richardson
T. Evans	C. Shillabeer
E. Gale	R. Tebby
H. Gwilliam	J. Vickery
J. Hole	

Source: Mr. Henry Witts, Llanharan, former Officer in Charge Section Leader.

Fire Drill Building.

Standing left to right: Oswald Thomas and Frank Russell
Sitting left to right: Egbert Butcher and Desmond Butcher.
The above photograph was taken in 1933. All of the above were regular soldiers recalled for action in France at the beginning of the War. Egbert Butcher was killed in action.

Emlyn Witts, Brynna, killed in action 9 September 1944
Witts. Emlyn. 3967585

ABLE SEAMAN GEORGE WORGAN

Able Seaman George Worgan was only six months into his war activities before he was sunk by a German attack while he was serving on a torpedo ship. His capture was to see him spend the rest of the conflict in a prisoner of war camp. Fortunately, despite his four years in captivity, he came home after the war relatively unscathed. After a period of recuperation, he took over as steward of the Llanharan Constitutional Club. Later, George left Llanharan and went to Swansea where he took over stewardship of the Mumbles Conservative Club. Later he was to take a pub in Swansea, which he held until he retired. Sadly, George died on 7 May 1994. His death provided full testimony to his popularity because his funeral saw a massive crowd in attendance to pay tribute to a respected and likeable individual.
Source: South Wales Echo

SOUTH WALES WAR CASUALTIES

PRISONER OF WAR

Mrs. M. Worgan, of Bridgend-road, Llanharan, has been officially informed that her son, George Worgan, who was serving on a torpedo ship, is a prisoner of war. He had been previously reported missing. He is 20 years of age and a brother of Syd Worgan, the well-known boxer. He has two other brothers serving with the Forces.

Left to Right: Front: Fred Merry, Guardsman J. Vivian Kuner, Wally Pritchard.
Back: Joe Basso, Glyn Pascoe, Goff Gore, Arthur Worgan. (c.1942) Guardsman Vivian Kuner was sadly killed in action not long after this photograph was taken. Source: Mr. Sid Worgan, Dan Caerlan, Llantrisant.

RICHARD GRIFFITH MARTIN

During the month of November 1940, convoy HX84 consisting of 37 merchant ships was proceeding westward through the Atlantic bound for various British ports. The convoy was under the sole escort of HMS *JERVIS BAY*.

Also steaming westward bound for Liverpool with a refrigerated cargo from Jamaica was a single merchant ship, the S.S. *MOPAN*. The *MOPAN*, because of her better speed, overtook the convoy and thus continued unescorted. On board was Able-Seaman Richard Griffith Martin, seconded from the Royal Navy to man the ship's guns.

In this same month of November 1940, the German pocket battleship *ADMIRAL SCHEER* entered the North Atlantic and 300 miles west of Liverpool sighted the S.S. *MOPAN*. The merchant ship took a shell below the waterline and was quickly sunk. Fortunately, all 68 of the Mopan's Officers and Crew were taken prisoner on board the *ADMIRAL SCHEER*, and they were kept imprisoned below for 5 months.

Having sunk the *MOPAN*, the *ADMIRAL SCHEER* then proceeded to harass the oncoming convoy of 37 ships and, of course, HMS *JERVIS BAY*. She was no match for the German battleship and was soon sunk. The convoy scattered, but not before the loss of 5 merchant ships.

The *ADMIRAL SCHEER* sailed all over the Atlantic sinking merchant ships at will, all the time the MOPAN prisoners being kept below decks. Eventually, she returned to a German port, but not before putting ashore her prisoners in the French port of Bordeaux.

The 68 prisoners were then sent by train to a prisoner-of-war camp in North Germany and Richard Martin was to spend the next 4^1/$_2$ years there.

Within a short time of his ship being sunk, the family of Richard Martin received a War Office telegram stating he was "missing on war service" only for him to turn up in Germany 6 months later.

During his 4^1/$_2$ years of imprisonment Richard Martin was largely involved in camp activities, both sporting and welfare, something he was to continue with on his return to civilian life. As many people will remember, Richard Martin spent much of his spare time on community and local government work.

Source: Mr. Randall Martin - son.

Able Seaman Richard Griffith Martin

The family of Richard Martin received a telegram from the War Office stating that he was "Missing in War Service" only for him to turn up in a prisoner of war camp in North Germany six months later. Martin was to spend the next 4^1/$_2$ years there.

D/JX 140408 GUNNER EDDIE ALFORD.

Mr. Eddie Alford hails originally from Coetrahen near Bridgend. As a young lad he enlisted in the Navy as a cadet recruit which was to eventually lead to a 15 year service with HM fleet. During the Second World War Mr. Alford spent six months in the University College at Cardiff involved in a pre-entry training programme. His service record shows that throughout his naval career he sailed on such distinguished ships as HMS *DUKE OF YORK*, HMS *KING GEORGE V*, HMS *NORFOLK*, HMS *DROMEDE* and of course the HMS *RODNEY*.

As a gunner Mr. Alford served in a number of naval campaigns. He took part in the memorable action in the sinking of the German Pocket Battleship *BISMARK* in 1941 while serving on the HMS *RODNEY*. The *RODNEY* also took part in the D Day landings and survived the war only to be scrapped in Inverkeithing, Scotland, in the March of 1948. It was a sad ending for a battleship which saw such distinguished action. She weighed 40,000 tons, was 710 feet in length and 108 foot beam. Her crew comprised up to 1,600 men.

Mr. Alford left the Navy in 1948 carrying the rank of Petty Officer. He married and settled in Llanharan where he resides today. His wife is Florence (*née* Pascoe). Mr. Alford is another serviceman who we honour in our Llanharan historical records.

The war rages on but the boys in the thick of the battles still find time to make a little bit of history through the eye of the camera. Sadly, we cannot name all the lads on this print, but we know that the soldier second right, back row, is Mr. Mel David of Brynna.

Note the writing on the tank.

'Alamein Tripoli Tunis'.

Again we are unable to give any information on the boys in this print only that Mel David came home to Brynna after the war.

Source: Mr. Sid Worgan, Dan Caerlan, Llantrisant.

Guardsman William Pascoe (Billy Guardy)
William Pascoe was well respected in Llanharan. His outgoing personality made him a popular figure everywhere. He was quite simply described as 'one of the characters of the village'. During the Second World War he served in various countries and finished up in the Normandy Campaign. When he came home, Billy started work on the railway with the Llanharan main line gang. Sadly, while working on the main line near Llanharan Colliery, he was struck by a train and died from his injuries.

Mr. George Williams CBE., MC., TD., lays a wreath on the Llanharan Monument during an Armistice Parade.
Mr. Williams, formerly of Llanharan House, served six years in the Royal Fusiliers in North Africa, Italy, Greece and Iraq and was awarded the Military Cross at Anzio.

Royal Ordnance Factory, Bridgend.

No. *R33710*   Name *V. m. John*

is not allowed to come in contact with

T. N. T.   6 F   Ful of mer. Lead Azide

If asked to go on such work please show this card.

J. Davies   Foreman.

BRIDGEND FORM 9.   (4963)—W875/P.223/2—5M (4)—11/39. P.P. **654.**

When constructed in 1938 the Royal Ordnance Factory at Bridgend was one of the largest munitions factories in the country. In the early part of 1940 the factory was in full production employing people from most of the local areas and as far afield as Swansea. At the end of 1941 the Royal Ordnance Factory employed a total of 37,000 people, mainly women. Many of our Llanharan inhabitants worked there on a three shift basis. Trains were laid on daily and the siding at Tremains, Bridgend, resembled a football crowd each shift. During an interview with a number of the Llanharan ex-munitions workers, they spoke of the discipline procedure which took place at the plant. Before going to your workplace all jewellery, rings, necklaces etc., would have to be removed. Lockers were numbered and a key given to each section employee. All clothing would be supplied along with shoes. The women would also have to remove hair clips and a hair net would be put on. It was certainly a nerve racking place to work. Many of the girls spoke of having to leave their place of work and go into the shelters when a raid was imminent. The German Luftwaffe made a number of attacks in an attempt to destroy the factory. It was a difficult task for the Germans because the whole of the munition area was fitted out with a network of steam blast pipes. When the steam was released the whole of the Bridgend Factory would be misted out! By 1945 the factory was run down and closed. Today the area is called the Bridgend Industrial Estate.

MR. LEWIS COGBILL

A touch of moral decency during the time of adversity.
This photograph was taken at Stalag 4B Muhlberg on Elbe,
Germany, 1942. Sixth from left is Lewis Cogbill.

The late Mr. Lewis Cogbill like many other serving soldiers, was, during the war, imprisoned in a P.O.W. Camp. After travelling in a cattle truck for four days Lewis was put into Stalag 4B. At the camp the prisoners were encouraged to make their own entertainment and pastimes, thus alleviating the desire to escape. Lewis himself chose to encourage rugby football in the camp and even managed to form a 'Welsh Team'. Red jerseys were created by dyeing vests and soon other prisoners took patriotic views by forming a country team. Very soon a South African Springbok team had been formed and an 'International Match' was played in front of a noisy but enthusiastic camp of supporters. Prisoners of all nationalities surrounded the pitch. Even the Germans, who were bemused by such hysteria, came to witness the spectacle.

Our photograph above shows a burial in progress of a Sergeant, who was prisoners 'Stage Show Entertainments Officer'. The Kommandant of the camp was so impressed by the Sergeant's work and with the various stage shows arranged, that he himself attended most camp productions, also insisting that a number of his fellow officers attended. Suddenly the Sergeant died, leaving the whole camp stunned. To show his sympathy and gratitude, the Kommandant arranged all the funeral formalities and also provided a military escort squad to fire a salute over the Sergeant's grave as a tribute. The service was allowed to go ahead under British military direction and the Kommandant himself put a wreath on the grave on behalf of himself, officers and soldiers. For Lewis Cogbill that burial service was the strangest and most touching experience of his lifetime.

Source:
Interview with Mr. Lewis Cogbill 1970.

RAINHAM COUNCIL SCHOOL CHILDREN EVACUATED TO BRYNNA, MID GLAMORGAN IN 1940.

Eileen Akehurst
Ron Baker
Frank Bartlett
John Beer
Colin Bolton
Bob Castle
Joy Chapling
Roy Chapling
Dave Cumberworth
Ivan Driver
Iris Edwards
Thelma Edwards
Ken Ford
Reg Ford
Albert Hammond
Jean Harris
Vic Hazon
Peter Henderson
Sheila Hinch
Joan Howard
John Knight
Maria Knight
Doreen Lambourne
Eric Latty
Betty Laurie
Maureen Laurie
Jill Lewis

Dick Lindsell
Norman Lindsell
Godfrey Longley
John Matthews
Peter Milner
Barbara Moore
Cathy Moore
Pam Moore
Harry Nicholls
Patrick Pattenden
Sally Pattenden
James Pawsey
Joan Pawsey
David Payne
Eileen Payne
Ilan Payne
Ron Payne
Bernard Shepherd
Teresa Shepherd
Peter Simpson
Vera Skinner
Daphne Skofield
Derek Skofield
Eric Stringer
Graham Stringer
Pam Tree
Dennis Tuckwell

Tony Lewis
Joyce Woolman

Edward Wilmot

This is not a complete list.

ONE TEACHER'S MEMORY OF THE EVACUATION OF SCHOOLCHILDREN FROM RAINHAM IN KENT TO BRYNNA, SOUTH WALES.

(Mrs. H. Thomas, *née* Cheeseman)

The war was going badly - our army was in retreat from Dunkirk, and we expected it to be followed by an invasion by the Germans. An earlier evacuation of school children in our area had failed; they had been moved to villages near the Kent coast, which was now our most vulnerable region. It is a measure of our fear that loving parents were now prepared to allow their children to be taken - without them - to Wales, a faraway country where, as we believed, the people didn't even speak our language.

On 3 June 1940, the children of Rainham were directed to assemble at their schools to await transport to Wales sometime during the day. They were to bring a small case containing night attire and a change of underwear, enough food for the day and their gas mask. No drink was to be carried as the containers,

Rainham Evacuees settle at Brynna School 1940.

usually glass, were considered dangerous. Our train arrived about mid-day and we hurried the children, aged from 3 to 11 years, ten to a carriage with one adult for each group.

There was so much movement of soldiers and children all over Kent that our journey around London was constantly held up and it was about 8 o'clock in the evening when we arrived, dirty and tired, at Llanharan.

We were met by the kind folk of Llanharan, Llanharry and Brynna who had offered, or been persuaded to offer, homes to our children. As far as we could make out they seemed to be speaking English which was a relief. They had waited a long time and were concerned that the enormous meal they had prepared for us would be spoilt. They needn't have worried as the children had been eating all day from the generous supplies packed for them by anxious parents. They were not hungry but very thirsty and wanting nothing so much as a drink and their own beds. We were taken to a large hall where pandemonium reigned for a time, while foster parents looked for likely children, most of whom were looking far from their best. The lady in charge tried to control affairs by constantly ringing a bell and calling for order. It was midnight before the last child was settled in its new home.

Then arose an unexpected problem. Our party was designated as a group of unaccompanied schoolchildren and no provision had been made for the teachers and helpers who had, of necessity, come with them. All the prearranged billets were full and most of the people gone home. We laughed about it afterwards but were too tired to care that we were mostly offered armchairs and sofas in people's front rooms. The lucky ones used the beds of miners on night shift. I spent the rest of the night very comfortable on the surgery bed of the local doctor.

Our party of about 60 children were all billeted up the hill in Brynna so we spent the next day visiting our charges, sorting out problems and trying to pacify those who were already homesick. Fortunately many of them were already making friends with the local children and enjoying the adventure.

After the first day we had very little trouble. Brynna people did their utmost to make us feel welcome. There were one or two small problems. One was that we were on double summer time and it was almost impossible to get the children indoors and in bed at what we considered a reasonable time. Mr. Griffiths, school master, solved the problem for us. At 9 o'clock each evening he walked up the street, whether or not, as was said, he carried his cane, it certainly had the desired result. No child risked being caught by 'Master'. Another small problem was that our children had no Sunday clothes. The custom had very largely died out in our area, but was still a part of Welsh life. In most cases the parents either sent or brought different coats and hats for Sunday but I know that some of the foster parents bought them themselves rather than send their charges to Sunday School in their everyday clothes. The children were soon assimilated into the school routine and with books and other necessary apparatus supplied by the home school and the extra teachers, things ran very smoothly; we even learned a bit of the Welsh language and to this day I can say 'Nos Da' and 'Bore Da' at the right time even if I can't spell it correctly.

We all, children and teachers alike, enjoyed our stay in Brynna. We found it was not a typical Welsh village but had been invaded by the English before. Miners from the Forest of Dean had come from the worked out pits to work in the newly opened ones in Glamorgan. By the time we had arrived, however, the Brynna pit had already closed and the men had to travel to work. There were no pithead baths at that time and our children had to get used to the sight of black men coming home from work.

One thing that surprised me was that whist drives and other social functions were sometimes held in the mornings for the convenience of the night shift.

We loved the country around Brynna. We went for long walks. On the first of these, we teachers made our way over the hill looking up all the places around on our maps.

Some vigilant farmer spotted us looking and pointing in the direction of Coity, near which, although we did not know it, was a branch of Woolwich Arsenal which was used for making bombs and other explosive material. He did his duty and before long we found ourselves accosted by police who wanted to know what we were up to. We did our best without any document proof, to assure them we were not spies and were allowed to go back and report ourselves to the Brynna policeman - taking our identification papers. Our first opportunity to do this was early the next day, Sunday, and I remember a very indignant policeman viewing us from his William Street bedroom window - telling us he knew all about it and had already vouched for us.

We had two favourite walks, one down a lovely little lane to St. Mary Hill and the other down past the church and up the mountain to Llanbad.

Although we had been sent to Wales to be safe from air-raids it didn't work out quite like that. Brynna lies between Cardiff and Swansea and was often flown over by the Luftwaffe, and one plane perhaps having been turned back from bombing Swansea unloaded its bombs, one of which fell near the school in Brynna. Fortunately it fell late in the evening; for the next day, the corridor we had used as a safe place for children not living near enough to be sent home during an air-raid alarm was covered in glass. For a time there could be no school so we took the children for walks through the snow and tried to keep them occupied during the days. We were often reminded that the war was all around us. For several days a pall of smoke covered our hills by day and a red sky at night after the destruction of the Port Talbot oil tanks, also, after a raid on Cardiff it was possible to see the glow of fire in the east.

It seems ironic that although we were bombed out of our Brynna school, at home the school survived unscathed. The worst incident at Rainham was when a flying bomb exploded under a bridge just as a train was crossing it.

It's all a long time ago now and many people will not remember it, but there are still folk in Rainham who recall their stay in Brynna as one of the happier memories of the war.

We were fortunate in our reception in Wales and at this time I cannot help thinking of the thousands of poor people fleeing from wars in Africa and other parts of this unhappy world, who do not receive the kind welcome in a strange place that we found in 1940.

Source:
Mrs. H. Thomas (nee Cheeseman).

Street party in full swing on Southall
Street, Brynna.

Street Party V.J. celebration at Argoed
Avenue, Llanharan.

Brynna inhabitants enjoy the V.J. Day
Street Party.
*Right to Left: Frank Merry, Jack Tomlin, Burt
Dykes, Albert Hawkes,
Milly Witts, —?, Maud Green, Lily Williams,
Mrs. Merry, Martha Tomlin and David Watkins.*

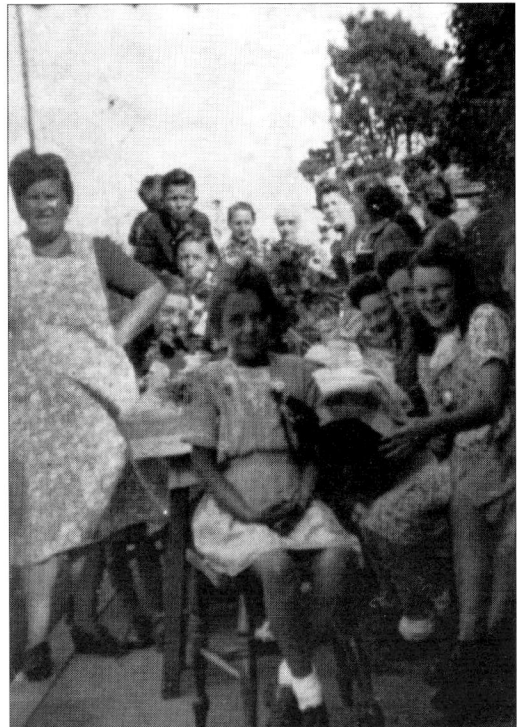

Brynna children enjoy the V.J. Day Party.

TOM SHEPPARD

The first Sheppard to find his way into Llanharan was John Sheppard. He was one of nine brothers, four of whom eventually settled in and around Llanharan. Before coming to the village, John worked for the gentry class in Wiltshire. He was a driver of a four in hand (four horses pulling a coach). It was in Wiltshire where the generations of Sheppard originated. It was while taking his employer to Cardiff on a visit that John met his future bride, and later on marrying her found employment with Thomas James Masters of Lanelay Hall, Talbot Green (former Meiros Colliery owner.) Settling in Llanharan, John Sheppard died a young man, killed as a result of an accident. His widow, after a number of years, married John's brother, Tom.

Tom Sheppard was a keen businessman. He first of all kept a small shop on the Dolau, then for a while kept another shop on Bridgend Road which in later years became the property of the Lusardis. Behind the shop there was a corrugated roofed extension in which Tom put his own 'pop' or as it was generally called 'Aerated Water'. Tom covered quite a large area selling his pop, transporting it on a large cart. He owned a lovely show pony called Rosy and a natty low trap which he entered in agricultural shows in the Vale of Glamorgan.

For some unknown reason, Tom Sheppard packed in the pop round and started a roller skating rink in the hall. The new project went well for a while, but Tom was a man with entrepreneurial ideas and another brainwave saw the introduction of billiard tables in the hall which really took off on a grand scale. So much so that Tom saw that a larger hall was required. Soon the Arcadia Billiard Hall came into being and Tom immediately moved into it. History already shows that a number of very good players materialised at the new Arcadia. In later years, under the ownership of Mr. Gwyn Howells (Welsh Champion) a number of top world class professional players gave exhibitions there. While raising funds to publish my first book on Llanharan entitled "Forgotten Years" Vol.I, the World Champion of the time, Mr. Ray Reardon, came and played for my cause, not only giving the crowd a memorable exhibition, but he gave his fee toward the publication of my book. Something I will never forget.

Tom Sheppard was in his day one of Llanharan's truly outstanding personalities, who without doubt brought many amenities to the village. The late gent is still talked about today amongst the older folk who used the facilities after a hard day working in the mine.

Source: Mrs. Amy Inglis – *née* Hutchins

THE REVEREND TOM JONES

Although not a good print, this is certainly an important one. On the left of the picture is the late Reverend Thomas Jones, Vicar of Llanharan with Llanilid. Throughout my researches I was unable to find any other prints of the reverend gentleman. Also in the picture are the two Sheppard brothers. Tom in the middle, Arthur on the right.

During an interview with Mrs. Amy Inglis (*née* Hutchins) she described the Reverend Tom Jones as "An old saint if ever there was one, gentle and soft of speech, and a shepherd of his flock".

The Reverend Tom Jones visited his parishioners on a regular basis, his means of conveyance was a pony and trap, he mostly took his daughter Alice with him on his visits for company. If a miner was injured underground, he called on the family often and gave the unfortunate individual every encouragement to make a full recovery. Alice was organist at Llanharan Church for many years.

The reverend gentleman was also well respected by the Blandy Jenkins household. On one occasion when an appeal was made for a carpet for the Church, the Llanharan house family came to the front and immediately footed the bill for a new carpet to be laid. During those early days, according to Mrs. Inglis, Harvest Thanksgiving was the most enjoyed. If you didn't get to the Church early you wouldn't get in. It was always packed with single seats put into the aisles. The Reverend Jones died in the 1920s and his place was taken at Llanharan by the Reverend John Evans Jones.

Source: Mrs. Amy Inglis *née* Hutchins.

The Jones Family ('Jones the Back') No. 8 The Square, Llanharan.
Alice and William - standing in the doorway.

RIVER ROW

This is a very rare photograph, it shows the Jones family who lived at No. 8 The Square, Llanharan (now demolished). Alice and William Jones were affectionately knows as 'Ally and William the Back'. This name materialised quite simply because their house near the river at the foot of Hillside Avenue, was one of a block of two which was back to back to the old Llanharan Church Yard. 'Ally' was famed for her ability to breed ducks. The river, which was adjacent to their house, was permanently dammed. This gave the small stream about two feet of water, enough for 'Ally' to bring up her families of ducks. The young ducklings were bred in an abandoned house which stood next door to theirs. When strong enough, the birds would be let out onto the river. Many of those ducks would be sold on, usually to Estate houses in the principality. 'Ally' in fact, made quite a name for herself, for we learn that many a squire came and purchased a number of her stock for their lakes and ponds. Sometimes, a number of ducks would be stolen off the river by local individuals.

When this occurred, 'Ally' would take vigil at the riverside and pity anyone caught near the river, they would indeed feel the wrath of Alice Jones. Apart from the ducks, she held a reputation for making excellent and succulent toffee. This she sold to the children of the area. Alice Jones was, without doubt, a well respected character of the old village. Her husband William, on the other hand, was highly respected in Church circles. He was Church Sexton for many years. During his working life, William was one of the head hauliers working the horses at Meiros Colliery. Alice died on 9 March 1915 and William died on 24 March 1917. Alice's daughter Mary married Mr. Phillip Penfold and they both kept the old house together for many years. Mr. Penfold worked for British Railways and was a prominent member of the local R.A.O.B. organisation. Mary, like her mother before her, kept a number of ducks on the river. Alan, their son, who sadly passed away recently, was married and lived in Cardiff, but made regular visits back to the village.

Source: The late Mr. Alan Penfold, Cardiff.

THE TEGWEN LEWIS MEMORIAL

When Tegwen Lewis died suddenly on Tuesday 8 March 1988, it was a numbing shock to all who knew her. Sadly, at the time of her death Llanharan village, like many other villages in the area, was changing rapidly and a large number of people only knew Tegwen as a lady who kept cats. We in Llanharan who remember Teg's productive years as a poet, knew her for her talented brilliance. Her achievements in Eisteddfodau will never be equalled. During her competitive years she amassed 29 Chairs and 3 Crowns.

Tegwen's interest in the miners of her locality was very close, this is obvious by reading some of her poems. During the 1950s she was a regular competitor at the Miners' Eisteddfod at Porthcawl. Everyone acknowledged Tegwen as an outstanding and likable individual. Her death evoked a deep feeling of loss.

From a report in the local 'Diary' in the September of 1990 by Mr. David Evans of Seymour Avenue, Llanharan, suggesting that some form of memorial should be made to remember Tegwen, a meeting was called at the Welfare Hall on 9 October. Llanharry historian Mr. David Francis and I had already subscribed a literary memorial on Tegwen entitled "Tegwen Lewis 1914-1988", with all the royalties from the sale of the book being donated to the Mid Wales Animal Sanctuary. The book was printed and produced by Pallas Press, Llanharan. On her death, Tegwen left 14 cats at her home including two blind kittens named Margaret and Elizabeth. Sometime later, after a donation of £100 was sent to the sanctuary, a letter returned stating that Tegwen's cats had settled well in new homes around the area and that one of the blind cats, Elizabeth, was well and living in Shrewsbury.

Following the October meeting, it was decided to form a committee with the aim of raising enough funds to erect a clock on the old blacksmith's shop wall on the Square (now the home of Mr. & Mrs. Tystyl Jenkins). They gave the committee permission to erect the memorial and the hard work raising the money began immediately. The committee working for the 'Tegwen Lewis Memorial Fund' were as follows:

Mrs. Gill Richards	- Secretary
Mr. Phillip Loomes	- Chairman
Mrs. Pauline Harris	- Treasurer.

County Councillors:
Gerald Harris
Gerald Waters

Clerk to the Council	- Mr. W. Westcott

Members:
Mrs. Joyce Riddler, Mrs. Val Harris, Mrs. Mary Brown, Mrs. Doreen Holland and Mrs. Sheila Green.

From the Memorial Fund formed in October, up until the February of 1992, it had reached the grand total of £2,000, an outstanding achievement. It would be proper of me to mention Mrs. Gill Richards, (nee Ray) the Fund's secretary. Gill and I went through our schooldays together, and spent many happy hours in 'Basini's Cafe' during our youth in the 1950s and early '60s. Even then Gill possessed a strong personality, a determination which gave her that leadership quality. This has been proved in recent times with her ability to organise carnivals and fetes. Today, she dedicates most of her time in trying to make Llanharan a better place for our younger generation. Trying to lay a platform where the youngsters can form some kind of identity for themselves. Knowing Gill as I do, and with a little help from us all, I think that in the not too distant future, the young folk of the village may well be saying that "Llanharan isn't such a bad place to live after all".

When purchased, the clock cost £1,750, it was provided by Joyce & Co. Ltd., Shropshire. A plaque was also manufactured. The unveiling dedication took place at the Bethlehem Chapel on Tuesday 23 June 1992. After the service Mr. George Williams, of Llanharan House, aptly summed up the moving occasion with these words:

"Tegwen would, I am sure, be delighted with it all and it is so nice there should be a permanent memorial to one of Llanharan's most colourful personalities. The Committee are indeed much to be congratulated for commemorating Tegwen in such a way".

Tegwen finds time to chat to Mrs. Blanche Salway at her home. Sadly, both ladies are now deceased.

Tegwen Lewis at her home in Chapel Road, Llanharan. During her competitive years she amassed 29 Chairs and 3 Crowns, an achievement which will now stand unequalled.

A proud moment for Mrs. Gill Richards (left) and Mrs. Pauline Harris as they pose for the camera with the Memorial Clock in the background on the former old Blacksmith's shop. 23 June 1992.

THE MINER
- Tegwen Lewis -

The weary hooter slits the silence wantonly
   And men go down into the night again.
And intimate within the world
   Beneath the fair familiarity of earth and sky they toil,

And in the light of comradeship
   The dark flame of courage
Glows within that twilight land.

And in my unlearned lethargy recollections come
   of binding intimacies
The common task shot through with laughter,
   And the swift aware-ness
When the blinding flash of grief
   Plunged the hours
Into long seas of weariness
   And the slow apathy of despair.

I hear them come
The rasp of hobnail in the genesis of day,
At noon,
And then the clanging stride
When darkness beings her fit-filled hours
   Within the night's distress.

I am not young,
Nor yet too old for dreaming,
But now there are no dreams
   Each day one long harsh prelude to the nights unrest.
O that the wine-sweet winds of autumn
Could wake the cancerous lung to health again,
That all unwholesomeness be purged,
And the dark fear unrealised.
   I am not young
Nor yet too old for dreaming....

Three Members of the Llanharan Scout Section 1928,
Ellis Williams, Ben Roberts, Gof Farnham.

Young Clifford Jacobsen, Cub Scouts, Llanharan 1927.
The flag was used to send messages using the morse code.

The Rover Scouts, Llanharan 1926 - 27.

Llanharan Ambulance Division 1927.

Although a number of the Ambulance Team were in local businesses, a number of the men were miners, some, participants in the mines rescue service. 3rd left, back row, Dr. Tucker, 4th left, Charlie Bailey, 7th left, Bill Richards, 8th left, Arthur Jones, 1st left, front row, Cliff Jacobsen, 3rd left, W. Perkins and 4th left, W. Wright.

1st Llanharan 9th Bridgend Scouts.

Top Row: Steve Witts, unknown, David Price, Paul Lewis

Second Row: Robert Newby, Vaugn Thomas, Bob Barbour, unknown, Gareth Edwards. Hugh Westcott, J. Summers and John Evans.

Third Row: David Wooloff, John Earp, Christopher Cory (Commissioner), Doug Summers, Jeff Evans, Vicar Frayne (Scout Master).

Fourth Row: Martin Cook, Michael Anthony, Andrew Horlock, Jimmy Druce, Gwyn Price, unknown,

Chris Edwards, Perry Hayes, Jeff Evans and Wayne Davies.

Front Row: Michael Gromwood, Martin Clarrige, Chrisopher Russell, Craig McInnon, Morgan Smith, Mark Hayes, Andy Witts, Mark Membrey

and Rhodri Thomas.

Llanharan Primary School Infants Section School Band 1936.

Schoolchildren during the early 1930s and 1940s.

Our opening pictures of 'Schooldays' show the children of the 1930s and 1940s. Unlike the children of the present day their lives were dominated by the local collieries. Most of the children seen here became miners and miners wives. School facilities were minimal and discipline was the operative word.

LLANHARAN SCHOOL-   JULY.1927

Opening of Dolau School 1928 - Dolau Infants Second Class.

Dolau Schoolchildren Class IV 1931.
Many of the young lands in this picture became a part of the mining industry.

Brynna School 1931.

Schoolchildren during the Forties.

Left to right: Brenda Lovel, Nora Williams, Betty North, Mair Evans, J. Maunders, Rai Baldwin. During the forties most of the village schoolchildren used the Welfare Ground as their play area. Note in the background of this print the colliery steam engine in the siding of the railway goods yard. (now demolished).

1964 – Llanharan Colliery had closed in 1962, this group of children seen here enjoying St. David's Day celebrations would not grow up under the influence of the mining era.

Llanharan Primary School Girls Netball Team 1974 - 1975.
Back Row: Left to Right: Kim Davies, Miss Hellis (Teacher), Catherine ?
Front Row: Left to Right : Jackie Huish, Lynne Callow, Donna Jenkins, Allison Perkins
and Alecia Ffloyd.

23 April 1971. Parent Teachers Association Presentation.
Our photograph shows Parent Teachers' Association Chairman, Mr. Waverly Lewis, presenting on behalf of the organisation a television set to the Llanharan Primary School. Receiving the set on behalf of the school is Headmaster Mr. Emrys Prosser, while some of the school pupils look on. The Parent Teachers Association was formed in September 1970.

Llanharan Primary Schoolchildren's Nativity Play, Christmas 1972.

Llanharan Primary School
St. David's Day Celebrations 1971.

Charlie Bundy was born in Cwmparc, Rhondda, 20 March 1912. He started boxing in an era when poverty was rife throughout the hard and difficult times of the coal unrest in the valleys. He lived most of his life in Llanharan becoming something of a legend in his own lifetime. The Llanharan people took him to their hearts (see "Forgotten Years" Vol.I, II and III).

Ben Foord, the South African heavyweight, finds time for a round of golf between training for his fight with Jack Peterson (1942). On the right waiting to take up the golfing challenge is our own Charlie Bundy who was chief sparring partner to Foord in the build up to the fight.

Llanharan Boxing Venue - 3 August 1942
Left to Right : Syd Worgan, Charles Bundy, Sergeant Turner, Tom Kelly (Trainer).

3 August 1942, our photograph records a wartime sporting occasion when 2,000 spectators witnessed a boxing tournament in aid of charity. The proceeds went to the Cardiff Royal Infirmary, the Red Cross and the Llanharan Soldiers Relief Fund. Our three local boxers starred on the bill that day.
Syd Worgan beat Benny Isaacs (Loughborough), Charlie Bundy beat Wally Bridgmond (Scotland). Ron Pritchard lost narrowly on points in a terrific scrap with Vivian Martin (Maesteg). The show at Llanharan was a remarkable one for the fact that it was successfully organised by a committee consisting of - a colliery manager, a cashier, a station master, a fight manager, a journalist and a collier. The tournament is still eagerly discussed in the village today.

Our photograph shows the Llanharan
Constitutional Club Committee in 1957, it
includes our three memorable boxers.
Left to Right: (Back Row) G. Butler, G. Gore, B.
Gardener, R. Martin P. Smith and D. Owen.
(Front Row) R. Pritchard, C. Bundy, F. Perry, S.
Worgan and S. Barkle.

N. 904   PROGRAMME 3d

BOXING - JULY 5th

Presented by Llanharan Sports Committee
at
Llanharan Welfare Ground
PROGRAMME TO COMMENCE 6.30 p.m.

Ronnie James   v.   Wally Downs
(British Lightweight Champion)   FOUR ROUNDS.

Syd Worgan   v.
(Welsh Featherweight Champion)

Vernon Ball   Phil Freeman
EIGHT ROUNDS.

Warren Kendall   v.   Jack Phillips
(Welsh Lightweight Champion)   THREE ROUNDS.

BRYN MORRIS   v.   RON COOPER
THREE ROUNDS

ROY KINSELLS   v.   REES LOVELUCK
THREE ROUNDS

CLARENCE TREGONNING   v.   RON PRITCHARD
THREE ROUNDS

GRAYHAM JOHN   v.   BILLY HALL
THREE ROUNDS

PERCY MODICAI   v.   KEN JONES
THREE ROUNDS

MOG DAVEY   v.   YOUNG LEWIS
THREE ROUNDS

M.C.: BILLY HUGHES, MAESTEG

D. Brown and Sons Printers, Cowbridge, Glam.

A Boxing Bill with a number of events which were organised by the Llanharan Sports Committee.
Note that Syd Worgan has no opponent on this bill. The reason being that an opponent in a charity
bout would normally be selected on availability on the night. Syd Worgan, Ron Pritchard and Charles
Bundy gave many charitable exhibitions during the war effort.

25 October 1937. Kid Simmonds, Featherweight Champion of Trinidad, takes a count in his
unsuccessful fight against Syd Worgan. The fight took place at the Colston Hall, Bristol. Referee F.R.
Hisll, Cardiff.

222

**GWYN HOWELLS
The Meiros
Colliery Coalface
Worker
who became
Welsh Champion.**

When the Workmen's and Public Institute was built after the 1st World War the caretaker in charge was a Mr. Dan Howells, formerly of Blaengarw. He became a popular figure because the new hall was furnished with snooker tables, and as Mr. Howells was a notable billiard player in his own right, the sport soon took on with the Meiros miners.

Mr. Howells' son Gwyn was also a keen enthusiast and spent many hours at his father's side learning the finer arts of the green baize. While working in the coalface at Meiros Colliery Gwyn received serious injuries being caught under a fall of rock. Such was the seriousness of his plight that it was believed at the time that he would not recover from his injuries. Thankfully he did recover and after a long pull of convalescence young Gwyn began his fight back by spending more time at his father's side in the Workmen's Hall. He never looked back and gained an impressive record. In my 'Forgotten Years' series of books I covered the successful years of this well liked and genial sportsman. When Gwyn Howells died on Saturday 23 September 1995, aged 89 years, the South Wales Echo paid a worthy tribute to our outstanding personality. It is worth recording as a final tribute to a sportsman who was much loved by many people throughout the area.

"Former Welsh Snooker Champion Dies.

Snooker fans in Wales will be saddened to hear of the death of former Welsh Champion, Gwyn Howells of Llanharan.

Gwyn aged 89, won the Welsh Snooker Championship as long ago as 1937 and was five times runner up in the Welsh Billiards Championship.

But playing was only part of his service to the sport. He was also a most able coach and among the players who passed through his once thriving snooker hall in Llanharan were former world champions, Joe Davis, Ray Reardon, Walter Lindrum together with Terry Griffiths, Mario Berni, Steve Newbury and Alwyn Lloyd."

Youngsters benefited from his coaching, both at snooker and billiards, and he developed a strong friendship with the legendary Joe Davis who stayed with Gwyn at Llanharan when he visited South Wales.

When Gwyn, also a lover of cricket, made trips to London, it was Joe who arranged for a ticket to Lord's and invited him to stay at his home. It was during a billiard-snooker exhibition with Joe in Pontypridd that Gwyn potted the final black off its spot to win a best of six frames challenge, but Joe had his revenge in the billiards event and made a 1,000 plus break.

Up to the time of his death, Gwyn was still enjoying his game of snooker with his friends at 'Snooker World', Church Village, and was making breaks of 50 plus.

Source: South Wales Echo 29.10.95
Also notes from "Forgotten Years" early volumes.

Llanharan Bowls Club.

The Llanharan Welfare Hall Bowls Club was made up mainly of mining and ex mining personnel. This particular photograph shows one of the finest teams ever produced at Llanharan. This team were winners of the Welsh Indoor Bowls League for five consecutive seasons.

A Colliery Sporting Occasion 1951.

Soccer, rugby and cricket thrived during the mining years and were encouraged by colliery management. During the early 1950s Llanharan Colliery cricket team won the coveted South Western Division Knockout Cup.

Our photograph above shows a number of colliery officials and team players during a Llanharan carnival sporting cricket competition. Sadly not all of the above can be named. We record the following: Left to Right: Mr. Ivor Prosser (Engineer), County Councillor Mr. Cyril David, Mr. Stanley Hughes, M.E. (Colliery Manager) Mr. Sid Sedgebeer, Mr. Billy Griffiths, ——, Mr. Mansel Cogbill.

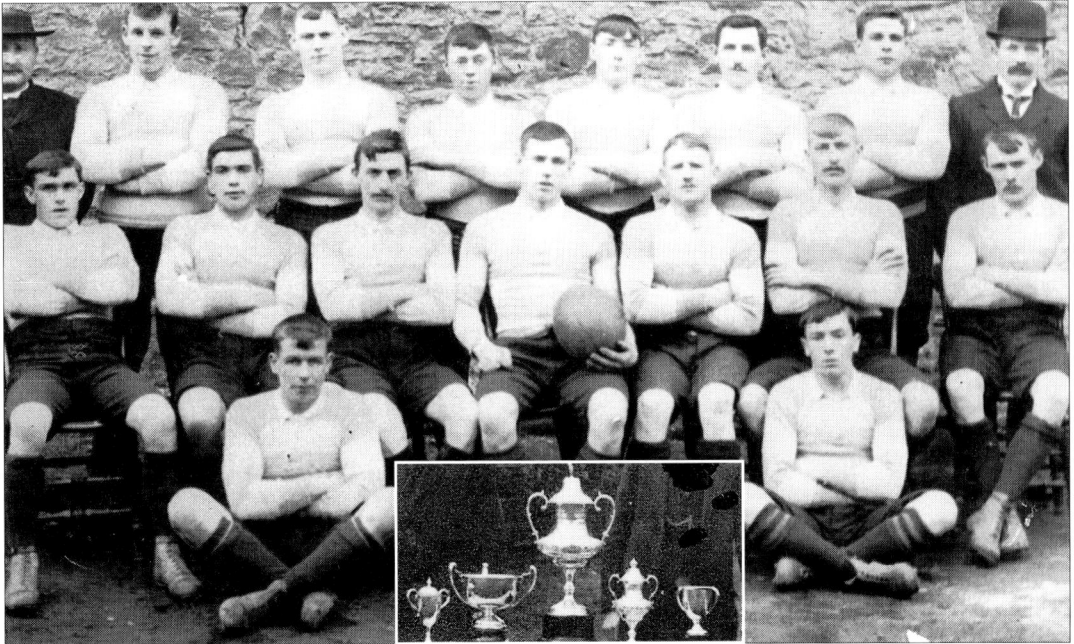

The Brynna Drainpipes played for and won the Meiros Cup on three occasions. The cup was played for between local collieries. The Meiros Colliery team won the cup on seven occasions. Our photograph shows the cup which was presented during the finals.

Above – the Eagle Hotel, Brynna   Below – Meiros Rugby Team 1921.

Meiros Rugby Team 1921

'The Village Princess' bus was owned by the Griffiths family who were licensees of the Turberville Hotel during the 1920s. Many trips were organised by the various pubs in the village. Above is a trip to a Cardiff International in 1924, organised by the officials and Meiros Colliery Rugby Team.

1970 Llanharan Rugby Football Celebration. Fifty Years in the Welsh Rugby Union.
Back Row: D. John, J. North, E. Harrison, C. Howe, A. John, N. Roberts, A. Ware.
Second Row: C. Shellibeer, R. Pick (Chairman), E. Lewis (Referee), M. Davies, M. Thomas, L. Ponton, M. Davey, T. Benjamin (Secretary), H. Perkins, R. Jenkins, E. Evans (Fixture Secretary), L. Harris (Treasurer), D. Hughes, J. Hughes (Social Secretary), C. Jenkins, N. Clarke (Trainer).
Seated: W. Watkins, C. Coles, P. Benjamin, S. Sedgebeer (Life Member), C. Jones, (Captain), J. David (President), A. Jarvis and M. Russell. Front Row: K. Smith and R. Williams.

PERSONAL VIEW OF A GREAT RUGBY CLUB

Having credited those early pioneers who introduced rugby to the village, I am satisfied and more than confident that my files over three volumes have well and truly documented those exciting years in the development of what was described in the early days as 'A Family Club'. There is no doubt that sometime in the future some enthusiastic author will compile a complete history of the club. My work is done, hopefully leaving enough foundation in photographs and text to allow the connoisseur to make a thorough and complete work in the outstanding climb to success of what after all is a great club.

I do not profess in any way or form to have any intellectual knowledge of rugby football. The only time that I played the game was at school under the guidance then of that inimitable teacher, the late Gwyn Williams. I played scrum half for Llanharan Primary for two seasons only, and enjoyed that period in my sporting youth. However, while in the Army I tried again and played three games in a Regiment fifteen, but failed to gain rugby enthusiasm and joined the soccer side instead. This sporting move was to be my undoing, because while playing in a South Wales Borderers trial, I broke my leg which saw me hospitalised, never to participate in either sport again.

Having explained my short and questionable association with rugby, I make no excuses for the following article, it is my personal tribute to two individuals who have established themselves over the years with Llanharan R.F.C.

From the days of the 'Meiros Cup' up to the present time, the village has been blessed with an enthusiasm for the game of rugby far beyond the call of duty. Before Heineken League status, Llanharan gained a most impressive record in the East District, and one can look back to those early days in the W.R.U. Cup when teams like Pontypool and Pontypridd come to mind, giving the village at that time games which will forever be brought to mind and making Llanharan a name which no first class side wanted to know when the Cup draw came around. Talking of 'First Class' it was teams such as Llanharan, Blaina and Dunvant, who, in their 'Giant Killing' capacity, made the lower clubs over the years, realise that the gap wasn't all that big between first and second class. More effort was made by the smaller clubs and over the past three seasons, Heineken Leagues have turned the sport into a completely new ball game. For Llanharan the Heineken League has been of mixed fortune. It was believed that our village side would be the first second class side in the Heineken League second division to carry the standard into the 'Elite' section. However, Dunvant were the honourable bearers, with Llanharan losing out as runners up to Cross Keys on try count. Dunvant are more than worthy of their honour and are a truly outstanding side.

I stated earlier that my intention was to credit two Llanharan R.F.C. individuals. I have during the compilation of my 'Forgotten Years' series given credit to many people who gave their time and effort in building up a sound footing to the club. However, having already mentioned the establishment, I wish to finalise my contribution by offering a few words about two people who, in my opinion, gave Llanharan R.F.C. the required impetus in their approach to Heineken League status and survival. The first individual is Mr. Chris Davey.

When Chris Davey resigned as coach to Llanharan in the mid season (December 1993) it came as a great shock to members and officials of the club. Leaving for personal reasons, the former skipper of both Llanharan and Maesteg had an impressive record. Davey started his playing career with Llanharan Youth and went on to captain the English Colleges. He played for Llanharan before joining Maesteg, which he captained. Returning to the village he also captained Llanharan before taking over as coach. Under Davey, Llanharan gained promotion to Division Two Heineken League from the East District (1990). On promotion, Chris Davey's ability was being noted by a number of clubs. It is my opinion along with many other people far more knowledgeable than I that Chris Davey was destined for higher honours in Welsh Rugby Union circles. His contribution put Llanharan over the bridge onto the first class platform, that is unquestionable. The village club had a successful centenary year (1993) and only missed promotion on try count. Chris Davey was, in my opinion, a front line contributor to the club's climb into the Heineken League.

Postscript: Since leaving the Llanharan Club, Chris Davey, as coach, has taken Caerphilly R.F.C. into the Premier Division. At this present time, he is also on the Welsh coaching staff, and coached the under twenty one side, to win the Grand Slam in the 1998-99 season.

My second individual is Mr. Hugh Smith. As a player Hugh was one of the keenest and most reliable players in the game. One thing is certain about this amiable schoolteacher, his heart and soul lies in the fortunes of Llanharan R.F.C. Since Llanharan's step into the Heineken League, the birth of the new playing arena, the Dairy Field, has seen the emergence of a completely new set up at Llanharan. With the change the introduction of the club programme made an immediate impact to the supporters. Like all match programmes, Llanharan's contribution carried the usual advertising logos. However, the programme holds artistic dimension within its pages with each home game carrying interesting historical facts from bygone days with such items as: spotlight on today's visitors, down memory lane, bits of black and blue and even star profiles, adding humour to the interest. With 1993 being Llanharan's Centenary Year, the match programmes became 'collectors items'. There must be houses in Llanharan today where a collection is hidden away, treasured, to be opened and read in years to come. It has been said openly that the programme is a credit to the club. All this work is down to Hugh Smith who is the club's publicity officer, and known in the programme as 'The Scribe'.

Hugh has done tremendous work in his office. During one of our games at home against Maesteg, one of the Maesteg supporters pointed out that he had learnt more from the Llanharan programme about Maesteg than what he actually learnt at Maesteg. As people go, Hugh Smith is one of the best. His unassuming personality always shines on match days, he obviously relishes his position in the club and carries out his work professionally. He is, without doubt, a credit and an asset to Llanharan R.F.C. Long may his dedication reign supreme. And long may 'The Scribe' be a part of our Saturday campaigns.

Heineken League

Llanharan -v- Swansea 12 March 1994
Llanharan scrum half Graham Pritchard makes a quick release during this hard fought match at the Dairy Field. Swansea ran out victors by the narrowest of margins Llanharan 6 Swansea 8.

DANIEL PRICE

When Mr. Daniel Price died in the November of 1993, aged 80, we witnessed the passing of not only one of the villages most controversial characters, but also one of the longest serving farmers and sportsmen.

Mr. Price came from Bryncethin to farm at Argoed Edwin in 1939. While living at Bryncethin in his early days, he attended the Garw School. From there he gained 4 schoolboy caps playing in the position of prop forward. We also learn that while playing for Wales his reputation became stamped throughout the Welsh Club circuit, and had it not been for a leg injury, which forced him out of the game, Dan Price could well have gone on to gain top Welsh honours. However, it was not

to be and Daniel in later years turned his favours to the Llangeinor Foxhounds. He became in 1945 a member of the Hound Association and up to the time of his death was a life member of the Llangeinor Foxhunt.

There is no doubt that the likes of the inimitable 'Danny' will never be seen in the village again.

Work started on the new Medical Centre on Chapel Road on 6 June 1993. The new building was opened on 21 December 1993. The gate showing on the left of the picture is the house where the old surgery run by Dr. James Patterson (shown above) was held during the 1950s. It is ironic that after approximately 30 years a surgery should return to the area.

The New Medical Centre - Opened 21 December 1993.
List of Doctors on the opening of the new Medical Centre:
Dr. G.M. Gwilliam, MB. ChB. D(Obst) RCOG
Dr. G.W. Phillips, MB. BCh. D(Obst) RCOG
Dr. J.P. Jones, MB. BCh.
Mr. D.A. Ware, B.Sc. MB. BS. DCH. MRCGP
Practice Nurses - Sister Vivien Wright, Sister Lynne Jones. District Nurse - Sister Dilys Thomas. (April 1994)

The New Carmel Baptist Chapel built 1969.

Prior to the building of the first Carmel Baptist Chapel at Llanharan, meetings were held for worship at the home of Mr. & Mrs. J. Madge. The first Chapel was a zinc sheet building, but with the profound effect that the mining industry was bringing to the village, new faces were rallying to the cause. Two of the then village colliery managers, in the forms of James Lewis (Meiros) and Williams Thomas (Llanharan) were staunch members of the Chapel. In 1924, a large modern building was erected on Bridgend Road. The Baptist cause continued to thrive and even though the mining industry had disappeared by 1962, the Chapel following remained on a sound footing. However, the old building was giving cause for concern and by the September of 1969 a new modern Chapel had been erected. The opening of the new Chapel on 19 September 1969 was officiated by the Rev. T.T. Evans, B.A., D.D., the former Minister, whose ministry began during the opening of the previous Chapel. Today, Carmel still has a healthy following with a forty to fifty strong congregation.

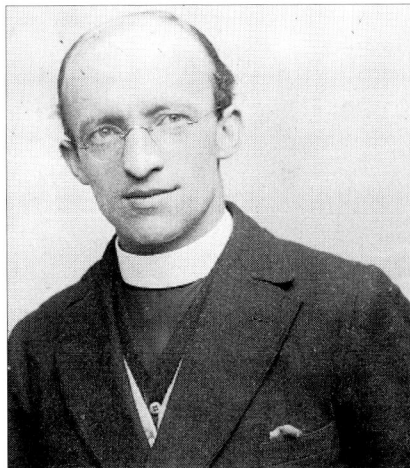

The Rev. Trevor Evans, B.A., D.D.

Parochial Church Council Members *c.1967*
Front from left: Rev. Derek Frayne, Mrs. Laura Pearce, Mrs. Violet David, Mr. George Williams, Mrs. Donovan, Mrs. Doreen Holland, Miss Merry and the Rev. Vernon Payne.
Back from left: Mr. Raymond Barbour, unknown, Mr. Lyn Cogbill, Mr. Idris Evans, Mr. Alf Humphries and Mr. Cliff Pearce, unknown.

Note:
While at Llanharan, Mr. George Williams, through his deep link with the Parochial Church Council, encouraged many fund raising functions on his Llanharan House Estate. As most people are aware, Mr. Williams became a highly successful businessman and South Wales industrialist. He was Chairman and Managing Director of Christie Tyler Plc until 1985, building up the company for thirty six years from very small beginnings to being the largest furniture manufacturer in the U.K., employing over 3,000 people when he left.

With this volume based entirely on Llanharan's rich mining past, it is fitting that Mr. Williams has always been very proud of his old coal mining family's skills who opened up many new industries in South Wales. Mr. Williams was awarded the C.B.E. in 1977 for services to industry.

FLASHBACK TO –
"THE FORGOTTEN YEARS"

I first began writing the "Forgotten Years" Trilogy in 1960. Since my first book, Volume I, published in 1975, I can now look back and say that it was a most invigorating experience. I must have met thousands of people during my researches – many of those good people long gone! Thankfully, through my books, not forgotten.

Often I am asked what subjects during research did I find the most interesting. I always reply by quoting two subjects, squires and mining. When you stop and think about it, both histories were responsible for the growth of both communities, Llanharan and Brynna. Looking back on my efforts in compiling a record of two villages, I regard it as a worthwhile adventure. Because now, the old places most of us grew up in when they were mining strongholds, have well and truly disappeared. New developments in the communities, some controversial, along with changing populations, have now seen the demise of our once proud identity. Nevertheless, I hope through my books some of our old ways of life are now 'locked' in the annals of history.

Encouragement forced my hand to writing in those early days. It is here and now that I would like to thank those very people who gave the encouragement and paved the way for me so to speak. I would like to thank those individual friends who have contributed financially throughout the compiling of my three book series – but wish to remain anonymous. Without their kind assistance I would not have got my work off the ground. Also, I wish to thank the Community Council who have never questioned my ability and have stood by throughout all my ventures. The faithful band of people from Llanharan and Brynna though small in number, who regularly support and contribute to my books. Those many people far afield who, in reality, make my books financially viable. It is unbelievable that most of my sales come from English counties and abroad.

I will always be indebted to the Williams family of Llanharan House, who have stood by me from the very beginning. All of my books have been launched from their historic mansion. But most of all, something that will stay forever as one of the most rewarding highlights of my work was when I was allowed to organise a 'Squires Link' at the 'Big House' something which had never before occurred at the mansion. We made this link when Professor John Blandy and Colonel Hugh Poyntz came down for the launch of Volume III, on 17 November 1993. That evening, our link in the form of Poyntz–Blandy–Williams, saw three regions of squirearchy under the roof of Llanharan House which goes back to 1806.

Yes! I am proud of our squires who formulated a lasting and important history during the early years of our village. Proud also of our mining heritage which left its mark in our community. A heritage to which my own family contributed with pride and dignity. I look back with admiration and thank everyone for their efforts on my behalf. Moreso, my Historical Society members, who, over the years, have played a momentous part in bringing my work to fruition. Most of all, I am proud to have been the person responsible for recording our past history which I hope will leave a lasting image for future generations.

Our photograph shows Mrs. Kitty Bannister at her home 'The Lodge' which was situated on the main Llantrisant Road (opposite Llanharan House drive gates). She was house cook to Mrs. Blandy Jenkins for seven year, when in 1953, Mrs. Blandy died. Mrs. Bannister's husband Tony, was chaffeur to the lady of the Big House.
The old 'Lodge' was a primitive little building and water had to be collected in pails from a small spring near the Llanharan House parklands.

Mr. Tony Bannister
Chauffeur to Mrs. Blandy Jenkins.

Professor John Blandy, middle, T.J. Witts and on the right Colonel Hugh Poyntz. This photograph taken during the launch of "Forgotten Years" Vol. III takes the Williams, Blandy, Poyntz link of Squires back to the year 1806.

A visit from the past

Left to right: Mrs. Winifred Saunders, Mr. Owain Williams, Mrs. Bethan Williams, Miss Elizabeth Williams and Mrs. Alecia Witts.
On 16th October 1993 Mrs. Winifred Saunders returned to visit Llanharan House. From 1930 to 1936 she was Lady's Maid to the Llanharan household. The story of Mrs. Saunders is well documented in "Forgotten Years" vol. III.

Our photograph shows Mr. & Mrs. George Williams with their grand–daughter Elizabeth and Tiger the dog at the Garden House, Craig–y–Bwla, Crickhowell, Powys. Over the years the Williams family has given the author great encouragement in his endeavours.

Mr. & Mrs. Owain Williams, Llanharan House have allowed three launches of T.J. Witts' books at their mansion.

BIBLIOGRAPHY

Seam and Horizon Mining Records, Llanharan Colliery 1944-56.

Practical Coalmining, Edited by Professor W.S. Boulton, Vol. I. 1915 Edition

South Wales Coal Annuals 1908 - 1937

Modern Mining Practice, C.M. Bailes, M.E., M.I.M.E. Vol. I. 1915 Edition

Colliery Managers Handbook 1900 - 1950

Rhondda Past and Future, Life and times of Walter Coffin 1785-1867, Lincoln Wagon and Engineering Colliery Managers Book, 1923.

Coal Seam Analysis - Mr. Stanley Hughes, M.E., Llanharan 1955, Records - Guest Keen and Nettlefolds, Meiros Colliery Owners, Extract From Gwyn Thomas' High on Hope.

Llanharan Colliery Technology by H.C. Bisp.

Seam Analysis Charts and Diagrams 1950 (National Coal Board)

Celtic Energy - Notes and documents on the Llanilid West Revised.

Mines report by J. Macleod Carey, O.B.E. On the causes of the explosion which occurred at Llantrisant Colliery, Ynysmaerdy on 2 June 1941. Illustrated - 1947 edition (January)

South Wales Echo - Western Mail.

Llantrisant Observer - Glamorgan Gazette Early O.S. Maps of Llanharan and Peterston Super Montem.

Ambulance Division Records - 1940-1952 Taff Ely Borough Council, for early information on housing development.

Dros y Ysgwydd (Over My Shoulder) Sarah Holland Miles, 1950.

Glamorgan Education Committee, Coal Mines Act Certificate 1921.

Advertising - Cowbridge Rural District Council.

Carmel Baptist Church Documents 1945.

The Miners - Tegwen Lewis.

Verse - Hyperion.

Archive Film Library, Aberystwyth (Ms. Iola Baines)

Robert Merrill, Manager, Marleen Adams, D/Manager, Chris Rees, Curatorial Assistant at Cefn Coed Mining Museum.

Staff - County Libraries, Bridgend, Pontyclun, Llanharan.

Book Preparation Acknowledgements

I wish to thank the following:

Mrs. Olive Prosser, who undertook the task of correcting the first manuscript. I am also thankful for her sound suggestions which enhanced the content of my book.

Mr. Brian Davies, Curator of Pontypridd Historical Centre, who introduced me to the Cardiff Central Library, enabling me to research and formulate a clearer picture of the 'South Crop' mining exploration. Also for his efforts in carrying out the unenviable task of editing the final manuscript for publication.

Finally, a special thanks to my wife, Alecia Christine, who stood by me throughout all my researches. Also for her unstinting expertise in setting out the draft and manuscript for reading.

Llanharan Community Councilís tribute to that time of tears

Left - Chairman of the Llanharan Community Council, Mr. Bryant Perkins and Mr. Les Harris, former Llanharan inhabitant whose father died as a result of an accident in Llanharan Colliery in 1931, stand with pride each side of the monument dedication plaque which was designed and manufactured by Conway Memorials, Pontypridd. A fitting tribute to our past mining heritage.

ACKNOWLEDGEMENTS

Without the fullest co-operation from the following people, this book would not have been possible.

Mr. & Mrs. George Williams, Ludlow, Shropshire, who have supported and encouraged my efforts from the very beginning.

Mr. & Mrs. Owain Williams, Llanharan House, who have given me tremendous encouragement, and have allowed me the use of their mansion for all my exhibitions and book launches.

Llanharan Historical Society, who have worked so hard on my behalf.

Mr. Bryan Riddleston, Chief Executive, Celtic Group Holdings, for his help during research and for his foreword to this book.

Mr. Alan Reed, M.E., former Manager of Llanharan Colliery, who read the manuscript, provided technical advice and contributed an introduction.

Mr. Bernard Walters, Pencoed, for advice, technical information and photographs on the Dowty Engineering programme at Llanharan Colliery during the 1950s.

Miss. Jill Craigie, writer, producer, director, for her account and foreword relating to the period when she was on location at Llanharan Colliery while making the film 'Blue Scar'.

Mrs. Rachel Thomas, Rhiwbina, Cardiff, (Actress), for her invaluable information on the making of the film 'Blue Scar'.

Celtic Energy who have always assisted me in my endeavours and especially Mr. Lewis Hands and Mr. Ioan Jenkins, concurrent Site Managers, Llanilid West Revised, for providing important details on the Opencast Project.

Ex Mining Officials, Llanharan, who gave invaluable details on old mine workings in the Llanharan District.

Mr. Clifford Jacobsen, Prestatyn, Clwyd, for providing many old photographs from his late father's immaculate collection. Also for his warm foreword and account of life in Llanharan Village during the early 1930s.

Mrs. Amy Inglis, Cardiff, who gave me a clear insight into the way of life in Llanharan during her early days.

Mr. Brian Donovan, Brynna, former Llanharan Colliery Official, who afforded me hours of his time in the study of old maps and documents. Without his vigorous efforts many important facts would have been missing from this volume.

Mr. Jack Hutchins for his account of the Meiros Colliery Inundation.

Mr. Teddy Freeman (Freeman's Funfair) who provided an excellent account and photographic records appertaining to their early visits to Llanharan from the early 1900s up to the Miners Fortnight 'Holiday at Home Weeks' during the mid 1940s.

Mr. David Evans, Llamedos, Craig Melin, for his unstinting support from the very beginning.

Mr. John Tomlins, Brynna, for lending his father's mining memorabilia.

Mr. Ted Worgan who gave me a guiding hand on facts and progress of the Royal British Legion.

Notes and tapes on the life and times of Mr. Edgar Hole and Mr. Harry Sheppard, Llanharan.

Mr. Steve Evans, my photographer, who remarkably revitalised many old and battered prints, and overcame most of the difficult tasks that I have thrown at him over the years.

Mr. Wyndham Smith, a true and faithful friend.

Douglas and Roy Pine, Hendrewen Garage, whose patronage has been of enormous help.

Mr. Brian Perry, Mountain Scrapyard, Brynna, whose support and loyalty has remained strong over the years.

Mrs. Kay Bater, for her useful contribution of her father's collection of photographs.

Mrs. Gill Richards, for her important file on the Tegwen Lewis Memorial.

All the people of Llanharan and Brynna who provided information during my researches.

Mrs. Flye and the staff of Llanharan Pharmacy, who have stood up to all my impossible demands.

To 'Busty' and the Guides at the Rhondda Heritage Park whose mining information proved invaluable.

My mother, Violet May, whose sound advice and information on Meiros and South Rhondda Collieries during the strikes provides a fuller account of our mining history.

Mr. David Preece, Mining Historian, Treharris, (photographs and maps) who allowed me access to his impeccable file.

Mr. Ian McCarthy for his invaluable assistance in the setting up of this volume.

Mrs Mair Howell, Brynna Mill, for her valuable photographic contributions and support over the years.

The late Mr. Alwyn Williams of 9 Bryn Heullan, Brynna, Llanharan, whose computer expertise enabled me to set the early chapters of my book. He was a true and faithful friend.

Llanharan Community Councils tribute to that time of tears.
Chairman of the Llanharan Community Council Mr. Bryant Perkins (left), and Mr. Les Harris, former Llanharan inhabitant whose father died as a result of an accident in Llanharan Colliery in 1931, stand with pride each side of the monument dedication plaque, which was designed and manufactured by Conway Memorials, Pontypridd. A fitting tribute to our past mining heritage.